Conversations about Space and Time
Early Mediterranean Scripts

EGE YAYINLARI

Conversations about Space and Time
Early Mediterranean Scripts

**Frederik Christiaan Woudhuizen and
Eberhard Zangger**

© 2021 Eberhard Zangger
ISBN 978-605-7673-93-0
Publisher Certificate No: 47806

All rights reserved. No part of this publication may be reproduced, stored in a retrieval system, or transmitted in any form or by any means, electronic, mechanical, photocopying, recording, or otherwise, without the prior permission of the copyright owner.

The publication of this book was made possible by Luwian Studies.

Cover illustration: Joe Rohrer; bildebene.ch
Layout Design: Aydın Tibet / Guido Köhler
Index: Jochen Fassbender, Bremen

Printing
Fotokitap Fotoğraf Ürünleri Paz. ve Tic. Ltd. Şti.
Oruçreis Mah. Tekstilkent
B-5 Blok No: 10-AH111
Esenler - İstanbul
Serticate No: 47447

Production and Distribution
Zero Prodüksiyon
Kitap-Yayın-Dağıtım San. Ltd. Şti.
Abdullah Sokak, No: 17,
Taksim, 34433 İstanbul/Türkiye
Tel: +90 (212) 244 7521
Fax: +90 (212) 244 3209
E.mail: info@zerobooksonline.com
www.zerobooksonline.com

Conversations about Space and Time
Early Mediterranean Scripts

FREDERIK CHRISTIAAN WOUDHUIZEN AND
EBERHARD ZANGGER

Contents

Research Means Looking at Things from a New Perspective	**9**
Speaking Luwian Today	10
Scripts Are Related	11
Science in Transition	11
How Does Decipherment Work?	**13**
The Generalist's Approach	15
Combining an Internal and an External Approach	18
Why Decipherings Are Needed	20
Talking about Methods	21
Schools of Thought	23
Understanding Linear A	24
The Notorious Phaistos Disc	26
Arthur Evans Caused Some Harm	28
Waves of Indo-Europeanization across the Mediterranean	**31**
All Emerged from the Steppe	33
It All Began 5000 Years Ago	35
Another Wave of Indo-European Speakers	38
Of Indo-Aryans and Hyksos	41
Minoan Crete Was Multiethnic	44
Immigrants Tended to Be Hostile	45
How the Languages Arrived	46

The Earliest Cretan Scripts — 53
- How the Script Came to Crete — 54
- Linearizing Hieroglyphs — 56
- Cretan Hieroglyphic and the Phaistos Disc — 59
- Looking across the Border — 64
- Let Atlantis Rest! — 66

The Lasting Success of Luwian Hieroglyphic — 73
- Two Forms of Luwian — 76
- Step by Step towards a Decipherment — 77
- Why Not Read Luwian? — 79
- Some Signs Are Polyphonic — 84
- No Sign for i Anymore — 88
- Recent Finds – Questionable and Unquestionable Ones — 91
- Yet More Inscriptions Appear — 98

Byblos Needs Its Own Script — 105
- The Byblos Script — 106
- What the Documents Say — 109
- The Road to Decipherment — 110

A Cypriot Admiral Calls for Help — 115
- Different Approaches — 116
- All about Business — 121
- Hittite Ambitions — 126
- A Spectacular Discovery — 127

Origin and Motives of the Sea Peoples — 133
- How the Situation Evolved — 134
- Famines in Anatolia — 135
- Where Was Haunebut? — 138
- Weshesh, Sherden, Shekelesh – and All the Rest of It — 141
- What Fred Thinks Happened — 144
- Some Discrepancies — 148
- What Eberhard Thinks Happened — 151

The Etruscans Came from Asia Minor — 157

- Connections with Anatolian Languages 159
- The Pyrgi Tablets 161
- A Whole Book: The Liber Linteus 164
- The Enigmatic Lemnos Stele 166
- Where Do We Go from Here? 168
- Don't Forget the Rhaetians! 170
- What Are the Consequences? 170

Other Luwian Dialects, Such as Lydian, Lycian and Carian — 173

- Lycian Can Be Read and Understood 175
- Three Signs in Lydian Should Be Corrected 177
- Sidetic Contains Signs from Cypriot Script 180
- Carian Has Not Been Deciphered Correctly 182

Southwest Iberian Is Celtic — 191

- The Alphabet Becomes Semi-Syllabic 192
- They Spoke Celtic, What Else! 193
- The King Is Named after the Silver 195
- Phoenician Port Towns Were Not Harmed 196
- The Celts Enter Iberia 197
- Iberia as a Sideshow 199
- A Dedication to Reinforce a Bilateral Treaty 201

Etymology or No Etymology – That Is the Question — 205

Appendix — 221

- Endnotes 221
- Further Reading 224
- Picture Credits 232
- Index 233
- About the Authors 255

FOREWORD

Research Means Looking at Things from a New Perspective

It all began with one word: Tarhunt. The young Dutchman Frederik Christiaan Woudhuizen, a student of Mediterranean pre- and protohistory at the University of Amsterdam, recognized in a text written in Etruscan – a hitherto undeciphered language – the name of a well-known Anatolian god. Thus, the idea took shape in his mind that Etruscan could be related to Luwian, the predominant language in Anatolia in the second and first millennia.* Both languages, Etruscan and Luwian, belong to the Indo-European language family. So the young researcher began to identify the roots of the Etruscan words. Then he exchanged them for their Luwian equivalents. Suddenly the scales fell from his eyes, and he could read Etruscan – all of it! Today, he said, there are no more open questions as far as Etruscan is concerned. With his translation key, all of the several thousand documents can most likely be understood.

This was the beginning of an amazing journey that would lead from one discovery to the next – an intellectual effort that stretched over four decades. Along the way, Fred Woudhuizen wrote 25 books and over 100 scholarly articles. Once he was able to read Etruscan, the first thing Fred did was to apply this newly acquired skill to Luwian, the language he had initially exploited. If, as it turns out, Etruscan is essentially a Luwian dialect, knowledge of Etruscan can help us better understand Luwian, the key language of Anatolia in the Middle and Late Bronze Age and the Early Iron Age. This reasoning subsequently worked even better than expected. However, Fred found that there is a discrepancy between the way Etruscan expressions are used in Luwian and how Luwian is transcribed among researchers today.

The study of early Mediterranean history is divided into two main disciplines: archaeology, which deals with material remains, and linguistics,

---

* The indication BCE/CE is omitted when it is obvious.

which studies ancient documents. Fred Woudhuizen's core competence is undeniably linguistics, yet he belonged to the small group of scholars who are courageous enough to consider quite different aspects of past cultures. This path inevitably leads to considerations of epistemology, with questions such as how we actually know what we know. It turns out that important foundations of Aegean protohistory were laid early on at a time when there was not yet sufficient evidence – or, even worse, when archaeology was strongly influenced by political and ideological goals and wishful thinking. The birth of Aegean prehistory also occurred between colonization and the terrible war between Greece and Turkey, both inevitably favoring Eurocentric interpretations. This was followed by the increasing specialization of the sciences, which led to a division of the legacy of past cultures into chronological periods, geographic regions, research areas and methods. Knowledge thus became in some ways fragmented. It is now time to bring it together again by way of an intensive dialogue.

Speaking Luwian Today

As for opinions on how to read and transcribe the picturesque Luwian hieroglyphs, a passionate debate prevailed for about half a century (c. 1920–1970). This ended with the New Reading of Luwian hieroglyphs proposed in 1972. From Fred's point of view, however, the discussion could have gone on a bit longer. For him, progress – in research and elsewhere – meant looking at things from a new perspective. He was still at the very beginning of his professional career when he noticed a discrepancy in the New Reading. However, this could be resolved by combining the New and Old Reading of the Luwian hieroglyphs – creating the best of both worlds, so to speak. At the same time, he came to the conclusion that the understanding of Luwian is limited if the terms are first transcribed into Latin words – as is customary today. Since about 90 percent of the phonetic values of Luwian symbols are now known, hieroglyphic texts can actually be read in Luwian. This made Fred pretty much the only person in the world who actually spoke Luwian – and he even liked to do so because it helped him to better understand an otherwise dead language and the thinking of the people who spoke it.

Scripts Are Related

For Fred Woudhuizen, career planning never played a role. More important to him was practising the researcher's craft as it was originally intended. He collected clues and arguments, searched for explanations, substantiated earlier ideas – and was not afraid to question existing doctrines when new evidence became available. This also applies without reservation to his own models, which he has willingly revised when new evidence has made this necessary. However, this has very rarely been required. It is actually more the case that established scholarship has come closer to Fred's ideas than the other way around.

There is no one who has worked so much on Luwian and come so far in that pursuit. Fred lived through the way the language was spoken and began to recapitulate the thinking of Luwian speakers more and more. The fascinating thing about his life's work is that the individual topics he has dealt with – from the origin of the Indo-European language to the decipherment of fragmentary scripts – are so different, but they are all ultimately related to each other and new, plausible results can be brought about by this insight. It is rare to find a scientist whose fields of work complement each other so beneficially as in Fred's case. He was the first to translate not only the hieroglyphs but also the cuneiform texts in which Luwian has been handed down to us. This showed that these cuneiform documents contain many references to celestial aspects: sun gods and goddesses, the moon god, heaven and earth, the months and the year. This insight comes at a time when new light is being shed on the Hittite and Luwian cosmovision. So the latest research in archaeoastronomy and the ritual incantations Fred studied, which have survived in Luwian cuneiform, supplement each other.

Science in Transition

Fred's professional career coincided with a period of fundamental change in the academic system. In the 1980s, financial resources became scarcer at universities around the world. One might be led to believe that the goal of research – at least in the humanities – was less to break new ground than to cut costs. When resources become scarcer, so do academic posts. And when there are fewer posts to fill, selection committees prefer to play safe. Eccentrics like Fred Woudhuizen no longer had a chance to find a permanent position. However, he made do with a modest lifestyle and found ways to make ends meet. In fact, by not having a job in academia, he gained ultimate academic freedom. Without teaching duties and administrative tasks, without the compulsion to sit on committees, without the time-consuming writing of third-party funding proposals and the need to supervise students, Fred was able to immerse himself fully in his research and thus got further and further ahead. He reached a point that many scholars aspire to: the lofty vista from which one sees how everything is connected. He inhabited a universe of ideas and insights largely alone, as hardly anyone could comprehend his thinking.

In the summer of 2020, Fred and I embarked on the writing of this book. It takes an unusual approach to unlocking complex models of thought in archaeology: the interview. When experts have to express themselves in writing, they tend to choose a matter-of-fact, technical mode of expression. However, when they talk about their work, they will inevitably do so in much simpler terms. A conversation is therefore an excellent means of communicating new ways of thinking – something that has been known for a long time. While the famous dialogues of the history of science were invented, this is not the case here. The interviews reproduced in this volume are transcripts of actual conversations. Through the spoken word we get to know Fred Woudhuizen's thinking much better, at a time when its importance is increasing.

A few months after we had begun with the interviews, Fred was diagnosed with leukemia. From then on our conversations were paced to some extent by the treatments. Despite this ordeal, Fred remained cheerful and satisfied until the very end. He passed away in late September 2021. His research and theories make an important contribution to the scientific discussion of protohistoric scripts, and his legacy is a plea for the freedom to tread new paths – and an invitation to dialogue, to weigh the pros and cons of the other's arguments.

October 2021, Eberhard Zangger

How Does Decipherment Work?

What is Mediterranean pre- and protohistory? The perks of interdisciplinary work. Combining the evidence. How Michael Ventris deciphered Linear B – and why Alice Kober would not have succeeded. One can learn from each breakthrough, but a recipe for success does not exist. Each time a different tool kit is required. What comes after the decipherment is more important. Etruscan has the largest number of documents – and all can be read. Challenges in dealing with Luwian hieroglyphic. An overview of the scripts covered in this book. Arthur Evans's successes and failures. The chronology ought to be fixed.

Eberhard Zangger: You describe yourself as a specialist for Mediterranean pre- and protohistory. Could you please elaborate on that? What are pre- and protohistory? And what does it mean to be a specialist in these fields?
Fred Woudhuizen: In simple words, prehistory covers the time before documents existed, so there is no written evidence for any scripts that may reveal the languages spoken at the time. The historic period comes later when we do have plenty of documents. And protohistory lies in between: it covers a time with relatively few surviving documents which may give us some hints regarding the scripts and possibly the languages used at the time. The field that used to be called "Aegean prehistory," the period roughly from 3000 to 1200, has been relabeled "the Aegean Bronze Age," because it is a typical protohistoric era, a time from which we do have some but not enough historical documents. We need to combine these with the archaeological record and with the historical and historiographic sources that may exist, for instance, in the account by Herodotus.

My education was interdisciplinary involving archaeology, linguistics and history. In the Netherlands, during the 1980s, this was a new approach to archaeological research, but it was unfortunately later discontinued. At the time, the idea and terminology had been introduced by Italian schools. The first congress of Mediterranean pre- and protohistory was held in 1950 in Florence, the second in 1980 in Amsterdam, as an inauguration event for the newly founded field of study.

Your core competence is in linguistics, but you also make much use of the archaeological record. How would you describe your daily work today?
The transmitted evidence is so scarce that you need to combine a number of sources in order to achieve anything. The ultimate aim will always be to acquire a better understanding of what happened in the past. The further we go back in time, the more we need to integrate all the evidence that has come down to us.

The Generalist's Approach

Is it fair to say that few people use such an integrated approach, because the more specialized a scholar is, the more scientifically solid their research will appear to be?

Frederik Christiaan Woudhuizen in his apartment in Heiloo near Amsterdam, Netherlands, on September 5, 2020, during the conversation with Eberhard Zangger about the Sea Peoples.

Yes, but specialization also has its downside – you simply do not get the desired results by using only one line of evidence. For example, if you want to answer the question, when did the Hittites come to Anatolia? Or when did Greek speakers come to Greece? It will be impossible to get a correct answer by purely using linguistic evidence, because you will not be able to date such an event, since linguistic evidence will not yield a date. Only archaeology can provide this, but one has to be sure that the archaeological finds actually record the arrival of a new group of people in the region. For example, the shaft graves in Mycenae are a completely new phenomenon and Robert Drews is attributing it to the arrival of Greek speakers in the southern Balkans at around 1600.[1] The language alone could never yield such a date.

You very much advocate an interdisciplinary generalist approach to reconstructing the past. You once said that it is necessary to understand how a past society functioned, what its culture was, and perhaps even what the thinking and beliefs of the people were at the time.[2] The more one knows about an ancient culture, the easier it will be to understand the elements it consisted of.

Indeed, for periods where there is little material recorded, it is crucial to combine all the evidence that exists to get a better picture.

The subject here is, of course, decipherment – and there are basically two kinds of decipherment, one regards the script and the other one the language. If we look at the history of research in Aegean and Near Eastern protohistory, there have been five major successes in decipherments: cuneiform, Egyptian hieroglyphs, Hittite language, Luwian hieroglyphs and Linear B. Hence, all the scripts for which many documents have been recovered are pretty much deciphered. What is left now are those scripts and languages for which we have fewer records. Is this a fair characterization?

The proper term is *Trümmersprachen* – an extinct language which is attested only in a very small *corpus* and whose structure is therefore considered not reconstructable.

Reading what you wrote in your books about successful decipherments, one gets the impression that you scrutinize the approaches taken at the time to extrapolate from them to your own research. If we look at these five successful decipherments, which approach do you think is most useful and should be considered today? In other words, what can we learn from successful decipherments?

I think from every decipherment you can learn something. Most of the decipherments benefited from bilingual documents, but if you look closely at the approaches taken by the decipherers, it turns out that they also profited enormously from studying all aspects of the ancient culture in question. For instance, Jean-François Champollion acquired extensive knowledge about Egypt in general, including its archaeology. He also studied the Coptic language that was known at the time. Eventually, he began looking at the royal names in the cartouches and was soon able to recognize the names of Caesar and Cleopatra; but that might not be helpful since you need to know the language. Champollion learned the

The famous Rosetta stone from 196 BCE is inscribed with a decree in Egyptian hieroglyphs, Egyptian Demotic script and Greek. This trilingue helped Jean-François Champollion to develop a complete translation system for Egyptian hieroglyphs in 1822.

language from other documents, especially the Coptic ones, that were at his disposal, and then came the Rosetta stone. With the values he got from the cartouches, he was then able to fill in the text and could thus read hieroglyphs.

The so-called Tarkondemos seal belonged to king Tarkuntimuwa of Mira, according to Fred Woudhuizen. It is probably the top of a sword hilt and was inscribed in cuneiform and in Luwian hieroglyphs around a figure of an Anatolian king.

So it is crucial to know the context in which a certain text was conceived; for instance, whether it was a ceremonial liturgy. We have bilingual documents, of course, in Luwian hieroglyphic as well, most importantly the Karatepe inscription that was discovered in 1946.

Yes, but the interesting thing is that much of the deciphering of Luwian hieroglyphic had taken place before Karatepe was found. If we go back to the Tarkondemos seal, for instance, that was first published in the 1860s, it features a short bilingual inscription, in Akkadian cuneiform and Luwian hieroglyphic. At the time, scholars knew a sign from inscriptions found at Carchemish, which also occurred in the legend of the Tarkondemos seal. Since this is a bilingual seal, it could be determined that it stands for "land." Using this information for its occurrence in the texts from Carchemish, it could be guessed that in these texts this sign is associated with the name of the town and that this should be read *Ka+r(a)-ka-mi-sa*. All these signs could then subsequently be used to read more of the text, only by trial and error, of course.

By the time Karatepe was found, however, many signs had already been correctly identified. The difficulty of Karatepe is that the second text, in addition to the Luwian hieroglyphic, is the longest Phoenician text in existence. Hence, scholars dealing with this document faced trouble even understanding the Phoenician part of the inscription.

Combining an Internal and an External Approach

Eventually, we get to the decipherment of Linear B, which may be the most interesting of them all – because it is the latest that occurred, in 1952, and at the time neither the script nor the language was known. Michael Ventris thought for a long time that Linear B reflected Etruscan. He started out, when he was only 18 years old, with an article in the *American Journal of Archaeology*,[3] in which he compared the Linear B signs with the much later classical Cypriot syllabary. This did not work out, because so much time had passed in between – a whole millennium – and, of course, the signs can change their form during such a long period. But then Alice Kober recognized the doublets and triplets, which brought the evidence for declension, such as in *me-di-cu*(s), *me-di-ci*, *me-di-co* in Latin. The *c* remains as the consonant, while the vowel is changing. One can put this into a grid, where a certain consonant is placed on a vertical axis, and then associate it with vowels 1, 2 or 3 on a horizontal axis. This in turn permits predictions about sound values. Ventris then plugged in a comparison with a known script which he knew well, namely Cypriot syllabic, and ultimately recognized that two signs are the same in Cypriot syllabic: *ti* and *to* – they had the same consonant and a different vowel. In other words, he used Cypriot syllabic to verify his interpretation.

Did he benefit from his knowledge of Cypriot syllabic after all?
Yes, but he needed Kober's doublets and triplets to make the comparison valid. All things considered, the deciphering of Linear B proves how valuable the combination of two different approaches can be: one is internal – doublets and triplets – the other one is external: the comparison with Cypriot syllabic. We need to bring these two approaches together and then … bingo!

Do you think if Alice Kober had lived longer, she would have figured out Linear B herself?
No, because she was not willing to take external evidence into consideration. If you want to read a text, you need sound values. You need to have the value for a sign, otherwise you cannot read anything. But you must be sure that the value is right, because if you fill in a wrong value, your whole translation will get mixed up. It is a dance on a high wire.

Michael Ventris also launched a questionnaire that was later dubbed "The Mid-Century Report," with which he consulted experts all around the globe, requesting their opinions on certain matters regarding Minoan culture and Linear B. In principle, he thereby anticipated grounded theory in qualitative studies.

His motivation was simply that he wanted to know everything about Crete, not just the script and language. Only if you know a lot about the lost culture you will be able to actually interpret correctly what you read. At the time, almost every expert whom he had approached participated in the survey; but Alice Kober did not, she considered it "a waste of time."

Michael Ventris was, of course, not even an academic, so that may have made it harder to find acceptance for his deciphering attempts. On the other hand, his biographer, Andrew Robinson, writes that at no time in his life would Ventris regard the decipherment of Linear B as a competitive race.[4] It sounds as if for him it was more like an intellectual exercise.

Ventris actually wanted to have as much information as possible, yet at the same time he was very willing to share information. However, he would certainly not have liked the idea that somebody else deciphered Linear B first. He wanted to be the one who did it – and he worked relentlessly towards this goal.

Why Decipherings Are Needed

Beyond being the first person to have solved a certain riddle, to what extent is using your achievement by applying it to other open questions in archaeology part of your motivation?

I would say that this is the ultimate aim and actually a highly desirable situation when you achieve it. It gives you a tool for archaeological reconstructions – and so you get new information, and you can use that information to figure out what happened in the past. The decipherment is thus the beginning of a sequence of events.

If we now turn towards your own contributions to decipherments, what are the topics you have dealt with? I am aware of your work on Linear A, the Luwian hieroglyphic, the Byblos script, Etruscan and the Phaistos disc. What did I miss?
The Southwest Iberian script: that is Celtic. Then there are some languages of which we have even smaller evidence; for instance, Sidetic, from Side in Pamphylia, which is also a Luwian language.

This is really what makes your work stand out, since nobody else in the world would claim to know all these unknown scripts and languages. Did you make a key discovery, or did you have some kind of magic wand that helped you with all these decipherings?
There is no such thing since every script and every language is different. Etruscan, for instance, is written in a known script, the alphabet, so it can be read. The question is only in what language it was composed. Basically, every script needs an approach of its own.

Obviously, in your case, the decisive factor is the tool kit that you were provided with early on and that you now have so much practice in using. You are applying this tool kit to different issues, right?
Yes, there is a tool kit, but you need different tools for each subject. In Etruscan you can read the text, but you have to find the roots and the meaning of the words. For the Byblos script, on the other hand, you first need to get values for the signs.

Which part of your work do you think will be hardest to challenge?
Well, in Etruscan, there are several thousand documents that can be used to test my transcription.

And what would be the second most important problem that you have worked on?
Clearly, the second most important problem is the reading of Luwian hieroglyphic.

Let's talk about that, because this is really a subject that has much contributed to your isolation in this field, since the few people who deal with Luwian hieroglyphic, maybe 20 to 30 throughout the world, have for the most part agreed on a common methodology which you also share but only to some extent.

I am a little bit of a loner.

Talking about Methods

The method you use is a combination of the now common standard with elements that go back to the time of the initial deciphering in the 1930s, thus to Ignace Gelb and Helmuth Bossert, but also to Emil Forrer and Bedřich Hrozný.

Yes, indeed. If you go back to the initial signs to be deciphered, it turns out that the first verb which Ignace Gelb was able to read in 1931 was *aia-*, a very common verb that stands for "to make," for instance "to make an offering" or "to make a house." According to the current textbook standard, it ought to be read as *izi-*; but if it was indeed *izi-*, Gelb would never have been able to read it in the first place. The vowels are frequent signs and therefore deciphered first. As opposed to this, *zi* is a much less frequent sign, and therefore only deciphered later in the process.

What I find most impressive, and what you have put much evidence on in your latest publications, is that you do have bilingual evidence that supports your reading. Bilingual, of course, means that certain words occur in Luwian hieroglyphic and in Luwian cuneiform.

Or Hittite! There are, for example, names of persons in two different scripts – in Luwian hieroglyphic and the same person's name in Hittite cuneiform. I call this bilingual evidence. The place-name *ī+r-ha-nu-a-*, for instance, occurring in a Luwian hieroglyphic text from the reign of Kamanas of Carchemish in north Syria, is well defined, since *ī+r-ha-* is the Hittite word for "frontier." As *-nu(wa)-* means "new," the whole expression denotes "the new frontier." In the New Reading, this would be read as *za+r(a)-ha-nu-*, which really stands for nothing. So, the situation is obvious, the term *ī+r-ha-nu-a-* is bilingually documented with the meaning of "the new frontier."

You have published a couple of papers providing lists with such bilingual occurrences of terms that confirm your reading. How is it possible that people ignore this?

It is an inconvenient truth! I recently published a paper about the Ankara silver bowl in which I provided everyone's transcriptions and translations and then naturally concluded with my own transcription and translation.

And in this case, your reading actually confirms what other experts, such as Piotr Taracha and Jacques Freu, had concluded.

As you know, the word for "house" in Luwian is *pa+r-ná-* – and as such, I use it in my transcriptions. According to the school of thought advocated by others, however, it must be transcribed with the word *domus*, which is Latin for "house." In my opinion, it is completely irrelevant whether you write *parna* or *domus*, what matters is how we manage to comprehend the text.

It just means you have to know Latin in order to understand Luwian. I fully understand the motivation at the time, that they wanted to establish a standard that is internationally applicable rather than it being in a certain language such as French as was suggested back then. So, some leading experts agreed on a neutral transcription and that was Latin, and it may make sense for the words where we do not know the reading in Luwian.

Of course, there are problematic terms where I use Latin just like everybody else. And then there are challenges when the word for house becomes a determinative for a barn, and you have another word following it. So *parna* became the determinative and not the term itself. But the main thing is that you rob yourself of essential information for a proper understanding of Luwian hieroglyphic texts if you use Latin circumscriptions instead of the real Luwian values of the signs.

Furthermore, if there is something fundamentally wrong with the current translation system, it must be legitimate to point that out. A good alternative is to use another form of transliteration, one that is less inaccurate, so to say.

Schools of Thought

In this case, you obviously suffer from the fact that you are not a faculty member and that you do not have students and therefore cannot create a school of thought with followers who would use your approach. For these reasons, you have no institutional power. All you have is the argument, but first people have to understand the argument. And secondly, they also have to make a career and if they do not follow the convention, it will be challenging for them to make a living in the academic system. People prefer to be wrong along with everyone else – rather than being right, but all by themselves.

If we talk about Hittite, there are over 30,000 documents and fragments of text, and I am, of course, not suggesting other readings for Hittite or something like that. But if you take Lydian, on the other hand – how many inscriptions do we have? Maybe 50 to 100 – in any case very little. Even in this case, the conventions how the signs have to be read are considered gospel. If there is so little material, however, nothing can be sure. Besides, who is making a career in Lydian … Come on! If anyone suggests that another reading for any of the signs is conceivable, that person will be ostracized. Yet, there is absolutely no reason to outcast scholars who suggest alternative readings. Trying to pretend that one can be sure about these readings is simply nonsense. We need to discuss them if we want to make progress! This is indeed a clear case of too much dogmatism in an early stage of the field.

With respect to Lydian it is still early days, but everybody agrees that Lydian is derived from Luwian, right?

No! The current view is that it is closer to Hittite and that the language represents a separate branch from Indo-European Anatolian. In other words, Luwian, Hittite and Lydian are separate branches of the Indo-European Anatolian language.

That is a bit strange though, because just in terms of geography it makes a lot more sense for Lydian to be Luwian.

Yes. It would indeed be very strange if it were Hittite, because the Hittites were rarely ever so far west, maybe occasionally with a conquering army, but never for very long. Of course, there were marriages between

Hittite rulers and western Anatolians. So influences from Hittite language cannot be denied. But that does not make the language itself Hittite.

Why do you think Lydian is derived from Luwian?
Well, I suggested that some of the signs are read incorrectly. If I fill in what I think is the right value, I get all kinds of Luwian forms, such as verbs ending in -*vi*, for example, which render the first person singular of the present/future tense: "I will do" this and that.

Understanding Linear A

Let's talk about Linear A a bit.
Linear A is a more difficult story, since the script is used for more than one language, just like the alphabet is used for lots of languages. In Linear A we have only 10 to 20 workable inscriptions, so almost nothing compared to Etruscan. If the evidence is so small, it will inevitably be difficult to gain acceptance for any proposed deciphering. In comparison, in Linear B the texts are not really very informative on syntax, but there are thousands of them.

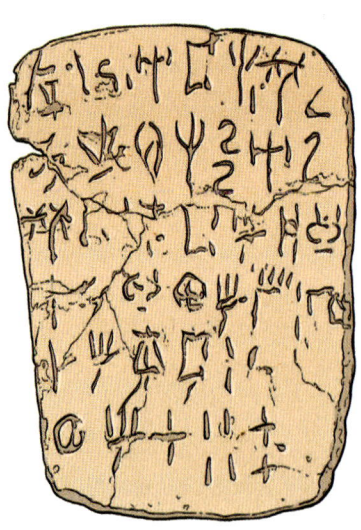

A Linear A tablet from Crete.

I think that the work by Jan Best in 1980/1981 was indeed a breakthrough, when he read the Asherah inscription with its recurrent formula in Linear A, because he could explain it totally in Semitic: "I have given and my hand has made as an expiatory offering, oh Asherah." This is a complete sentence with a verb etc., and the term *ja-di* "my hand," for example, is feminine and the ending of the verb *ki-te-te* is feminine as well. Come on! This is what makes the language tick. As it turns out, most of Linear A is in Semitic.

But Best's deciphering of Linear A is not accepted!
No, but he published it. The classicists who only know Greek do not understand it; however, they form the majority, and the majority decides what is accepted. If someone is a classicist or an expert in Indo-European languages, these people will naturally have a hard time accepting or even recognizing any parallels with a Semitic language, simply because they do not know anything about it. Fortunately, the Semitists, on the other hand, have no problem recognizing the parallels.

Basically, you follow a path that was set by Jan Best?
And Jan Best followed the path that was set by Cyrus Gordon. My work in Linear A follows in the line of Cyrus Gordon, Jan Best, Robert Stieglitz, Roberta Richard and Gary Rendsburg – a lot of people have said that Linear A is Semitic. It was not my idea. Most scholars who work on this arrived at the same conclusion. I am only providing more material in the line of thought that was already established in the 1950s.

And it is still not accepted?
No, because the classicists do not know Semitic languages.

What about the people who are indeed experts in Semitic languages? What will they think of this?
There is so much material in Ugaritic, for instance, where even today new tablets are found, that they have thousands of documents that need to be worked on. The specialists put their priority on texts found locally.

They do not pay attention to Linear A?
Not much. Some did write comments or reviews. Jan Best's work got one review in which the expert concluded that his translation reflects correct Semitic.

But you say that some Linear A inscriptions are also in Luwian?

Yes, but very few.

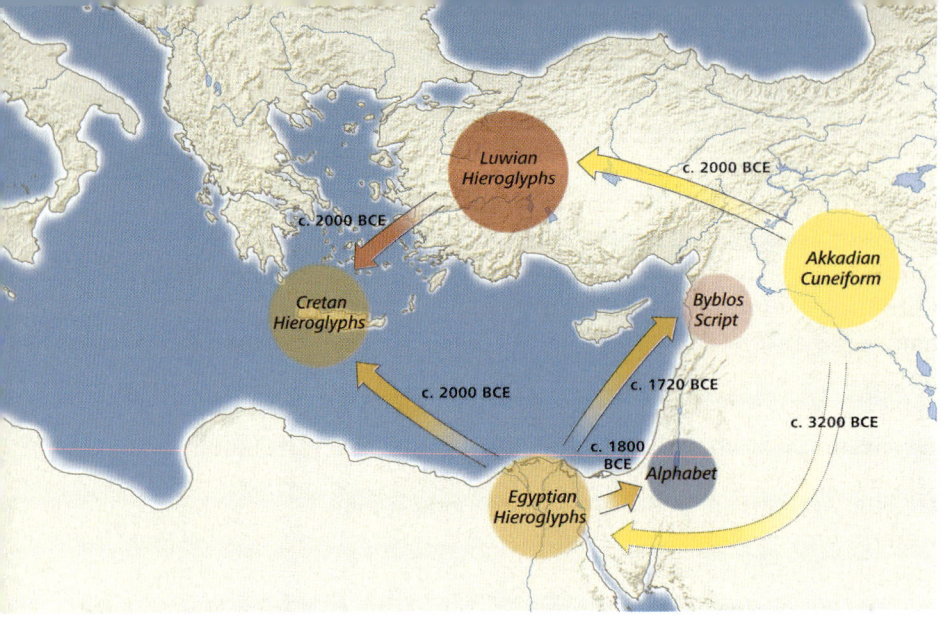

After Akkadian cuneiform and Egyptian hieroglyphic had been invented around 3200, it took one thousand years until Luwian hieroglyphic arose, almost simultaneously with Cretan hieroglyphic. The latter incorporated signs and sound values from Luwian hieroglyphic as well as from Egyptian hieroglyphic.

The Notorious Phaistos Disc

During the course of this book we will inevitably speak about the Phaistos disc, because it is such a formidable artifact – and in a team effort you provided a full translation of it.
The Phaistos disc is certainly connected with the problem of Cretan hieroglyphic in general. It is not an isolated object; it is part of the Cretan hieroglyphic script.

Which is for the most part earlier?
It is earlier but it continues. The Phaistos disc is one of the latest objects written in Cretan hieroglyphic using Luwian language. Again, there are not many inscriptions in Cretan hieroglyphic. We only have a few longer ones; for instance, the double axe from Arkalochori, an altar stone from Malia and a very large seal, but that is about it. The rest is just seals with titles and personal names and no phrases.

Does the Phaistos disc consist of Cretan hieroglyphic signs only?
Cretan hieroglyphic is actually related to Luwian hieroglyphic but includes signs originating from Egyptian hieroglyphic as well. Luwian hieroglyphic also contains signs which are reminiscent of Egyptian

hieroglyphic, but fewer. Crete is closer to Egypt and had direct contact with Egypt, and that is how the Cretans acquired some signs from there. Even though we have no evidence, it is obvious that Cretans had contact with Egypt and thus had seen the use of hieroglyphic script there for many centuries, actually a thousand years. Eventually they employed the same concept to Cretan hieroglyphic, though this is essentially based on the model of Luwian hieroglyphic; 75 percent of Cretan hieroglyphic signs were derived from Luwian hieroglyphic and 25 percent came from Egyptian hieroglyphic. Therefore in the end it is a combination of both.

Cretan hieroglyphic by itself would be impossible to decipher because there are too few documents, correct?
That is what they say, but if you know where the signs came from – from Egyptian and Luwian scripts – you can fill in the sound values and actually start reading the documents. It does not matter anymore whether you have many documents or only a few. You can read them; you can read personal names and you can read their titles on the seals.

In any case, the Phaistos disc is the longest text in Cretan hieroglyphic. In terms of the date, it still fits into the framework of the use of Cretan hieroglyphic.
From what we know today, Cretan hieroglyphic was in use from 2000 to 1350 – and the Phaistos disc coincides with the latest date of this period. It was found together with a Linear A tablet in a collapsed magazine. The archaeologists saw that the magazine's sherds date to the sixteenth century, but the Linear A tablet and the Phaistos disc were both from an upper story and had fallen into the magazine. They belong together – and the tablet can be dated to 1350, which thus also yields the date for the disc.

And what was the decisive factor that made it possible to read the Phaistos disc?
There are doublets and triplets! Employing these, we could verify a connection to the Luwian hieroglyphic script. In our team we made a grid with the doublets and triplets in which the consonant is the same, while the vowels are changing. Proceeding in this way, we came across the endings -*tu* and -*ti*, which are already known from Luwian hieroglyphic. So we could validate the connection.

If you consider your life work, what do you think will have the biggest impact in the long run? I assume it is your work on the Luwian hieroglyphic including your adjusted reading.
Luwian hieroglyphic entails the largest amount of text, with about 150 documents containing entire sentences. In Etruscan we have longer texts, including a book, but it is still much less than Luwian hieroglyphic; Lycian is still less, Lydian even more so, Linear A is the least. If, however, we are able to read Linear A as Semitic, this will inevitably have implications for our understanding of the Minoan culture, since important Semitic influences are then obvious. Of course, not everybody in Crete was a Semitic person at the time; after all, we know that there were many Luwians on the island too. It was simply a mixed culture.

It would mean that palace administration was introduced all at once as a system coming from Syria.
Yes, and that they used a Semitic language because it was economically important to furnish the trade with Egypt and the Levant.

But this is not what European scholars want to hear.
No, recently I read a book by Brent Davis.[5] He says the Cretan population arrived during the Neolithic on the island and never changed in thousands of years! Come on, I put names together of what you can read in Linear A and Linear B and there are Luwian names, Semitic names, you find Greek names, you find even Phrygian names, Thracians names, Egyptian names, Hurritic names – come on! This was a multicultural society!

And Homer says that there has been a mixture of languages in Crete![6]
Not to forget the Pelasgian language – we have three Linear A inscriptions which must be Pelasgian, because they are Indo-European, but not Greek or Luwian. This was a highly cultured society and not just farmers living there from the sixth millennium onwards, who never saw anybody from a foreign country. That is a modern myth!

Arthur Evans Caused Some Harm

I am afraid that Arthur Evans did not just establish the principles of Aegean prehistory with its chronology and the distinction of three cultures, the Minoan, the Mycenaean and the Cycladic, but also the approach towards the investigation of these cultures: rather authoritarian and with an academic economy whose currency is access to material and whose asset is a potential monopoly of interpretation.

But you should read Arthur Evans's early work! I read his book about Cretan pictographic, as he calls it, *Scripta Minoa I*. This appeared in 1909, and at the time he was still quite open-minded. He tried to make connections with Egyptian and Luwian, even though not much was known about the latter at that time. He was more flexible in 1909; however, as he became older, he became more narrow-minded.

Evans prevented the publication of the Linear B tablets for 40 years!
Yes, that is true – and against the principles of science. Scholars should share new material with their colleagues as soon as possible. Still, I was surprised by how open-minded he initially was. His investigations began with the seals. At the end of the nineteenth century, he found seals which at the time were called "milk stones" and worn by Cretan women as jewelry. Evans went to the peasants' homes to ask whether they had some "milk stones." He was interested in the signs on the seals and sought connections back then. In a book dating to 1895, he even called the signs pre-Phoenician.

In the 1950s, with Helmuth Bossert's discovery of Karatepe and Michael Ventris's deciphering of Linear B, the field of Aegean prehistory had gained momentum and was much en vogue. People may have been arguing and disagreeing, but it was an exciting field! Ventris's deciphering of Linear B took place in 1952, thus about 70 years ago. Since then, apart from your work, there have been no other breakthrough decipherments. I think that for these reasons, this research discipline has lost some momentum.
Yes, it is not exciting anymore – they are repeating the same arguments over and over. I keep a copy of Ventris's and Chadwick's book on Linear B and that is all I need. Very little new information has been produced, apart from some tablets found in Thebes.

One could wish for more!
That is what you say.

Also, I think that there are two different approaches. There are some people who work on ancient texts rather mechanically, almost as if they are dealing with Legos. Things either fit together mathematically, or they do not fit – there is nothing in between. On the other hand, there are scholars who want to assimilate past societies and cultures to acquire a position which allows them to understand what people were thinking at the time. Hugo Winckler and Emil Forrer thought along these lines, and so did Jan Best – and I think you are using a similar approach.

You want to understand how people thought back then. From what I can tell, however, there are very few people using such an approach. The majority of scholars is rather rigid in their thinking.

There are indeed huge issues; for example, when was Knossos destroyed? This is, of course, a very important issue. According to the current textbooks, the destruction of Knossos is dated to the end of Late Minoan IIIA1, c. 1350. The destruction layer, however, contained Linear B tablets with personal names occurring in combination – so-called "linkers" and "big linkers." These are officials which frequently occur together in the administration because they were simultaneously in function. The same combination of personal names occurs in a Linear A tablet found in Hagia Triada, but there the destruction is dated to Late Minoan IB, c. 1450. Hence, there appears to be a century between the two destructions, even though they evidently occurred synchronously – in Late Minoan II/III. The Minoan chronology is completely messed up! This is one reason why there has not been a comprehensive monograph on Minoan archaeology in half a century.

Interview conducted on June 14, 2020.

Waves of Indo-Europeanization across the Mediterranean

Why Indo-European studies are not obscure. First movements within the steppe. The horse, wagons and bronze come into use. Pelasgians spread across the Aegean. Two groups of Indo-European speakers disperse at 2300. The Luwians arrive in Anatolia – the Hittites too. Indo-Aryans and Hyksos in the Levant and in Egypt. Greek speakers arrived in Greece as late as 1650. And a multiethnic society thrived in Crete. Conflicts with immigrants are not new. The oldest languages in Iberia, Italy, the Balkans and Anatolia.

Forgive me for saying so, but my feeling is that – even amongst archaeologists – the field of Indo-European studies seems a bit obscure. Let's briefly review how this discipline arose.

Well, it goes back to the English judge Sir William Jones, who was posted to India in the late eighteenth century. He had a background in classics and thus knew Greek and Latin. To work with local laws and to conduct trials in India, he familiarized himself with Sanskrit. Jones then recognized many parallels between Sanskrit, Latin and Greek.

And he knew classics because that was part of the traditional education of the British upper class at the time?

Yes, of course. As you know, the word for *father* in Sanskrit is *pitár-*, which is close to *pater* in Latin and *Vater* in German. And parallels like this go on and on.

How come we still speak of Indo-European and Indo-Germanic studies?

That is typically German! It is basically the same. "Indo" represents the far eastern geographic extension of the language family, whereas "European" marks its far western extent. German scholars argue that English is part of the Germanic family; they therefore prefer to use the term

"Indo-Germanic," but in English this term is no longer used. "India" is also the name of a subcontinent, just like "Europe."

Since a common root for the Indo-European languages was obvious, the next step must have been to search for the earliest records written in such a language – and this takes us right back to the Luwians.

I have re-examined a seal from Beycesultan with a Luwian inscription that dates back to 2000. But there is even earlier evidence in the Ebla tablets, dating to the twenty-third century. Ebla is, of course, in Syria, and the cuneiform tablets found there mention a town called Armi on the northern frontier, most recently identified as Samsat. The tablets list Luwian and Hittite personal names, but also what I call "Old Indo-European" personal names. This might indeed be considered the first epigraphic evidence of Indo-European.

When was this published?

Well, I have yet to publish it! The names from the tablets have been published by Alfonso Archi, and other scholars also refer to these names, but they did not examine them closely. So they found some connections with Indo-European Anatolian, but only in a few instances, and I think there are many more.

If you are aiming for a complete picture regarding the earliest references to Indo-European, then we should also mention that *ūmman-manda* – *ūmman* is the Akkadian word for "horde of barbarians" and *manda* is the word for "pony" in several Indo-European languages. This appears to have been a horde of people coming from the north, who entered the Levant, apparently using ponies. Their appearance coincides with the Ebla tablets. These *ūmman-manda* are also first attested for the border region between Syria and Turkey – in the exact region where you would find the Armi personal names. So there's a connection between *ūmman-manda* on the one hand and Armi personal names on the other.

Seal from Beycesultan dating to around 2000, providing the first thus far known mentioning of a word ("Mira") written in Luwian hieroglyphic.

If this were not considered to be the earliest mention of Indo-European names, not even the seal from Beycesultan, then would Luwian still be the earliest epigraphic evidence of Indo-European writing?

There is also the archive of Kültepe-Kanesh, dating to the nineteenth and eighteenth centuries. Alwin Kloekhorst recently wrote a book about that.[7] He sees a dialect of Kanesh that is closely related to Hittite and calls it Kanišite Hittite. Ilya Yakubovich has also drawn attention to Luwian onomastic elements in those archives, dating to the earliest twentieth century, 25 of which I consider valid.

All Emerged from the Steppe

If we look back over the last half-century or so, there have essentially been two competing models to explain the movements of the Indo-Europeans: one was introduced by Marija Gimbutas, the other by Colin Renfrew.

They actually worked together in excavations. Basically, Gimbutas suggested that the Indo-Europeans were nomads with horses, cattle and sheep who came from the north Caspian steppes and went westwards – and this occurred in several waves, beginning around 3000. Her theory rests on pillars reaching further back into the nineteenth century, to Otto Schrader and Victor Hehn.

Colin Renfrew, on the other hand, suggested that the Indo-Europeans were a product of the Neolithic Revolution, that they had been farmers in Anatolia and had brought agriculture across southeastern Europe. This would have happened much earlier, starting around 6000. However, recently Renfrew officially abandoned this idea, because of the evidence now coming from ancient DNA. It became clear that the Indo-Europeans were indeed people coming from the steppes and entering Europe around 3000.

In 2007, David Anthony's book *The Horse, the Wheel and Language* already presented overwhelming evidence against Renfrew's model.

It did. To be honest, Renfrew used an archaeological approach that all along did not match up with the linguistic evidence. I think it is very honest of him to admit defeat and do this publicly – and his books were,

Movements of peoples of the Khvalynsk culture to the western shores of the Black Sea and the northern Caucasus around 4200.

in fact, quite entertaining. He was pushing the argument further and further, but I never believed him.

Yet Renfrew led archaeological research in the wrong direction for several decades.

Indeed he did. And migration was really considered to be "out" for a long time; the whole concept was simply unfashionable. Migration is very difficult to find in the archaeological record. What you see is destruction, with no positive argument proving any migrations. As an archaeologist, Renfrew was against the idea of migrations. Instead, he favored the concept of a Neolithic Revolution that moved forward incrementally, perhaps 20 kilometers per year or so; he called this "demic diffusion."

So the Gimbutas model has prevailed: the Indo-European languages can be derived from people who lived in the north Caspian steppes and who migrated in distinct waves to the east, but also to the west. When did the first migration occur?

Well, the first one took place within the steppes. The people living there at the time are not yet considered real Indo-Europeans; currently, they are called "Indo-Hittites." In the late fifth millennium, people from the Khvalynsk culture in the middle Volga region moved westward to settle on the western shores of the Black Sea around Varna in what is now

Bulgaria. These people may be called "Proto-Luwians." At the same time, other people from the Khvalynsk culture went south to the Maykop region just north of the Caucasus. These might be considered "Proto-Hittites." This diffusion is archaeologically recorded by the dispersal of scepters with horse heads. Around 4000, Varna was, of course, the place to be, because that is where archaeologists have found so much gold. The same is true for Maykop about 500 years later.

Why did the people move into these particular areas? Were they highly fertile or rich in minerals?
Maybe they were advantageous for trade!

The Maykop region north of the Caucasus.

It All Began 5000 Years Ago

So the initial wave of migration was still limited to the Black Sea region. When did the second phase occur?
Around 3100 or 3000.

You say that the effect of migrations becomes visible through innovations. Initially, we see the dispersal of mace heads. At the transition from the fourth to the third millennium, we see that the use of arsenic bronze is becoming customary, and long-distance trade with cargo vessels also increased at that time. What are the other innovations?

The bronze is important, but also, where Indo-Europeans go, you will find that the horse was utilized. What makes this wave of migration stand out is that it appears to have occurred all over Europe. Hans Krahe and his students reconstructed it from Old Indo-European river names.[8] One can find those even in Anatolia and in Syria. Research in Iberia is lagging behind a bit; however, recent evidence has sprung up from there as well. In Iberia, the arrival of Indo-Europeans coincides with the memories of the Lusitanians. In Italy, they are remembered as the Ligurians. From Italy, we have evidence for the use of the horse, and also for the introduction of the catacomb grave, brought by people coming from the steppes. The same type of grave is found in Bab edh-Dhra in the Levant near the Jordan River, and in the Conca d'Oro culture in Palermo, Sicily. The catacomb is very typical of Indo-Europeans.

In Greece, the immigrants were called Pelasgians. With their ships, they went all the way to Crete and, of course, as they passed, some settled on the mainland too. Pelasgians also settled along the coast of Anatolia. Troy, for instance, was founded at the time of the early Indo-European migrations. Even the Bible mentions a Philistine king, Abimelech, from the time of Abraham.

In addition to the catacomb, another type of grave is associated with the movements of the Indo-Europeans. For instance, in the Messara Plain in Crete, you find tholos graves – and we see the same type of tholos used near Pai Mago in Portugal and in the Los Millares culture in southeast Spain. The archaeological site of Shintasta in the steppes also contains tholoi, but they were made from mudbrick. Thus, they were not recognized by archaeologists for quite some time.

We must not forget that the earliest known evidence of a wheeled vehicle dates to 3400 and was found in a village called Flintbek in Northern Germany – which is where I grew up!

Okay! But you are right to point out that the main innovations for this early period are wheels and wagons! The wagons allowed the nomads to travel faster across longer distances while taking their homes right across the steppes.

Right page: A wave of Indo-European speakers reached several regions north of the Mediterranean around 3100–3000.

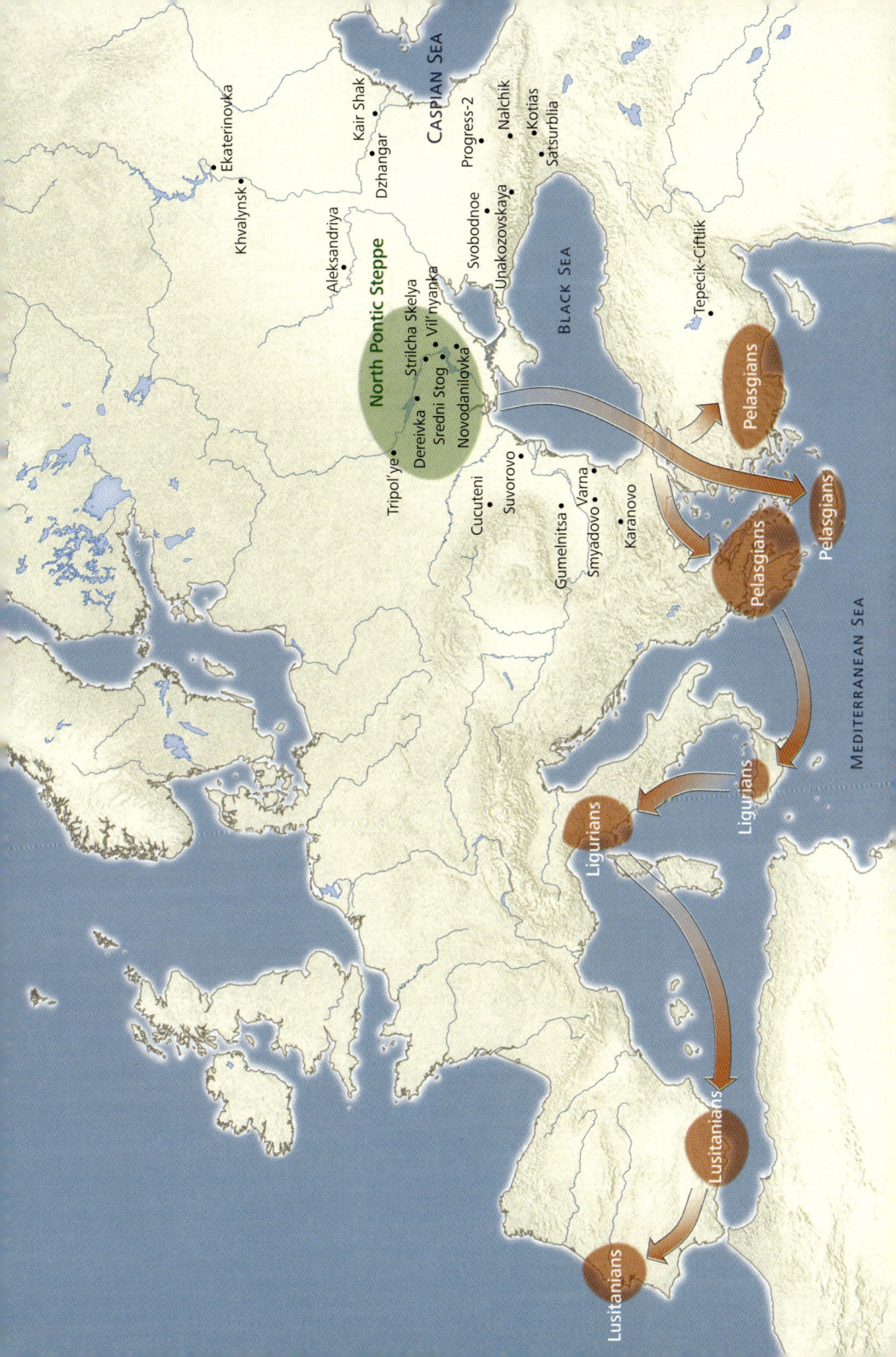

And in Greece the immigration of Indo-Europeans triggered the transition from the Neolithic to the Early Bronze Age?
Yes, indeed. This early wave of migration was accompanied by the introduction of place-names with the ending -*st*-, such as Lykastos in Crete. I recently published a paper in the *Journal of Indo-European Studies* in which my argument started in Holland with a theory regarding the so-called Nordwestblock, a concept introduced by Hans Kuhn.[9] This goes back to very ancient Indo-Europeans producing names such as Soest, with the -*st*- ending. I found out that there are also a lot of these place-names in Anatolia. They occur in many places around the Mediterranean, indicating the oldest phase of Indo-European migration.

The Indo-Europeans were highly innovative. Long-distance travel must have been done by boat, and the Indo-Europeans actually took some horses and cattle with them.

Is it not a contradiction to say that the Indo-Europeans were nomads, on the one hand, but skilled seafarers on the other?
I do not know how to answer that! All I know is that the only way to go to Sicily is by ship! Of course, you can rent ships.

And they may also have brought the plague with them?
That is true! We know that the corded ware in eastern Europe was introduced by steppe invaders; in that case, the archaeologists found out that the local population became extinct, while the invaders from the steppe went on. The same was happening in England.

In any case, the immigrants did not usually replace the indigenous population.
No, during this initial phase, we are talking about very small population groups which were on the move. The indigenous population and the newcomers normally coexisted.

Another Wave of Indo-European Speakers

The next big wave of migrations occurred around 2300, correct?
Yes, then things got a bit more complicated, because some of the Indo-Europeans – I call them Group A – can be characterized as being conservative. These included people speaking Hittite and Luwian, but also

Germanic, Baltic, Celtic, Italic and Tocharian. Another branch of Indo-European speakers – which I call Group B – introduced verbal augmentation, putting an *e* before the root in the past tense. This is typical of Indo-Iranian, Greek, Thracian, Phrygian, Armenian and Illyrian.[10]

Around 2300, we see movements of Indo-European speakers from the steppes to the Mediterranean, with some belonging to Group A and some to Group B. Group A arrives in Anatolia, with Hittite speakers coming from the Maykop region across or around the Caucasus. They eventually settled, for instance, in Alaca Höyük. The famous graves found there are typical of the Maykop type.

And in western Anatolia, you see Luwian speakers coming in. They must have come across the sea, because some went on to Crete and Cyprus. The Luwians settled in the western and southern part of Anatolia, initially only in the coastal regions, but with time, more and more also in the interior.

In Greece, on the other hand, we see the innovating Group B arriving, for instance, in Lerna. They were immigrants coming from the Balkan Peninsula, mostly Thracians and Phrygians, who brought with them Minyan ware, a typical Balkan ceramic style, and apsidal houses, also with Balkan antecedents.

Group B Indo-Europeans from Thrace and Phrygia settled in Greece, while Group A Indo-Europeans settled in Asia Minor – for example, in Boycesullan – and these were the Luwians. Therefore, while Greek, Luwian and Hittite speakers were to some extent related, were they also distinct in certain ways?

This is an interesting point! If you consider Alaca Höyük to be an early form of Hittite culture, which I would do, then the Hittites had graves in the style of Maykop. The Luwians, however, can be correlated to the catacomb graves around the Aegean. Christoph Bachhuber wrote a book about this early period,[11] but he understandably limited his scope to Anatolian sites and did not take the Aegean into account. For instance, in Euboea there is a catacomb grave from this period, and there are catacombs also in Crete and Cyprus. And where we find catacomb graves in Cyprus, we will see single-horse burials in the same region. So, the deceased person was buried with his horse. This custom dates to the time before chariots came into use, because when chariots were customary, people were buried with two horses!

One of the princely tombs at Alaca Höyük, dating to the time around 2200–2000 when the Hittites arrived in Anatolia.

On the Greek mainland, in Marathon, another single-horse burial was found, and one grave in Crete even contained a royal seal with the depiction of a horse. Therefore, the Indo-Europeans took their horses with them into the grave. Wherever Indo-Europeans went, we find the horse. We have to look at the entire Aegean coast all the way up to Cyprus to recognize the Luwian migrations, because if we do not, all you see in Anatolia is destructions. James Mellaart talked about that. Around 2300, every place was destroyed, and afterwards everything we find records the presence of grazing nomads. We only become able to identify the invaders when we look at the Aegean. They were the people who introduced catacomb graves and single-horse burials, and both are characteristic of Indo-European speakers.

And this is the time when place-names ending in -ssos or -nthos were introduced?
Yes, those endings are typically Luwian: *-nthos* is the Greek variant of Anatolian *-anda*, as in Puranda, Millawanda, Wianawanda and so on.

Can you say what happened in Troy at that time?
The earliest settlement in Troy goes back to 3000 and is Old Indo-European. Then there is a destruction layer in 2300, and after that we see the

use of a kind of Grey Ware, but apparently this is only full-blown after 1800. It is quite possible that Indo-Europeans may have settled in Troy in 2300 but were then dislodged in 2000 or 1800 by Phrygians or Thracians. As I said, the Grey Ware is Thracian and Phrygian – and it occurs in Greece and in northwest Anatolia as well.

In Greek mythology, we hear of a king with a typical Thracian royal name, Tēreús, ruling in the town of Daulis in ancient Phocis near the frontiers of Boeotia. Also, Pélops is a Phrygian name – the émigré the Peloponnese is named after.

Can you think of any more names which were established at this time?
Yes, on vases with Linear B legends from Thebes we find the ethnic adjective *o-du-ru-wi-jo*, which is a name for the Thracian tribe "Odrysians." These vases were imported to Thebes from Crete, to be sold in the hinterland of Phocis – where you find Tēreús in Daulis, an Odrysian royal name. So the Linear B record fits the myth.

Of Indo-Aryans and Hyksos

We come to the last big wave of migrations which occurred during the seventeenth century. This brought the Greek speakers and the shaft graves to Greece.

The Greek language, the shaft graves, chariots, pairs of horses – these are some of the most important innovations on the Greek mainland. At the same time, we see migrations of Indo-Aryan speakers into the Levant. Indo-Aryans are a linguistic group of people in northern Syria who later went to Iran and India. The royal names of the Mitanni are Indo-Aryan and connected with the introduction of chariots. I think the movement went across the Levant, all the way to Egypt, where the Indo-European speakers formed the Hyksos rulership. At that time, the Hyksos introduced the horse and chariot to Egypt.

The conventional wisdom is that the Hyksos came from Syria and Canaan.
I think it is a combination of Indo-Aryans coming into the region, together with the Hurritic population and Semites who lived there. This mixture made up the Hyksos. The technology of chariots and horses lives on, for instance, in the later Kikkuli text, the earliest document describing

how to train horses. Not just the Egyptians but also the Hittites learned it from the Mitanni.

And in Greece we get the Mycenaeans!
Yes, we get the Mycenaeans! The interesting thing is that the Greeks themselves believed that Danaus, the king of Argos, originally came from Egypt. Cadmus, the founder and king of Thebes, was a prince from Tyre in Phoenicia. Cadmus is indeed a Phoenician name, or if you prefer to use another term for the Late Bronze Age, a Canaanite name. The Canaanites were the forerunners of the Phoenicians, but it is the same population. Basically, we have a movement of people who ultimately came from the region around Shintasta in the steppes, then went across the Caucasus into Syria and Canaan, where they introduced the chariot and, with it, the use of two horses. In the Levant, they established the Mitanni kingdom, from where they pushed further south all the way into Egypt, where they established the Hyksos rulership. The movement went on from Egypt, joining others who came directly from Canaan, into Crete and further onto the Greek mainland. That is why we speak of "Minoization" – elements of Cretan (and Egyptian) culture during the formation stage of the Mycenaean period. All kinds of Minoan artifacts were found in the shaft graves at Mycenae, so evidently the Mycenaeans had looted Crete.

Is there any archaeological evidence for the Hyksos arriving in Crete?
No, all we see is a level of destruction. They went there, destroyed it, and left. We have, of course, the Chian lid, which also dates to 1650. It is a lid with the cartouche of Chian, a Hyksos pharaoh. This is very important for the dating of the destruction; however, it could have reached Crete through trade.

So, the coming of the Greeks is the end of a migration that proceeded clockwise all around the eastern Mediterranean, and in which the last stepping-stones were Egypt and Crete?
Yes, indeed. Actually, this idea had already been introduced by my teacher, Jan Best, who said that the Proto-Greeks were Hyksos. Their migration was distinguished from the earlier wave around 2300, when Thracians and Phrygians had moved into the Greek mainland. The Greeks were clearly latecomers since they were not in Greece at an earlier stage.

WAVES OF INDO-EUROPEANIZATION ACROSS THE MEDITERRANEAN • 43

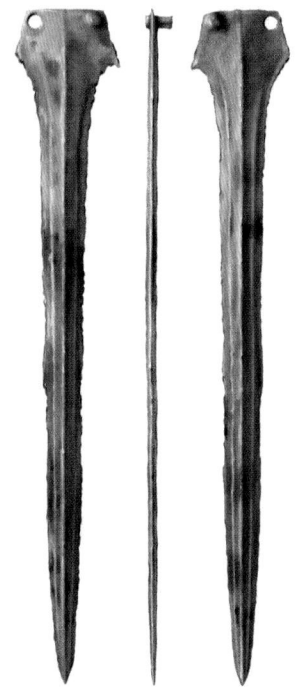

Long swords (rapiers) occur in the shaft graves in Mycenae as well as in the Caucasus.

This is also what Robert Drews discusses in his latest book.[12]

Drews only sees one wave of movements and uses this to explain all Indo-European migrations. He also argues in favor of a different route. He says that rapiers (that is, long swords) occurring in the southern Caucasus are exactly the same type as those found in the shaft graves in Mycenae. Drews thinks the migration proceeded by ship along the southern shore of the Black Sea. This would be an alternative route, which is also possible. In my opinion, the Levant would have been more attractive, though, because of its rich trading towns. If you possess superior weapons, including the extremely fast chariot, you might feel tempted to plunder the rich cities in the Levant. The southern coastal region of the Black Sea is rather dull by comparison. You go where the wealth is!

The chariot was a completely new weapon! It was like having a tank. The invaders could beat everybody, as long as the fighting took place in plains, since in the mountains, chariots are less useful. Danaus in Greece, for instance, who only had daughters, saw that they got married to local men, men bearing Thracian and Phrygian names. Accordingly, the immigrants interacted and intermarried with the local people. If you want to rule a region in Greece, you are forced to make a deal with the people living in the mountainous hinterland, and at the time those were of Phrygian and Thracian descent.

And since the newcomers were also of Indo-European stock, there was a good chance that local people and immigrants understood each other. Yes, linguistically they were closely related because they all spoke the augmenting language of Group B. Phrygian and Thracian are very close to Greek. I think, at the time, the different parts of the population could understand each other.

Drews points out that, even before the coming of the Greeks, graves in Kolonna on Aegina, in Thebes and in Ayia Irini on Keos already contained rapiers and thus belonged to men with a military function. Apparently, these warriors were forerunners of the actual Greeks, who came from the Caucasus and may have been hired to fulfil a military function. If these people maintained a connection to their homeland, they may have encouraged their compatriots to take a closer look, for instance, at the silver mines in Laurium, right next to Keos.

Minoan Crete Was Multiethnic

What was the effect of the movements around 1650 on Minoan Crete?
We see a destruction layer between 1650 and 1600 all over Crete. The invaders evidently hated the local people's religion: the intruders destroyed libation altars with hammers. But Crete very quickly recovered and then entered the high civilization of Late Minoan IA/IB, which is really the peak of the Minoan culture.

How would you characterize this culture?
It was a highly civilized, multiethnic society, trading all over the Mediterranean, especially with the Levant and Egypt. The Minoan culture was so successful because it was able to incorporate cultural achievements from all around the eastern Mediterranean, such as palace administration and writing. During the first migrations, we saw the Pelasgians coming to Crete. During the second wave, the Luwians arrived in Crete. So there were two different types of Indo-European speakers right from the beginning. After 2000, we also see evidence for the use of the Semitic language. And if you take the names in the Linear A and Linear B tablets from Knossos into account, you will find people from pretty much all shores around the eastern Mediterranean.

What was the political organization like?
I think in Late Minoan IA/IB a great king ruled from Knossos all over Crete. His power was based on the navy and on maritime trade with the Levant and Egypt. That is where the wealth came from. I also think

that Minoans were involved in the tin trade. Tin was, of course, the most important metal for the production of bronze weapons.

And it is hard to come by!
Yes, it is hard to come by, because you have to go all the way to the west or the east.

So you think that Minoan Crete was politically unified. But don't we see major differences in the material culture between, let's say, Knossos, Malia, Phaistos, Kato Zakros and so on?
I think that during the protopalatial period, aristocrats ruled independently over each of those kingdoms. This was indeed transmitted in the myth of Sarpedon, Minos and Rhadamanthys – the three brothers who ruled over Crete. But in the later period, after 1600, we see that the royal names from the Knossos dynasty are most important. Also, in terms of archaeology, Knossos is the most important place in Crete at that time.

Immigrants Tended to Be Hostile

In summary, we have not one migration of Indo-European speakers, but actually four – and these occurred in distinct intervals between 4000 and 1600. How should we imagine those migrations to have taken place? Did the newcomers gently blend in, or were they rather hostile?
If there was nobody living in the region, the immigrants just settled on virgin soil. If there were settlements, we often find destruction layers. Being nomadic or semi-nomadic, the Indo-Europeans were prepared to defend their cattle and sheep. They had weapons and could be very hostile. As horse riders, they were also quicker than others on foot. In particular, the phase between 2300 and 2000 was marked by all kinds of destruction.

Of course, we have explicit accounts and even graphic illustrations of what such migrations might have looked like from the time of the Sea Peoples' invasions around 1190. Do you think that these accounts might be characteristic of what also happened during earlier migrations?
I am convinced that the same story repeated itself over and over again, and this is indeed very much the story told about the Sea Peoples'

invasions. On each previous occasion, the same thing happened: you see the light go out, then we get destruction levels, new people arriving and so forth. In addition to the migration aspect, there is always also a looting aspect, a military aspect, a nautical aspect ...

In the mortuary temple of Ramesses III at Medinet Habu, the different phases were condensed in one picture: first come the raids, conquering, plundering, the destructions, and then after a while settlers come in to establish a new kind of culture, bringing their wagons and household items.
Yes, indeed! In addition to the land and the sea battles, the murals in Medinet Habu also show a picture of a cart with a woman and a child, thus symbolizing migration.

As you know, there is currently a debate as to whether these migrations may have been triggered by climatic change. It is indeed quite conceivable that the nomads in the steppes had a problem with the changing climate and therefore started to go on the move.

This discussion goes back to a paper from 1966 by Rhys Carpenter, which in my opinion was based on anecdotal evidence. I have taken cores for palynological studies near Tiryns and near Pylos. Both produced consecutive vegetation histories for most of the Holocene – and both record a major human impact on vegetation throughout the ages, but virtually no climatic change. In addition, from the detailed accounts of commodities listed in the Linear B tablets in Pylos the calories available for the population could be calculated, and there was no indication of starvation. From what I can tell, there are no convincing arguments for significant climatic changes taking place in the Aegean during the Bronze Age.
But why should there only be one reason behind all those diffusions of Indo-European speakers? I do not see that as a solution either.

How the Languages Arrived

What we have said so far basically summarizes the current state of knowledge in this field, with which the majority of scholars would most likely agree. You have recently published a book about Indo-Europeanization in the Mediterranean, providing many more details. About half of the book is dedicated to fragmentary languages and how they fit into this model. When you talk about fragmentary languages, you mean documents found on the peninsulas on the northern side of the Mediterranean – the Iberian, Italic, Balkan and Anatolian Peninsulas.

Yes, and the languages are "fragmentary" in the sense that we do not have much material.

Let's talk about these regions one by one. What about the western Mediterranean?

The earliest movements into the western Mediterranean relate to the appearance of Lusitanians, which are Old Indo-Europeans. There is one inscription in the Lusitanian language, even though it was composed rather late, during the second century BCE, but it is littered with Indo-European words. Without a shadow of a doubt, Lusitanian is Indo-European of an old type. These people came during the initial phase of migrations and

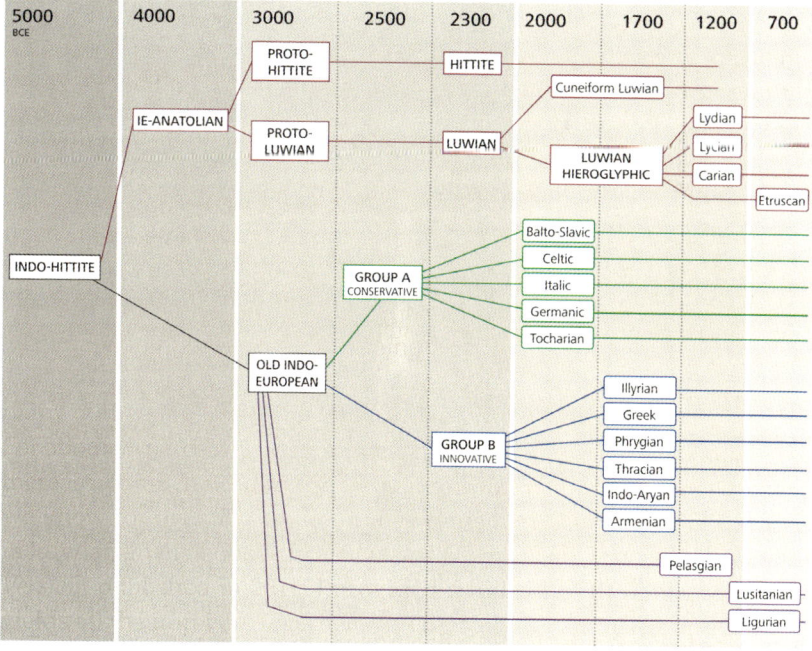

The development of Indo-European languages according to Fred Woudhuizen.

settled in by 2800. Strabo has a story about Lusitanians; he says well into the Iron Age, they were still fighting with bronze weapons.

In Iberia, the situation is quite simple, because you have only two layers: the Old Indo-European immigration around 2800 and then the formation of the Celtic culture after 1200. We do not find any evidence of an early culture which was non-Indo-European and covered the whole Mediterranean. There is a little bit of Basque in Iberia, which is not Indo-European, and in Anatolia we have Hattic, Hurritic and Semitic, which are non-Indo-European languages. The idea of a pre-Mediterranean culture from the time before the Indo-Europeans is vanishing. It was based on the misinterpretation of texts, such as Eteocyprian, Eteocretan, Southwest Iberian and Etruscan. They had all been misinterpreted as non-Indo-European; however, if you translate those texts, you inevitably end up with Indo-European languages. So it has become a non-issue.

And is there agreement on this?
No (*laughs*)!

What about the Italic Peninsula?
On the Italic Peninsula, we see the early group of Old Indo-Europeans coming in around 3000 and these can be correlated with the Ligurians. Speakers of this language occupied most of Italy. They are accompanied by Indo-European-style graves with horse burials, and in one case a wife's skull was broken so that she could be buried with her husband. That is a typical Indo-European grave already at 3000.

The river Arno also has a typical Old Indo-European name. The Tiber was then called Albula, another typical Old Indo-European name emphasizing the color white, which is where the Alps got their name from. For these reasons, there is no point in claiming the existence of an old non-Indo-European Etruscan residual group if the rivers have Indo-European names going back to 3000.

The second layer is the Italic branch, with Latin, Faliscan, Umbrian and Oscan, entering the peninsula after 1200. You see the Proto-Villanovan culture coming across the Alps, that is a cremating culture of the European Urnfield type, and in this period it extends all the way south, as far as Sicily. I personally think this may have been one of the triggers which started the migrations during the time of the Sea Peoples' invasions, because local residents were then displaced from their habitats in southern Italy and had every reason to go east. But during the Bronze Age, we only have two phases of migrations in Italy. In the Iron Age, we then get the Etruscans from about 700, who are Indo-European/Anatolian – and that marks the third phase of migrations.

And regarding the Balkan Peninsula, we have already discussed what happened, with the Pelasgians coming in around 3000 ...
... and then the Thracians and Phrygians around 2300, and the Greeks at 1650. So there are three phases of migration.

In Anatolia, we have, of course, the endemic Hattic culture ...
... and then Old Indo-Europeans coming in at 3000, introducing their typical place- and river names at that time. Then, around 2300 – perhaps, because of the Ebla texts, even a bit earlier – we get Hittites and Luwians. And from 1500 onward (in the Troad even earlier), we see Thracians and Phrygians moving into Anatolia. Of the Kaska, who lived north of the Hittites on the southern coast of the Black Sea, some bore Thracian and Phrygian names. I think the whole movement from the Balkan Peninsula went on and on.

After the Sea Peoples' migrations, we see Phrygians moving on a massive scale into Anatolia. They basically take over the whole northern part of Anatolia and thus much of the former Hittite territory, which then becomes the Phrygian kingdom.

Whereas the Lydian kingdom evolved out of the local Luwian population. Yes, there is no reason to look for the effects of migration because the language of Arzawa, from what we know from cuneiform Istanuwa texts, is simply Luwian.

Of course, the recent advances in analyzing ancient DNA have brought confidence where we previously only had competing models of thought. DNA works well in a clear-cut situation, where the newcomers replaced the indigenous population. If you are in the Mediterranean, which has been occupied by a mixture of different populations, and the newcomers marry local girls, you are bound to get a completely mixed picture already in the second generation. You need to know exactly what you are doing with the DNA. Because if you take the wife, you will get another DNA compared to taking the husband's. In Iberia, they found one

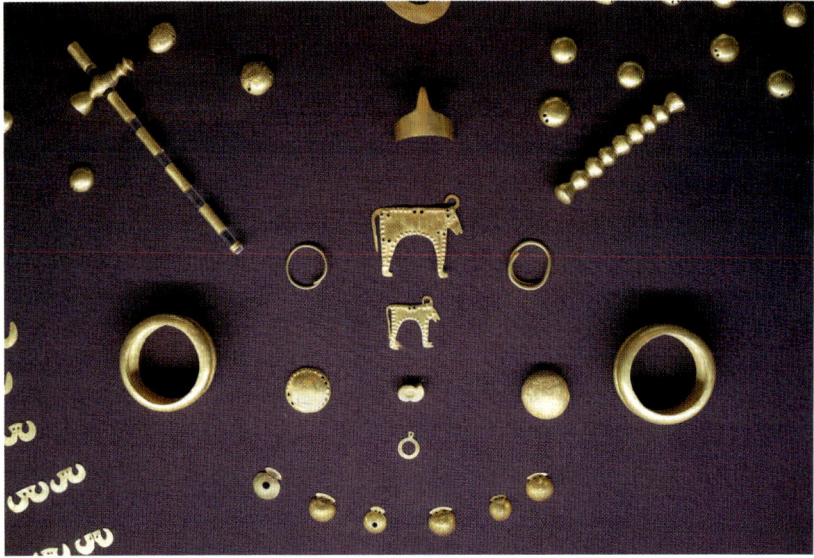

The Varna Museum of Archaeology in Bulgaria exhibits what is considered the oldest human-processed gold in the world, dating to 4550–4320.

The Historical Park in Neofit Rilski, Bulgaria, contains a reconstructed Neolithic settlement, thereby making it possible to experience the living conditions over six thousand years ago.

skeleton from a man who came from the steppes, but the rest were just indigenous people. If you take Crete, the situation gets very complicated. It depends on which graveyard you are looking at, and which person within the graveyard. The same applies to the cattle. That is why you can find indigenous Etruscan cows not far from cattle that may actually have been imported all the way from Anatolia.

Interview conducted on June 28, 2020.

The Earliest Cretan Scripts

First there were Akkadian cuneiform and Egyptian hieroglyphs. Thousand years later hieroglyphic scripts appear in Anatolia and in Crete. There is a relationship! Linear A is Semitic. The Phaistos disc is one late form of Cretan hieroglyphs. Research has lost momentum. A context for Atlantis?

Cuneiform writing was invented around 3200 and employed in Mesopotamia, eastern Anatolia and Syria. Very soon thereafter, hieroglyphs were invented in Egypt. For thousand years people all across the shores of the eastern Mediterranean and far back into the hinterland saw these writing systems in use, but they did not do anything about it, until eventually additional scripts started appearing in the eastern Mediterranean. What is the first evidence of writing in addition to cuneiform and Egyptian hieroglyphs?
From what we know today, people started to write using Luwian hieroglyphic around 2000 as documented in a seal found in Beycesultan. At the same time, a hieroglyphic script appeared in Crete. In general, however, the dating in Anatolia is better, because the settlement at Kültepe-Kanesh can be directly correlated with Assyrian king lists, whereas Cretan dating is a little bit vague. Some encyclopedias say that Cretan hieroglyphic appeared as early as 2100, but I consider this guesswork. I think Luwian hieroglyphic started in Anatolia and almost simultaneously writing was introduced in Crete.

Luwian hieroglyphic looks in some ways like Egyptian hieroglyphic. In fact, Herodotus mistook the inscription at the Karabel Pass for Egyptian.[13] While knowing about the existence of Egyptian hieroglyphs, people in Anatolia developed their own new local script. How does the Luwian language compare to Egyptian in terms of grammar, syntax etc.?
Egyptian is a totally different language from Luwian; there is no connection. Egyptian is connected with the Hamito-Semitic language group,

whereas Luwian is Indo-European/Anatolian. These are very distinct language groups. Egyptian hieroglyphic is also a consonant script; it has half-vowels, but no vowels. Luwian hieroglyphic, on the other hand, has syllabic signs: a consonant together with a vowel.

If Luwian hieroglyphic was pretty much available for anybody to use throughout the eastern Mediterranean, why was there a need to develop a new script, and several others soon thereafter?

It was common to use local scripts in addition to the international writing systems. Incoming letters were translated into such local scripts and languages. Consequently, there was an abundance of scripts and languages at the time. For instance, people in Ugarit used cuneiform Akkadian and Luwian hieroglyphic at the same time. Nevertheless, they devised an additional alphabetic script.

How the Script Came to Crete

So, the general pattern is that there were scripts which were used internationally, and in addition scripts which were used locally. In what context was writing used back then?

The first signs occur on seals and sealings, basically to indicate who people are and what they were doing. All goods in the palaces were secured with clay seals to hamper embezzling. I think the use of writing was initially connected primarily with international trade, more specifically with tin trade. The earliest seals from Crete depict ships, pots and oxhide ingots. So, the owners of those seals very clearly signaled what business they were in!

The tin mines in Anatolia apparently were discontinued around 2000. Ever since then, Anatolia was not a source of tin. I think that due to the geographic position of Crete, tin could be more cheaply introduced from the west, rather than from the east. Tin coming all the way from Afghanistan had to go through the Orient and must have gotten more and more expensive during transport. We do, however, have letters from Mari, on

Right page: The development of Mediterranean scripts during the second and first millennia according to Fred Woudhuizen. Dotted red lines indicate active influence (or borrowing of signs and sound values). The red star marks the emergence of western civilization – according to outdated Eurocentric models.

	3000 BCE		2000		1000		0	700 BCE
Iberia						Southwest Iberian (Celtic)		
Italy						Etruscan (Luwian Dialect)	Latin Alphabet (Latin)	Latin Alphabet (Latin)
Greece				Linear B (Greek)			Greek Alphabet (Greek)	Greek Alphabet (Greek)
Crete		Cretan Hieroglyphs (Luwian)	Linear A (Semitic)	Linear B (Greek)		*	Greek Alphabet (Greek)	Greek Alphabet (Greek)
Cyprus					Linear C/D (Luwian)	Cypriot Syllabic (Greek)	Greek Alphabet (Greek)	
Anatolia			Luwian Hieroglyphs (Luwian)		Luwian Cuneiform (Luwian); Hittite Cuneiform (Hittite); Luwian Hieroglyphic (Luwian)		Anatolian Alphabets (Luwian Dialects)	
Syria / Lebanon			Byblos Script (Semitic)	Proto-Sinaitic Alphabet (Semitic)	Ugaritic Alphabet (Semitic)		Phoenician Alphabet (Semitic)	
Egypt		Egyptian Hieroglyphs (Egyptian)						Coptic Alphabet (Semitic)
Mesopotamia		Cuneiform (Akkadian)		Elamite Cuneiform (Elamite)				Aramaic Alphabet (Semitic)

the Euphrates in today's easternmost part of Syria, indicating that Cretans were also engaged in tin trade from the Levant. In this particular case, an interpreter from Ugarit was involved. These letters date to the Zimrilim period (1775–1761), before Hammurabi the Great destroyed Mari in 1761. Tin from the west was coming from Cornwall and the Erzgebirge; the route to the first region was indirect through the Rhône valley and that of the Seine.

Virtually all documents with Cretan hieroglyphs were found in the eastern half of Crete. One gets the feeling that there was more going on in that part of the island.

Well, of course, the big palaces were Knossos, Phaistos and Malia. There may have been an orientation towards the trade posts in the east, but to be honest, there is no Akkadian cuneiform in Crete. There are some cylinder seals with cuneiform writings which were found in Crete, and those were very important in international trade, because a cylinder seal was an entry ticket to trade in the Levant – without it one could not trade. But no tablets bearing Akkadian cuneiform were found in Crete. Maybe people could understand it and documents were indeed produced, but on perishable materials. Of course, throughout the Levant interpreters were available, so the language barrier was overcome with the help of professional services.

Linearizing Hieroglyphs

You began to become interested in this field about 40 years ago, right?
I started in 1980 studying Mediterranean pre- and protohistory. I was in Amsterdam at the time when Jan Best worked on the decipherment of Linear A. It was very exciting to take part in his classes where we learned about the progress he made. This was perhaps the main reason why I became fascinated by the subject.

Jan Best published in 1981 a *Talanta* Supplement in which he provided the translation of the so-called libation formula, making up an entire sentence in Linear A: "I have given and my hand has made as an expiatory offering, oh Asherah." From this one sentence alone, it was clear that the language is Semitic. This was a major breakthrough!

What indicates that it is Semitic?
Take the verb *ya-ta-nū-tī*, for instance: this is genuinely Semitic *yatan*, which means "to give." The ending belongs to the first person, "I have given …" To be honest, the Mycenologists read *ya-ta-i* (sign 301). So they never get to *ya-ta-nū-tī*.

There is a little bit of a problem with the *nū*, because it is almost the same sign as the *i*. One inevitably has to decide in which case it marks an *i*, and in which case it stands for *nū*.

When Linear A was developed around 1700, simultaneously with the Byblos script, 19 signs were borrowed from the latter. Other signs were taken from Cretan hieroglyphic, and these in return were mostly derived from Luwian hieroglyphic. Therefore, signs which ultimately originated in Luwian hieroglyphic were then integrated into Cretan hieroglyphic to finally also occur in Linear A. Of course, during this transformation they were linearized and were thus no longer hieroglyphic.

Where do we stand today with respect to Linear A?
Jan Best only provided the first part of the first phrase of the libation formula. In several cases the inscriptions are much longer. And after his initial breakthrough, he did not continue to work on the longer inscriptions to unravel their whole text. I got engaged in the subject after 2005, initially to write a review article on the topic, but eventually it became my aim to complete the job. This work is concluded now – I have looked at every document.

There is no technical challenge anymore? You can deal with Linear A without any difficulties.
It is indeed very easy, there is no question about the values of the signs – they are almost the same as in Linear B. There are no challenges: you fill in the signs, look up the Semitic words, and then you are able to translate the text. Linear A documents are anyway reasonably short and thus easy to translate. I have a grid for the signs and collected all Semitic words and elements, prepositions, verbs and so on.

From your perspective, is Linear A taken care of?
Yes, it is.

The deciphering of Linear A has, however, not been accepted because scholars dealing with Crete typically have a background in Greek, whereas to understand Linear A it is crucial to know some Semitic – and Jan Best and you do so but others don't?

No, they do not. On the other hand, Jan Best and I also published in *Ugarit-Forschungen* – and the fact that our work appeared in this series indicates that Semitic scholars take it seriously. They are, however, absorbed with the work on thousands of texts in Ugaritic alphabetic, whereas we only have some tablets and longer inscriptions in Linear A. Overall the number of documents is not great. So, the focal point of research by Semitic scholars lies in the documents found in Syria.

You may have read that Linear B was decipherable because there were so many documents. The quality of Linear B texts is low though because they consist of dull enumerations of commodities coming to and going from the palaces. In Linear B, there are almost no sentences with a verb. In Linear A, on the other hand, even though we have much less material, it is of higher quality, because there are longer sentences including verbs. The verb rules the whole sentence. If you have the verb, then you can translate the sentence for sure.

And knowing Linear A is important, because it is a crucial link between Luwian hieroglyphic and Linear B.

Yes, of course, it is important, but in particular since it reveals a connection to the Byblos script and thus to the Levant. As it turns out, the language is identical to that used in Byblos. In Semitic there are all kinds of dialects and the one spoken in Byblos is closest to the language spoken in Crete.

What are the archaeological implications of that?

It must mean that people from the Levant went to Crete from 2000 onwards. They then settled there and introduced the whole set of palace administration, the sealing system and so on.

This is what many scholars have suspected all along, so your work is confirming existing assumptions. Was there anything that came as a complete surprise when you were able to read those documents?

Well, one never knows what will come up. Recently I worked on some silver pins from Knossos, and it turns out that they belong to religious functionaries. These pins were dedicated by officials of the cult; one of them even by a high official. Most of the Linear A inscriptions are indeed religious. They occur on libation tables and are of a general nature. We have only found Cretan hieroglyphic inscriptions on royal seals and only a few longer texts. One of the seals shows a winged sun disk indicating a great king. So there was once a great king ruling over Crete.

What you found makes perfect sense – evidence for aristocratic and religious rulers; those were the smart people, people who could read and write. There are no surprises, really – it is exactly what one would expect: names you would expect, deities you would expect and so on. Through the Linear A texts, we learn about the Cretan religion at the transition from the protopalatial to the neopalatial period. Religiously the culture was quite simple. Most of the time we find evidence for a cult of a holy triad: the male storm god, whose name in Semitic was Hadu, and in Luwian it was Tarhunt. Then there are three female deities: Asherah, Astarte and Tinita. Astarte and Tinita, however, are two appearances of the same goddess – Astarte is overlooking the celestial realm, while in the form of Tinita she is ruling the netherworld. The root on which the name Astarte is based is the same as that from which our word "star" is derived; indeed, her personal symbol was a star.

Cretan Hieroglyphic and the Phaistos Disc

Let's now briefly go back in time to 2000, to the first appearance of symbols of writing in Crete. What characterizes Cretan hieroglyphic? Cretan hieroglyphic is very much influenced by Luwian hieroglyphic – almost 75 percent of the signary of Cretan hieroglyphic consist of Luwian hieroglyphic. For example, in Cretan hieroglyphic there is a sign in the form of a goat head; the same sign exists in Luwian hieroglyphic. The remaining 25 percent of the Cretan hieroglyphic signary were taken from Egyptian hieroglyphic. Thus the bee sign in Cretan hieroglyphic can be derived from Egyptian hieroglyphic, where it was used for the title of king. In such cases, there is no chance of confusion. Obviously, if people on Crete made use of Egyptian hieroglyphic signs, they had to change them from consonants to syllabic values to accommodate the system.

When I asked you to define ten topics that would encompass your life work, you did not choose the Phaistos disc to be one of those, because ...

… it is part of Cretan hieroglyphic and it is not a big deal from today's perspective, just the longest document.

And there is no reason anymore to regard it as a potential forgery, because the signs from the Phaistos disc occur in a number of other documents from Crete as well. There is no doubt that it is genuine. In fact, there is a good chance that one day more documents of a similar type will be found, considering that stamps were used to produce the Phaistos disc.

Yes, the stamps most likely were made of metal and were custom-made to produce this one very important letter. There must have been several

The Phaistos disc, side A, as displayed in the Archaeological Museum of Heraklion, Crete.

copies of this document and one draft was in fact retrieved far away, in Vladikavkaz in the Caucasus.

The disc of Vladikavkaz is not a forgery that appeared and then mysteriously disappeared?
It surfaced in 1992 and indeed disappeared in 2001 but had been photographed and published in the meantime. On this item the script is not stamped, instead the signs were inscribed with a stylus. The fragment appears to be a preliminary draft of the Phaistos disc. Since the text had to fit nicely on the disc, it would make sense for the scribe to first make a draft to evenly divide the signs.

Jan Best assembled a team of five people to investigate the Phaistos disc. For many years we worked on its script, which clearly consists in part of the Luwian hieroglyphic syllabary. There are also signs on the Phaistos disc which are not paralleled in Luwian hieroglyphic. The work was very complex. Employing our knowledge of Luwian hieroglyphic, we were eventually able to read the text, which was another breakthrough. The disc turned out to be written in Cretan hieroglyphic; it is a letter to king Nestor of Pylos. After that we could straightforwardly read the other long texts in Cretan hieroglyphic since they consist of the same sign types. These are the inscriptions on the bronze double axe of Arkalochori and on the altar stone from Malia.

What do those inscriptions say?
The double axe of Arkalochori is part of a whole set of double axes. It has three vertical columns on its shaft, incised with an inscription consisting of 13 individual signs, saying these axes were dedicated by such and such. The inscription on the Malia altar is quite similar: "This inscribed altar stone for Baluzitis." Both artifacts are object bilingues in the sense that the items themselves are referred to in the texts.

In principle, however, the signs consist of Cretan hieroglyphic.
Yes, in Crete you only have Cretan hieroglyphic. There is no imported Luwian hieroglyphic inscription in Crete that we know of. Unfortunately, the dating of the Cretan hieroglyphic documents is difficult since they were not found in a clear stratified archaeological context. The Phaistos disc is more or less datable thanks to the context and the contents of the translation. In addition, the man's head has a bulbous skull in an

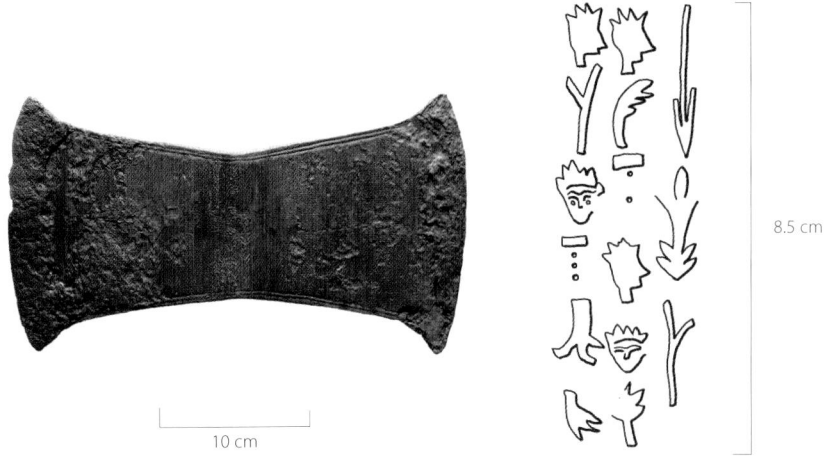

The axe of Arkalochori is inscribed with Cretan hieroglyphs that are reminiscent of the Phaistos disc. Today it is on display in the Archaeological Museum of Heraklion, Crete.

Akhenaten style. It is thus depicted in a fashion dating to the Amarna period around 1350, when Akhenaten ruled in Egypt.

How did you continue after the work on the Phaistos disc?
The Phaistos disc is, of course, the longest text. There is an overlap with the signs you find on seals, but this is not complete. There are also signs on seals that do not occur on the Phaistos disc. The challenge was to find the right connections for the Cretan hieroglyphic signs that only occur on seals, and this took me many years.

What is the current status regarding Cretan hieroglyphic? Are you able to read all documents?
All texts that are well preserved are readable according to my method.

Let me recapitulate: at about 2000 people from the Levant reach Crete and settle there, introducing the palace administration, including the system of using seals as well as Cretan hieroglyphic as a combination of Luwian hieroglyphic and Egyptian hieroglyphs ...

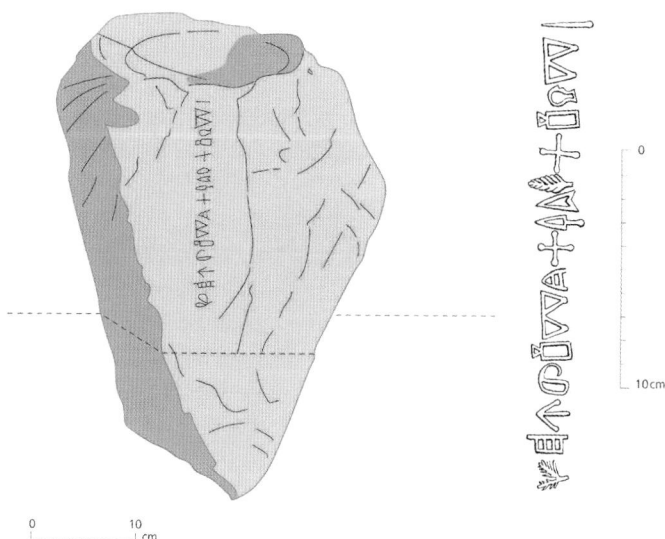

The Malia altar stone inscribed with Cretan hieroglyphic (after Chapouthier 1938).

... after 2000 we find Cretan hieroglyphic inscriptions on seals mentioning the Levantine goddess Ashcrah. At that time, people from the Levant, most likely from the area of Byblos, arrived at the island. I worked on six scarabs and scaraboids from Crete dating to 2000, some of which were clearly locally made, yet they bear Egyptian hieroglyphic inscriptions. So, at the time there were scribes in Crete who understood and wrote Egyptian hieroglyphic. The same is true for the Levant, where we also find scribes writing in a local variant of Egyptian hieroglyphic.

By 1700 the people in Crete introduced a linear script that consisted of a combination of Cretan hieroglyphic signs and signs from the Byblos script. In 1650 it appears that the Hyksos conquered Crete and destroyed the altar stones. Crete then recovered quickly, and its culture reached a zenith between 1550 and 1450 in the form of the Minoan civilization, more precisely Late Minoan IA and IB. At that time, the society on the island was multiethnic and multilingual, but politically united under one king whose palace was at Knossos. The Greeks conquered Crete around 1450, and the first conquerors came from the western Peloponnese; that is, from Pylos. While the Minoans had ruled the sea with their navy, the Greek conquerors came with chariots. We know this because chariots are mentioned in the Linear B documents. They take residence at Knossos but leave Phaistos under the rule of local administrators – these were the two most important palaces at the time. Malia had peaked during the protopalatial period and was not so significant at the time of the new palaces. Kato Zakros, at the far eastern tip of Crete, on the other hand, thrived during the new palatial period. Yet, it was an extension of Knossos, with its port facing the shores of the eastern Mediterranean. With the Greeks reaching Crete at 1450 comes the adaptation of the Linear A script to express Greek language in the form of Linear B, which remained in use until 1350 or even 1200. Mycenae takes over all of Crete after 1350. From then on we find standard Mycenaean-type megaron houses in Crete.

The Linear A documents from Hagia Triada, which are traditionally dated to Late Minoan (LM) IA (c. 1450), contain combinations of two, three or even five personal names, evidently indicating important functionaries who were active at the same time. The same names occur in Linear B texts from Knossos, which must therefore be synchronous with those from Hagia Triada. Yet the archaeological date given to these assemblages is the end of LM IIIA1 (c. 1350), so that they are currently a century apart from their counterpart in Knossos. Obviously, the whole chronology has not been worked out yet.

Looking across the Border

If I counted correctly, you and Jan Best have co-authored two books on today's subject of conversation in the 1980s, and then you produced three single-authored books on the same subject later on. The latest and most substantial one is *Documents in Minoan Luwian, Semitic and Pelasgian* that appeared in 2016. What is the difference between those five books?

Well, the books with Jan Best presented preliminary results. At the time, we started to tackle the subject, I think in a promising way. In *Ancient Scripts from Crete and Cyprus* (1988) we dealt with Cretan scripts in general as well as with Cypro-Minoan – and in *Lost Languages from the Mediterranean* (1989) I also dealt with Etruscan, the Pyrgi tablets and the Lemnos stele. This was all tentative and I continued to work on these subjects. Regarding Cretan hieroglyphic and Linear A, I was able to add a lot in the books which appeared in 2006, 2009 and 2016.

If one wants to get a general overview of the most current research on ancient eastern Mediterranean scripts, the obvious thing to do is to consult Wikipedia. I did this and was surprised to see that most of the research quoted there dates to the time between 1970 and 2000. Virtually nothing is mentioned that has been published since then. Is this a pattern or a chance find?

There was not much going on during the past 20 years. What has been published only repeats existing information – there is nothing new coming out! Most scholars want to focus on Crete and are not willing to look for parallels in Luwian or Egyptian hieroglyphic. Therefore, they are not able to read anything. Even the big names in the fields do not look across the border. They prefer to see Crete in splendid isolation! The approach of looking at Crete as being secluded dates back to Arthur Evans. As we know, some British people would like to see their home turf as an isolated island.

In summary, your recipe to success consisted of determining from which scripts individual signs can be derived?

The recipe for success lies in looking across the border. Scripts do mingle! Wherever we look, we will find scripts that have mingled. In Coptic, Egyptian hieroglyphs are combined with alphabetic signs. Some Medieval inscriptions in Britain even include runic signs within the Latin alphabet. Nevertheless, one should be careful when making these comparisons. First of all, the quality of the work has to be good. Secondly, the results have to be convincing. If I end up reading nonsense, I have gone off in the wrong direction. So much is clear! But using my approach to read Cretan hieroglyphic seals, I find personal names, geographic names and titles. What would you expect to find on seals? Personal names, geographic names and titles! Luwian hieroglyphic seals bear the same information.

Let Atlantis Rest!

And this concludes today's subject. Or is there anything else that you would like to discuss in this context?
There is one more thing that we might want to talk about. I do not know whether you have a problem with this, but I do know that you have your own ideas on the subject – the eruption of Thera and its effects on the people living around the southern Aegean. On the seals I found a standard formula which reads ta_5-ru-$nú$ and can be read phonetically as /*atlunu* /– and that could be taken as an equivalent of the name "Atlantis"! In other words, "Atlantis" is a derivation of /*atlunu*/, with Atlas being at its root. If we read this as an indication that Crete was at some point named "Atlantis," then inevitably Plato's story of the lost continent comes to mind. It may well be that Crete suffered significantly under the consequences of the eruption of Thera, which I place in 1450. I think the tsunami that was triggered by the eruption destroyed the ships in the harbors, and the Mycenaeans from Pylos ultimately took advantage of this weakness and eventually conquered Crete. This scenario basically goes back to the books written in the 1970s by the Irish classicist John Victor Luce, but others, including Spyridon Marinatos, had proposed similar ideas already much earlier.

I think the initial eruption of Thera took place in the spring of 1628.
There is a difficulty though, because Manfred Bietak has found in Tell el-Dab'a, the former Avaris, many pieces of pumice, most probably from the eruption of Thera. This stratum dates to an advanced period of the reign of Thutmose III, that is, 1450.[14] Bietak confirmed this date in a letter he sent me. So, if you date the eruption to 1628 you would lose some 175 years or so. There would be a black hole in the chronology and the Egyptian king lists, and that is a real problem!

Simply put, I only believe the interpretation of such a stratigraphic context when I see it myself. In 40 years of working as a geologist on archaeological sites, in my opinion there have been only few incidents where geological deposits or phenomena were correctly interpreted by archaeologists. If I visited those places in the field, I managed to come up with entirely different and much simpler explanations. Think of the

Fred Woudhuizen is making a point during many hours of conversations.

generations of archaeologists who proclaimed earthquake destructions across Crete, something that is neither geologically possible, because the fault lines are too short for that, nor archaeologically plausible, because in many places destructions occurred selectively. Or think of the tilted stone in the foundation of a building at Amnisos! One slightly tilted stone was proof for Spyridon Marinatos that Minoan Crete suffered a natural calamity.

Okay!

There is a paper describing tsunami deposits from Palaikoastro in eastern Crete [15] – and since this was written by competent scholars, it is often referred to as indisputable evidence for the destructive wave triggered by the eruption of Thera. Those conglomeratic deposits, however, occur at the farthest tip of a promontory which extends way into the sea. What you see there is debris produced by regular wave action and not by a tsunami of any kind. Tsunami deposits are, for instance, individual boulders, weighing a few tons, which have been carried several hundred meters inland. I have spent much time looking for these on the northern coast of Crete and have not found a single one. I have also taken cores from coastal swamps in Crete without finding any unusual deposits. And I inspected all exposed architectural remains of Minoan houses along the northern shore of Crete, and it turns out that they yield no indication of destruction by a massive tidal wave.

The tephra layer from the Minoan eruption is ubiquitously present in the stratigraphy at sites in southwestern Anatolia such as Iasos and Çeşme-Bağlararası, because the wind was moving to the southeast at the time of the outbreak. In my opinion, this is the best region to obtain a relative chronological date for the event. An absolute date may be achieved eventually with dendrochronology. As of today, both of these methods point towards a date between 1640 and 1600.

What is more, I would not even know a mechanism that could have triggered a tsunami. Thera is, of course, today a caldera, but this caldera did not form during the Minoan eruption, it is one hundred thousand years old. For a caldera to collapse, masses of volcanic rock have to be ejected first. Eventually a cavity forms below the cone of the volcano and at some point the cone collapses into this hole. On Thera there is no evidence for tectonic movement accompanying the Minoan eruption. The pumice that was thrown out covers the older surface like a wet tablecloth. If the caldera collapsed after the deposition of the pumice, this beautifully homogenous and bright white tephra deposit would have been massively disturbed. Besides, the multistory houses in Minoan Akrotiri would have been completely wiped out.

Without caldera collapse it is more difficult to explain how a big wave could have formed. The eruption of Krakatoa in 1883 caused such a devastating tsunami that may have been triggered by pyroclastic flows hitting the sea surface. These are currents of hot gas and volcanic material moving at high speed, certainly faster than 100 kilometers per hour. If they hit the sea surface, they can trigger a big wave. In the case of Thera, however, the pyroclastic flows were lighter than water, because pumice floats, and so rather than displacing and pushing the water, they would have slipped on the sea surface.

In my opinion, the eruption of Thera was an extremely impressive natural phenomenon which could be seen from the shores all around the Aegean. For the people living on the island, it had the effect that they had to move elsewhere, since they could not continue to live on Thera. The eruption was evidently not a sudden event, so the people saw what was coming and were able to evacuate the island in time. During excavations on the island of Therasia conducted under the direction of Ferdinand Fouqué in 1867, the skeleton of an old man was found below the Minoan ashes. Evidently this man either did not want or could not escape and thus became an eyewitness of the full-blown eruption; alas, not for very long.

The people who used to live on Thera resettled somewhere else and a sudden increase in population is evident, for instance, on the little island of Mochlos on the northeastern coast of Crete. Obviously, the eruption changed the lives of these individuals, but I do not see an effect on the Minoan kingdom as a whole.

Regarding the date I have drawn attention to sealings found in Akrotiri, Phaistos and Sklavokampo which were made with the same seal, belonging to a named functionary. In Akrotiri the sealing is dated Late Minoan IA, and in Phaistos and Sklavokampo they are dated Late Minoan IB. Scholars working on this item argue that this functionary had a very long life! This is, of course, nonsense. The person may have had his function for 10 or 20 years. This particular item by itself would date Akrotiri to have thrived during Late Minoan IB, that is, c. 1500–1450.

Sealing found in Akrotiri on Thera in a LM IA level and in Phaistos and Sklavokampo in a LM IB level.

So what is the bottom line? What do you think: Atlantis is Crete or Atlantis is Thera?

I think it is Crete! And Thera was part of Crete. The gist of the story is a war and that is paralleled in the legend of Theseus going to Crete to kill the Minotaur. This must have happened before the eruption. Plato recollects how Athens has done a great deed by overcoming the supremacy exerted by a force abroad, and afterwards, natural disasters took place. The Egyptian priests in Plato's account are recollecting how the countries around the eastern Mediterranean were threatened by a major power, and the Greek kings then united their forces in an attempt to overcome this power. Theseus had to go to Knossos because the Greeks were subservient to the Minoan thalassocracy. The latter consisted at the time of Semitic, Luwian and Pelasgian ethnic groups, making up the pivotal force in the trade with Egypt and the Levant. The Minoan influence extended to the north Aegean, including Troy, but also to Sicily and Italy – you find them everywhere! Until eventually, in 1450, the Greeks come in and attack Crete, toppling the aristocratic rulership. We know from the tomb of Rekhmire in Upper Egypt how the originally Minoan dresses of Aegean suppliers were painted over with Mycenaean kilts. So, the takeover in power in Crete may even be reflected in the wall paintings in Egypt.

And you think that this is basically a reflection of the war that is described in the Atlantis account, which would make sense in some way, because both, the wall paintings and the narrative describing Atlantis, came from Egypt.

I think that first the eruption occurred, and then the Greeks took advantage of the weakness of the Minoans. Somehow, they were weakened. Boats may have suffered from ash fall and the trade network may have been disturbed.

I can see all that, and yet I fundamentally disagree. From all we know in history, natural disasters trigger solidarity among people, even amongst enemies, rather than an opportunity to take advantage of the vulnerability. Besides, Plato's Atlantis account clearly puts the military conflict first and attributes all the significance to it. The natural disaster is only mentioned in passing and, quite opposed to conventional wisdom, it is Greece, above all, who suffers from the calamities. Atlantis is only said to have disappeared "in like manner."[16]

In addition, Plato provides so many details which cannot be accommodated with a conflict between Greece and Crete. Take, for instance, the location of Atlantis at some narrow straits – no such thing exists with respect to Crete. If one passed through those straits, Plato says, an entire sea would open behind them, and this sea was called Pontus, which is, of course, the name of the Black Sea. With respect to the war, Plato mentions 1200 ships, equivalent to the 1186 ships accounted for by Homer to have taken part in the Trojan War. There is no indication that a united Greek army was involved in the conquering of Crete; but we do know, if we believe Homer, that Greek forces united in the fight against Troy. There are so many other things that Troy and Atlantis have in common, including, for instance, a pair of hot and cold springs, prevailing strong northern winds, traces of an artificial port system, a peculiar type of bull sacrifices at the palace. If one wants to see a historic source for Plato's account, I still set my chips on Troy.

The beauty of your work on the earliest Cretan scripts, however, is that it finally leads to a coherent explanation of what has been going on in Minoan Crete, one that has been lacking for a very long time. **Yes, indeed, the destruction of Knossos is still wavering between 1450 and 1200, and everything in between!**

Clearly there is a need to overcome the lack of synoptic reconstructions of Cretan culture in the second millennium. One can only hope that someone will soon present an up-to-date comprehensive summary.

Interview conducted on August 7, 2020.

The Lasting Success of Luwian Hieroglyphic

Luwian hieroglyphic has been known for 200 years. The decipherment was incremental. A bilingual inscription at last. Different ways of transcription. An Old Reading, a New Reading, and an Adjusted Old Reading. The mystery of the large "Beyköy 2" inscription. A sign indicating forgery appears in the real world. Türkmen-Karahöyük and the question of its dating.

The topic of our conversation today is Luwian writing and language between 2000 and 700. Let's first talk about the research history in particular during the nineteenth century, at a time when scholars did not yet know how to read Luwian documents.
The first stones with Luwian inscriptions recorded by a western scholar were in Hama, on the Orontes river in northern Syria. The Swiss ethnographer Johann Ludwig Burckhardt saw them in 1812 and made a note in his journal. The stones were eventually retrieved from the building walls in 1872 and then taken to Istanbul where they are still on display in the Archaeological Museum.

Between those two dates much has happened, Hattusa was first seen by a European in 1834 and its "discovery" made a big splash in western Europe. How were the Luwian signs interpreted at the time when they could not be read?
Not at all! The first person who worked on the Luwian hieroglyphs was Archibald Sayce. He examined the Tarkondemos seal and recognized the determinative for "land." So obviously a place-name was mentioned in the seal. Sayce also correctly identified the triangle as the sign for "king."

The seal was purchased around 1850 in Smyrna. It contains a Luwian hieroglyphic and a cuneiform inscription that has been reinterpreted a few times over as Luwian hieroglyphs became better known. What is the most current translation?

The problem is that the person's name contains a sign with an animal head, and some experts have interpreted this to be a donkey head. In that case, the name reads *TARKASNA-wa*. In my opinion, it is a goat head, because it has a beard, a very distinctive beard – and then it becomes a different sign. The inscription then reads *TARKU-wa*, which is a shorthand variant of the royal name Tarkuntimuwa. Since the inscription is bilingual, it also contains the name in Akkadian cuneiform as ᵐ*Tar-qu-u-tim-me*. The name of the land is also given; it is Mira. Hence, we are dealing with the king of Mira, the same king we know from the Karabel inscription.

The Tyszkiewicz seal bears Luwian hieroglyphic signs, reflecting the high level of artistry that must have once existed in Luwian lands.

Then, in 1900, the first edition of Leopold Messerschmidt's *corpus* appeared – a compendium of all documents. What was its impact on the field?

As a collection of all the texts known at that time it is still important, even today; 32 major and 29 minor inscriptions were initially known. I am still using Messerschmidt's *corpus*. If I want to check the relevant texts, it makes sense to go back to the first drawing.

After Bedřich Hrozný deciphered the Hittite language in 1915, Emil Forrer managed to recognize eight languages altogether in the cuneiform documents from Hattusa.

Interestingly the languages are also mentioned by their names in the cuneiform tablets. So, there are many references to the main language *nešili*, designating what we now call Hittite, but was then named after the town Nesa. Then there is *pabili* for Akkadian or Babylonian. Forrer also saw that the scribes wrote in *hattili*, the language of the Hattian population who had already lived in the region long before the Hittites arrived, as well as in *hurlili*, the language of the eastern neighbors, the Hurrians. *Luwili*, the language of the Luwians, characterizes an ancient culture of the same name going back to the Bronze Age.

The Hittites did not call themselves "Hittites"; the people whom we now call Mycenaeans would never have considered themselves "Mycenaeans," neither would the Minoans think of themselves under such a name. Nonetheless, in Egyptian hieroglyphic they are indeed referred to as *Keftiu* and *Mnws*. Only the Luwians were called and considered "Luwians" all along.

The name *lu-wi-ya* that appears in the documents in Hattusa is, however, eventually replaced by "Arzawa."

Yes indeed, Luwiya is certainly another name for Arzawa. Still, it may have been a designation for a land that stretched more towards the east to include, for instance, the Konya region. We do not really know, since we are beyond the borders of the Hittite kingdom. In any case, Luwiya may have been more of an ethnic or language designation, whereas Arzawa was a kingdom or political state.

Did the Greeks refer to the Luwians at all?

Yes, they did! In Linear B we find, alongside *mi-ra* "Mira," the term *ru-wa-ni-jo,* which is likely to indicate Luwiya. And also in Egyptian texts *R/Luwana* is mentioned in the mortuary temple of Amenhotep III in Kom el-Hetan on the west bank of the Nile. The pharaoh provides three names which all refer to western Asia Minor: Arzawa, Assuwa and Luwana – people from all three regions are actually depicted as captives.

Emil Forrer also realized that the documents from Hattusa included texts written in the non-Indo-European Hattian language of the indigenous ancient Anatolian people.

Oğuz Soysal recently wrote a whole book about Hattic, but it is still difficult to interpret the texts, because we have so little information about them.

Two Forms of Luwian

If we summarize what is currently known about Luwian, one of the most remarkable things might be that it was written over a long period in two different scripts.

Don't forget Lycian and Lydian were written in alphabetic script, so Luwian was recorded in three different scripts. But the alphabetic Luwian, of course, occurs only during the Iron Age. Luwian hieroglyphic started around 2000 and continues until 700, and Luwian cuneiform was written from the sixteenth through the fourteenth century.

And the cuneiform Luwian that has been transmitted consists mostly of obscure incantation rites?

The documents are indeed ritual texts that are sometimes badly preserved, but the missing parts can be extrapolated since there is so much repetition. In an article for *Talanta* in 2017, I talked about the Luwian cuneiform documents we know today. The majority of the texts are in Kizzuwatna Luwian. Still, we also have the songs of Istanuwa, a city in the Sakarya basin, where Hapalla is situated – and Hapalla is one of the Arzawa lands. Thus, the Istanuwa songs tell us something about the language of Arzawa.

What do they tell us?

We can reconstruct the paradigm of how the words were reflected, the verbal forms they used etc. Cuneiform Luwian is common Luwian, but there is a distinction in my opinion, since we have, for example, the plural in cuneiform Luwian with the ending *-nzi*, nominative plural – and in hieroglyphic Luwian we get *-i* for the same ending. So the languages are very close to each other but there is a distinction perhaps comparable to High German and colloquial German. Cuneiform Luwian is high Luwian and Luwian hieroglyphic is colloquial Luwian.

What can you say about loanwords?

Concerning the Luwian hieroglyphic, it is interesting that after the collapse of the Empire, in the earliest phase of the Early Iron Age, we see many Hittite loanwords – very distinctive Hittite words in Luwian hieroglyphic. People who were part of the Hittite kingdom went south to northern Syria and Kizzuwatna to settle there, and they had some influence on the Luwian hieroglyphic vocabulary. Also, the names of the kings of the Neo-Hittite states are predominantly Hittite, such as a form of Suppiluliuma or Mursili – a continuation of Hittite royal names.

Before 1200 Hittite kings may have had Luwian names.
Muwatalli is a Luwian name for a Hittite king. There are many Luwian words in Hittite.

And there are also Hurrian loanwords emphasizing the Mesopotamian influence towards the end of the Hittite kingdom.
Yes, you know, of course, that at Yazılıkaya the deities bear names in Hurrian: Tessup, Hebat etc.

Writing was introduced in Hattusa by Hattusili I in the middle of the seventeenth century.
It was a concept that he imported from north Syria. We have to distinguish between different phases. In the Kültepe-Kanesh period, old Assyrian was used. After that, we get a phase of illiteracy and then Hattusili introduced writing again presumably from the Alalakh and Aleppo region in north Syria.

I find it fascinating that the same script was used for eight languages simultaneously.
At the same time, during the thirteenth century, we have in Ugarit several different scripts and languages, as is evident from the documents. It just was a very cosmopolitan style of life. In addition to Akkadian cuneiform there is the Ugaritic alphabet, then there are Luwian hieroglyphs, texts in Hurritic and even texts in Cypro-Minoan.

Step by Step towards a Decipherment

The decipherment of Luwian hieroglyphic happened over a long period of time, beginning with Archibald Sayce, as you said before, and then it continued ...

Ignace Gelb was the first one to make progress towards the decipherment in 1931. And after that we get Emil Forrer, Helmuth Bossert and Bedřich Hrozný. This all happened within a few years between 1931 and 1936. Gelb recognized, for instance, the word *a-i-a-* "to make."

They also had the determinative for personal names which helped finding values. A few personal names and place-names sufficed to derive some 20 to 30 values. Then Emil Forrer came along. He knew the Luwian language from his extensive work on the cuneiform tablets. Consequently, he became the first scholar who could read a whole section of the text: the "curse formula" that occurs at the end of many inscriptions. It says something like: "Whoever destroys this monument shall be punished by the gods!" Forrer first identified a part saying, "be it king or lord, be it prince or nobleman." As early as 1933 he read this phrase in every detail – and his reading is still valid today.

By the end of the 1930s many of the logograms had been identified …
… and many sound values. I think up to 40 sound values for those syllable-signs were already correctly identified before the war.

But also many mistakes were made, hampering the progress.
Yes, of course, one always makes mistakes in this kind of pioneering work. It was Piero Meriggi who was able to distinguish between the good and bad readings. He came up with a list of what worked – and simply left out what did not work. In the 1960s Meriggi produced a whole *corpus*, but he used his own system of transliteration, one that was closer to cuneiform. Nobody uses this anymore except for his former student Massimo Poetto. Meriggi's attempt at translation of the texts, however, was a little bit premature.

And then right after the war Karatepe was found in 1946 …
… and this discovery, of course, changed the whole ball game, because people then had a very long text in which they could read entire phrases thanks to the Phoenician version. But it was not so easy either because the Phoenician was not well known. This is the longest Phoenician text ever found. It brought a lot of new information to be digested even for the scholars working on Phoenician. Yet Karatepe was an important milestone. Then the texts from Ugarit came along; Emmanuel Laroche published these in the 1950s. Laroche made a wonderful book listing all

the Luwian signs and assigning them the numbers we still use today. He introduced French words for the logograms.

It was really the work of David Hawkins with the publication of the *corpus* of Iron Age texts in 2000 which made it possible to read all the texts including Karatepe in a robust way, thanks to the excellent photographs and drawings. There is little discussion about the Karatepe text today, because it is very well known. We have the bilingual version and everybody can read it today. You can have differences in interpretation for a not bilingual text, but the Karatepe text is very well founded.

I began as a student of Philo Houwink ten Cate in the 1980s, and at the time Philo said: "Wait till you do this or that, because the *corpus* is coming out!" But we had to wait until 2000, since it was David Hawkins's personal long-time project. He is not using computers and has been carrying the manuscript all over the world. It never got lost.

Why Not Read Luwian?

And now we are waiting for the *corpus* of the Bronze Age inscriptions to appear. You and David Hawkins are probably the two scholars who have dedicated more time than anybody else to the scrutiny of Luwian hieroglyphic. You have been using quite different approaches in this pursuit. Hawkins's approach became the standard, whereas yours is not being employed by anyone else. Obviously, we need to talk about this! You deviate from the standard in two ways; let us first speak about why you use the Luwian expressions for values, rather than Latin ones like everybody else. In 1996 Craig Melchert published a list of 77 Luwian determinatives, their meaning and their Latin transcriptions. If we take this list as a reasonably sized selection, can you say for how many of the signs we know the Luwian pronunciation?

For about 90 percent. The short message is: at today's level of knowledge there is not much need to use Latin terms for the transcription, because we know for over 90 percent of the words how they were pronounced in Luwian. In my book *Selected Luwian Hieroglyphic Texts – The Extended Version*, published in 2011, I provided a full list of the concordance. It yields all the numbers together with the values I am using and my colleagues' values.

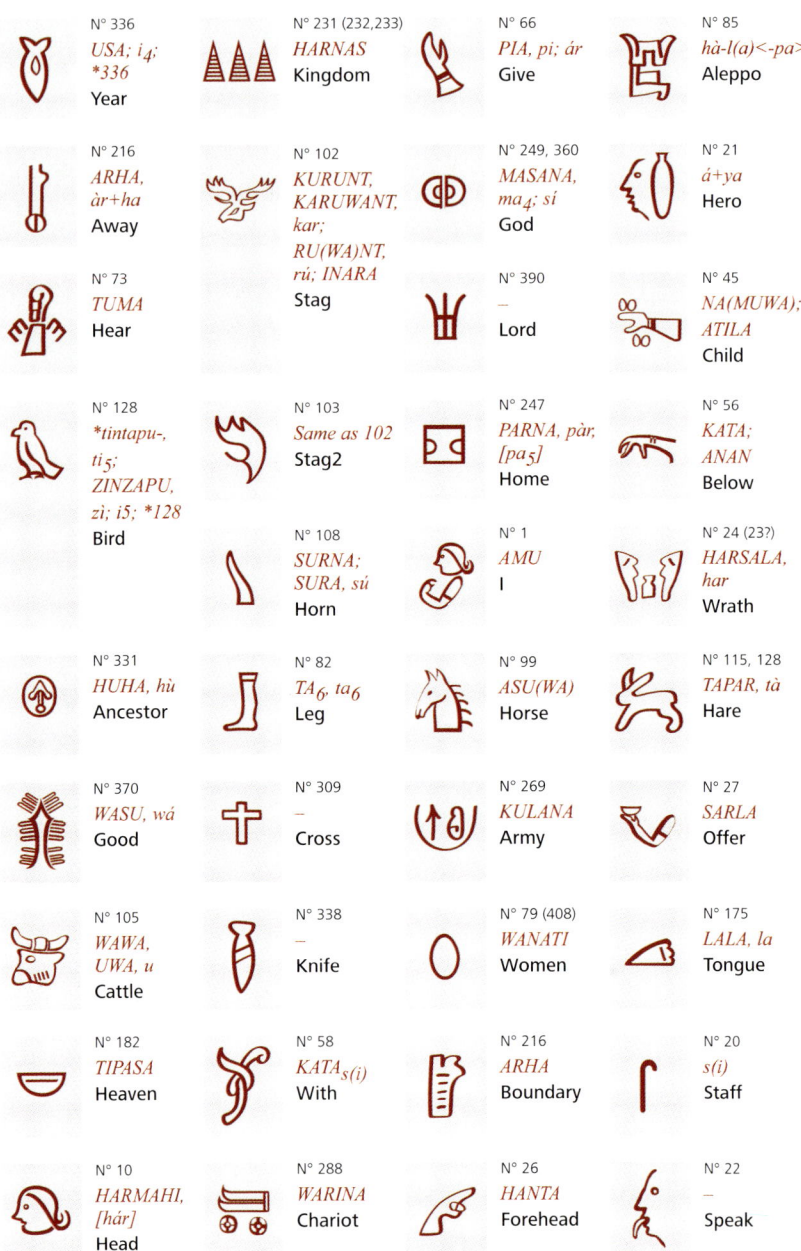

Craig Melchert provided this list of Luwian logograms in 1996 together with their Latin terms used in transcriptions. The chart shows that for almost all signs the original Luwian term (red italics) is known. Thus, there is little need to employ Latin words in the transcription of these determinatives.

THE LASTING SUCCESS OF LUWIAN HIEROGLYPHIC • 81

N° 193 *ARMA* Moon	N° 379 *APAMI*, a_5 West	N° 39 *TA*, *ta* Fist	N° 201 *TASKUWAR (LBA)*; *PÁTA* Land
N° 336 *URA*, *ur* Great	N° 366 *TANAMI* All	N° 228 *UTNA*, tu_5 Kingdom	N° 298 *ASATAR*; *WASA* Throne
N° 280 *WALA*, wa_5 Hammer	N° 192 *KISATAMI* East	N° 17 *HANTAWAT*; *HÁSU* King	N° 199 *ARMA* Thunder
N° 368 *ATUWALI (LBA)* Bad	N° 11 (518) *HAWA*, ha_4 Sheep	N° 80 *SARU+r+má* Sarruma	N° 225 *UMINA*, *um* City
N° 59 (44?, 60) *ASATAR* Hand	N° 181 *TURPI*, $[tu_6]$; pa_4 Bread	N° 268 *HUI*, *hù* Chisel	N° 341 *vas*; *ZARZA* Vase
N° 207 *WANTI*, wa_4 Mountain	N° 90 *TIWA*, *ti*; *PATA* Foot	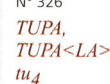 N° 326 *TUPA*, *TUPA<LA>*, tu_4 Clerk	N° 447 + 26 *TAWIAN*; na_5 Toward
N° 332a *NAWA*, na_4 Neg(ative)	N° 93 *TIWA*, *ti*; *PATA* Foot 2	N° 190 *TIWATA*, ti_6 Sun	N° 221 *HARWAN* Road
N° 332b, 332c *NAWA*, na_4 Neg_2, Neg_3	N° 65 *TUWA*, *tù* Put	N° 299 *ASA(NU)*, a_4 Seat	N° 160 *WIANA*, *wi*; *TUWARSA* Wine
	N° 34 *APA(NA)* After	 N° 267 *WANA*, wa_9 Stela	N° 313, 321 *ZITI*, *zí* Man
N° 300 *NA(MUWA)-HASU-ti4* Descendant	N° 14 (13) *PÁRANA* Before	N° 70 *SARA* Above	N° 200 *TARHA* Strength

What is the advantage of using Luwian values? How can it take you any further than if you are using Latin words?

Let's take, for example, my recent contribution to the proceedings of the European Association of Archaeologists' conference in Berne; the session you co-hosted. I spoke about how during the Late Bronze Age the biggest kingdom in western Asia Minor was addressed with different names at different times. It is well known under the name of Arzawa. The name is spelt with an eagle head, sign number *131. If you read this sign with the Latin word *avis*, it is difficult to recognize any combinations, because you have that particular sound in your mind. If, on the other hand, you work with the actual Luwian values of the sign, it becomes "ARA, ar, ra" – and you see that it is followed by the syllabi *sà* and *wa*. Then you can easily read the name *ar-sà-wa* "Arzawa" for the country. If you have *avis* in your head, you will not be able to see it: AVIS-*sà-wa* just makes no sense!

If I understand you correctly, Luwian hieroglyphic works much like a rebus – a puzzle consisting of pictures representing syllables and words. As such the letter *h* and the icon for an ear might be read as: "hear" or "here." If, however, you combine the letter *h* with the Latin word for ear, which is *auris*, the word would become "hauris" – and that would make no sense whatsoever.

Exactly! It is impossible to understand how the language works if you use Latin words for the transcription. In deciphering documents that are over 3000 years old, we need every bit of information that we can get – it's a real fight to obtain every Luwian sound value one can possibly get out of a text. Only if you do, you are able to read more and understand the texts better. Using Latin in this process is as if you pull a screen or a curtain in front of a window: you might be able to guess what is concealed behind the screen, but you're not able to see it clearly. Using Latin will deteriorate one's understanding of what is written in the text. Luwian hieroglyphic was written in word-signs, or logograms, where one sign stands for one word, such as "king" or "country" – and in syllable-signs, or syllabograms, where the sign stands for a syllable that is used to spell out a word. Sometimes, only the logogram was written, sometimes only the syllabogram – but many times they were both written together. So in Luwian the sign for house, number *247, might be followed by the syllables *pa+r-na*. This simply indicates that a house was called *parna* in Luwian. According to the current standard, the term is transcribed as *domus*, the Latin word for house, which quite frankly makes no sense. We have to use the syllabic cases to understand how the determinatives are formatted.

In ancient languages we find a lot of use of the acrophonic principle – and this has been routinely exploited in successful decipherings. The acrophonic principle entails that the phonetic value of a symbol is the first letter or syllable of the name of that symbol. Hence, if Luwian scribes wanted to use the sign for "house" for a syllable, they would simply write ⌂ to indicate the syllable *pàr*. If one transcribes this Luwian sign with *domus*, it won't take you anywhere. Believe me, I have a lot of cases like that! This is how the system works: the logograms and the syllabograms are tightly connected. Determinatives are not separate from the syllabary; they work together!

Could you give some more examples to show where your approach takes you further than the method currently used by other scholars working with Luwian hieroglyphs?
Some documents in western Asia Minor are connected with water basins, such as the long inscription at Yalburt – or Karakuyu, more towards the west in the district of Kayseri, which is associated with a sluice. In those inscriptions a combination occurs which I read MALIA-WAIA based on the Luwian meaning of the logograms – and this means "sacred water." So there's a connection between the object – that is, the water – and the inscription. One can call this an object bilingual – the object appears in the inscription as one might expect.

And if you transcribe that using Latin words, where would that take you?
Well, David Hawkins reads something completely different – he sees "the hunter" in it and thinks it's the title of a great king!

Why then are your colleagues not listening to your arguments?
In 1998, during a meeting on the island of Procida in the Gulf of Naples, they established a standard. I fully understand that to furnish a scientific discussion it makes sense to work from a standard if it already exists. In that way, people understand each other. The standard, however, is not a goal in itself, it is a vehicle to help us comprehend Luwian. If the

opportunity arises another standard would help us better understand Luwian hieroglyphic inscriptions, I think we should switch to this new standard. Because it's only a tool – and there's always a chance that a better tool lurks around the corner. But the colleagues are not willing to change!

I think what might help though is if you would show many graphic examples to illustrate how your reading works well and where the current standard does not deliver equally good results. From what I know you have already done that in your publications a few times, but those examples are quite distributed. It might be helpful to put all the evidence in one place.
Hm. The fact is, if you don't use the current standard, then you are a little bit of an outcast. It gives the others a reason not to read your papers in the first place.

Would it be possible that the current standard of transcription using Latin words is hampering progress in Luwian studies?
I'd certainly think so. It is very simple – if you have Luwian words and sounds in your head, you will better recognize a Luwian text than if you have the Latin vocabulary and sounds in your head.

Some Signs Are Polyphonic

We mentioned earlier during this conversation that there is a second aspect where your approach to transcription deviates from the standard. The discoverer of the Karatepe bilingual, Helmuth Bossert, in 1960, during the last year of his life and even posthumously, published three papers in which he indicated that Luwian hieroglyphic might not be fully understood.
Yes, he did! He spoke about one pair of signs, number *376 and *377, which were both read at the time as *i* – with a short and a long sound.

Bossert himself felt that the deciphering was not entirely correct. And then not too much later, David Hawkins, Anna Morpurgo-Davies and Günter Neumann – three highly distinguished scholars – picked up the argument and presented a new standard for the transcription which has ever since then been called the New Reading. They basically said that the symbols *376 and *377 should not be read *i*, instead they should be read *zi* and *za* – and this would apply every single time when they occur.

The idea sprang up after Emmanuel Laroche had found Urartian words written in Luwian hieroglyphic, where he argued the signs must indicate a sibilant. You will get quite another reading if you read *zi* instead of *i*.

Those were units for measuring volume ...
Yep! The word was *terusi* – which is written with an *s* and not with a *z*, but still it produces a sibilant. This is how the argument began. And then Hawkins, Morpurgo-Davies and Neumann worked it out by using *zi* and *za*. What they did at the time was very smart and indeed needed! Because the signs are used as *zi* and *za*. Unfortunately, they neglected to present a list of cases where the reading as *zi* and *za* is certainly correct.

You made such a list!
Yes, I was the first to come up with such a list, which is a little bit strange. Every time a new name was found to confirm the New Reading, they went like: "Hurray, the New Reading is confirmed!" This was true, for instance, when the name **Kuzi**tesup was first identified in 1986. There certainly is new evidence coming up all the time for the *zi* and *za* reading.

It was, after all, an ingenious move that advanced the discipline. Many people say that it kind of opened the flood gates for more progress in Luwian studies, because finally texts could be read correctly.
Well, that is a little bit of an exaggeration! Many occurrences of those signs are in endings, and if you read *-nzi* for the plural nominative – or *-i*: it is still the plural nominative. So we can understand the text no matter how. In the grammatical paradigm, in most cases, it does not matter at all for the function.

Hawkins argued that in the Late Bronze Age sign *376 can be *zi* and *za* as well, because there was no separate sign for *za*. In the Early Iron Age, however, *377 was used as a distinct sign for *za*.

At some point you began to argue that this interpretation is indeed correct. Still, it is not the complete truth, since you realized that the Old Reading (*i*), introduced by Helmuth Bossert and his colleagues, is still valid in some cases. The sign is thus polyphonic – an idea that was also already expressed by Bossert.

Yes! There are cases where the Old Reading generates a word, but the New Reading doesn't. It is as simple as that. For example, if you mention a place-name that you read as *zarhanua*, you will not find it mentioned in any other text. If, on the other hand, you read it *irhanua*, it becomes clear since *nua* is the word for "new" and *irha* for "border." So the place-name simply means "new border." As *irha* is Hittite, this is a good example of a Hittite loanword in an Early Iron Age text.

Would you have some more examples like this?
Let's take a personal name: If you read *mazikárhuha*, it has no meaning. If, on the other hand, you read *maikárhuha*, you'll find that *mai* means "great" in Luwian while *kárhuha* is the name of a god. So the name means "Kárhuha is great." It is totally clear!

Another example: Hittite texts mention a religious functionary called *minalla*, which is probably a handler of some sort, like an altar handler, since **men-* is the root for "to handle." The reading of the Luwian word as I propose it results in *miinala* – equivalent to the Hittite term. The New Reading, however, produces *mizinala* – a word that has no parallel. It has been suggested that *mizinala* is a mixer, somebody who mixes things, since it would rest on the Indo-European verb **meiḱ-* for "to mix." This is a possibility, but there is no parallel for it in any Hittite or Luwian text from Anatolia.

Where it really gets tough is when you look at the name Azatiwata, the regent of the king in the Karatepe text, which is, of course, a bilingual. In Phoenician it is written *'ztwd* – in which the *z* appears, thereby apparently verifying the New Reading. And yet, the sign in the form of the bishop's staff ʃ (*378; LITUUS) appears in the Luwian version of the name. The advocates of the New Reading then decided to take the LITUUS sign out of the name to put it in front of it, translating it as (LITUUS)*á-za-ti-wa/i-tà-ia-* (Azatiwataya). But the LITUUS is attached to the first sign, *á*, and if the Luwians attached one sign to another, it must be read in second position. So the correct order is *Á-LITUUS* … and then it goes on.

Right page: Chart indicating the effect of the Old Reading, New Reading and Adjusted Old Reading (proposed by Fred Woudhuizen) on reading Luwian hieroglyphic.

Sign	N°	Old Reading (Laroche 1960)	New Reading (Hawkins, Morpurgo-Davies, Neumann 1973)	Adjusted Old Reading (Woudhuizen 2011)	Examples where the New Reading works well	Examples where the New Reading does not work	Examples where the Adjusted Old Reading works well
←	*376	*i*	*zi*	*i/zi*	hi-la+(i)-**zi** (Hillarizzi) Ku-**zi**-tešub-pa (Kuzitesup) Mi-**zi**-r(i) (Egypt) á-**zi**-yà (Aziya) **zi**-m+r(i)-pa-lu (Zimribēlu) ha-**zi**-ï (Hazziya)	**zi**-ku-wa-na (Konya) a-**zi**-ya (to make) ar-ná-li-**zi** (Arnili) ma-**zi**-ká+r-hu-ha- mi-**zi**-na-la- etc. all without parallel	**i**-ku-wa-na (Konya) a-**i**-a (to make) ar-ná-li-**i** (Arnili) ma-**i**-ká+r-hu-ha- (CL *māya/i-* "great") mi-**i**-na-la- (Hit. ᴸᵁ*minalla*- religious functionary)
←//	*377	*ī*	*za*	*ī/zā*	**zā**+r-**zā** (heart) (Kültepe texts *zarza*-) ha-**za**+-ā)-na- (governor) URA(+r)-**za**- (great) **za**-pa- (to sacrifice) ta+r-**z**a-**za** (Terrusa) **zā**- "tnis" (CL *za*-) in princ ple possible	**za**+r-ha-nu-a (LITUUS)á-**za**-ti-wa/i-tà-ia- (Azatiwataya) *378 LITUUS unexplained	**ī**+r-ha-nu-a (Hit. *irha*- "border") á+s(i)-**ī** (CL ᵈ*Assiya* love goddess) ha-pa-**ī**-nú-wa- (Lyc. *χbai*- "to irrigate") TARHUNT-hu-**ī**-sa (Lyc. *Tarqqiz*) **ī**(à)- "this" (CL *iya* "these") Genitive plural -Ca-**ī** (Lycian *-ãi*, Lydian *-ai*)
⌒	*209	*a*	*i*	*a*	**i**-pi-na-á (Ibniya) **i**-la-n≀ (Ilanu) **i**-ni-TEŠUP-pa (Initesup) ma-sa-hú-**i**-l+u-wa (Mashuiluwas)	**i**-la-pa (Aleppo) **i**-ma-tu (Hamath) **i**+r-TEŠUP (Hurr. Aritesip) **i**-ru-na- "sea" (Hit. *aruna*-) Yariri	**a**-la-pa (Aleppo) **a**-ma-tu (Hamath) **a**+r(i)-TEŠUP (Hurr. Aritesip) **a**-ru-na- "sea" (Hit. *aruna*-) **a**-ara-**a**+r(a)- (Araras = "eagle man") IE *ara*- "eagle"
⌒⸗	*210	*ā*	*ia*	*ā*	*Ehliy***a** *Maziy***a**		Insignificant if following *i* as this is often the case, e.g. *a-i-a-* or *a-i-ā*- "to make"

How do you read the name then?

The LITUUS has a value – the sibilant is expressed through it, as further underlined by its interchange with *25 sa_8, and thus the reading is *á+s(i)*. Then we ought to read the following sign *377 as *-ī-*, so we get *á+s(i)-ī-*, which is closely paralleled by *Asia*, the goddess of love, and it means "to be loved." The king's name is thus Asiatiwata, "Beloved by the Sun God." Of course, there are exact parallels in cuneiform Luwian.

When you talk about them, I must admit that these explanations become very clear and convincing. Still, as I'm not a linguist, I often find your arguments unfathomable in your publications.

Those things are not easy to understand; I worked on this for 40 years.

Let's hear some more examples!

Take another personal name: Arnili (*ar-ná-li-i*) – it also has a parallel in cuneiform. But if you interpret it as *ar-ná-li-zi*, then there is no name in all we know from Hittite and Luwian texts like that. It does not exist! Sign *376 thus must be read as *i* in this case.

Or take the place-name *ikuwana* for Ikónion in the classical period and Konya today. You have to read the first sign as *i*, since *zikuwana* is simply not known to have been a name of any place. – It is the same story over and over again!

Concerning grammar it is very important that the genitive plural is certainly in **-a-i** or *-a-ī* and not in *-zi* or *-za*, because we have parallels in both Lycian and Lydian, where the genitive plural is *-ai*. Hence, the parallels between Luwian, Lycian and Lydian become immediately clear. You cannot read it otherwise!

No Sign for i Anymore

The New Reading deals not just with one pair but actually with two pairs of signs.

The real problem with the New Reading is that there are cases where the Old Reading remains convincing and clear, so the solution must be more complicated than has been suggested. If the signs *376 and *377 are always read as *zi* and *za*, there is no sign for *i* anymore! And this is indeed the Achilles' heel of the New Reading. Hawkins himself argued in his publications that it is a "basically improbable assumption" that Luwians only knew two vowels.[17] To compensate for the missing vowel *i*, it was therefore decided that sign *209 should not be read as *a* anymore (since there are other signs for *a*) but as *i* instead, so that it becomes the third vowel. Quite frankly, this makes no sense. Because we get the situation that *209, which I still read as *a*, interchanges freely with sign *19 *á* and sign *450 *à*. So there can be no doubt that *209 is indeed *a* and not *i* – you cannot make it *i*.

When you say it interchanges, it means that two different signs can be used alternatingly in one and the same place? For instance, in modern Greek the sound value of i and o can be produced with different letters.
Yes, indeed. If you have for example -*ha*, which means "and," the Luwians sometimes wrote it with *209 and sometimes with *450 *à* (-*ha*-*209/ -*ha*-*à*) – thereby making it extra clear that those signs must be read in any case with the value *a*.

And this has supposedly tremendous consequences!
This is deadly for the New Reading as we know it! It is simply not possible to read the script correctly with this transcription.
 Hawkins suggested a work-around that he hopes would compensate for the error. Sign *450 (*à*) has a diacritical mark on top – like a grave accent. Hawkins's approach consists of leaving out the letter *a* and its value completely, so that only the diacritical mark is left. For him, -*ha*-*à* must be read -*ha*-`, to rob the sign from its *a* quality. He even goes one step further and in the case of *209 (his *i*) transliterates -*ha*[i], with *i* in superscript as if it is almost not there! From my perspective, this is going one step too far: it is not tolerable anymore. Needless to say, the enclitic †-*hai* "and" does not exist in Luwian.

I saw that you used the Luwian spelling for Aleppo as an example, but wasn't the town called Halpa at the time?
No, there were two forms: ***a-la-pa*** and *halpa*. The latter is the Hittite Indo-European Anatolian form beginning with a *h*, whereas *a-la-pa* is the Old Indo-European form. In Indo-European the word is reconstructed as *h_2elb^h- – which always results in *alpa* – and never in *ilpa*. The latter possibility is simply excluded. From this root, by the way, the Alps got their name as well.

The same applies to ***a***-*ma-tu* for the town Hamath?
Yes, if you would read ***i***-*ma-tu* it would be without parallels in any other texts.

How about the personal name Aritesup?
There is a parallel in Hurritic for Aritesup, which means "Tessup has given" – much like Apollodorus in Greek means "the gift of Apollo." It is a typical theophoric name. But Irtesup does not exist at all.

Take the Indo-European root *ara*, for instance – the word for eagle. In Hittite, the word for eagle is *haran-* with a laryngeal sound. Hawkins does not give it the syllabic value and just transcribes it with the Latin word for bird: AVIS. So you never get to recognize the name Arzawa, as we said earlier. Moreover, the name *Araras* is specified in Luwian texts as the eagle man, which makes no sense in the New Reading *Yariri*.

Sign *209 comes in a pair with *210 of which the New Reading says that it should be read as *ia* or *ya*, whereas the Old Reading transcribed it with a long sounding *ā*.
There are a lot of cases where *210 is following an *i*. I argue that it is a long *a*; but if you say it must be *ya* that is easy to argue, because the *a* often follows after the glide *y*. It is thus mostly irrelevant.

If we summarize this discussion, where would you say Luwian studies stand today, and what needs to be done to make a big leap forward? Obviously, we need more inscriptions …
Let's take the Late Bronze Age inscriptions, for example: virtually all scholars complain that they are very badly known and understood. So researchers have a problem with them, but if you do what we have just discussed – putting in the Luwian values, the determinatives and the logograms – in other words, if you use the Adjusted Old Reading, you can read those texts. It is not very difficult, there are endings, not in every instance, but enough to use them. I was even able to reconstruct the grammatical paradigm for the Bronze Age texts; that is all possible!

From your perspective the case is clear cut: we need a new method for the reading!
I think that the New Reading as it stands today will not last. Call me overconfident, but I don't believe it can survive. If you live a lie, it will

not last. There will be somebody else, maybe in 20 years, who will say that this replacing of *a* with *i* must be wrong, because it contradicts the facts. If something contradicts the facts, it will not last. I believe in science.

It is remarkable that for many years I have been the only one who has scrutinized and discussed the pros and cons of the New Reading. Everybody is taking it for granted, but as scientists, we have to question the paradigms to determine whether they work or not. Everyone in the field can make a list with the words where the New Reading works and where it doesn't. It may be considered untouchable today, but it cannot last. I strongly believe in this.

Recent Finds – Questionable and Unquestionable Ones

We ought to discuss another issue in this context. Not too long ago, in 2018, a particular case regarding the Luwians made headlines in which we were both involved. To recapitulate what happened: I had the opportunity to obtain documents from the estate of the famous English prehistorian James Mellaart (1925–2012) which he had marked as being of particular importance. I met James Mellaart's son and only heir Alan Mellaart in his parents' former apartment in North London and I obtained a pile of about 500 sheets of paper consisting of unpublished manuscripts. The lion share of this material dealt with something James Mellaart had dubbed the "Beyköy text." According to James Mellaart's elaborate descriptions of the research history, this document provided English translations of cuneiform tablets which were found in the second half of the nineteenth century in western Asia Minor. During further scrutiny of Mellaart's study a few months later, I found indisputable evidence that the famous archaeologist had fabricated all this material from scratch.

Among the documents were also a number of sheets dealing with several Luwian hieroglyphic inscriptions of which James Mellaart possessed copies in the form of drawings. One of these inscriptions was extremely long; the drawing covered four sheets of A4-sized paper and the original document on stone must have been almost 30 meters long. James Mellaart related how this document had been found in 1878 by peasants from the village of Beyköy, from where William Ramsay had indeed reported a small Luwian inscription in 1884. When I had received these drawings, I scanned them and sent them to you for your perusal. You suggested calling the largest text "Beyköy 2," counting Ramsay's inscription as "Beyköy 1." Now that we know that James Mellaart had actually fabricated the alleged translation of cuneiform documents, it is more than likely that the entire elaborate story he provided about retrieving the hieroglyphic documents and their subsequent research history is also invented. What is more, we cannot be sure that the drawings of Luwian hieroglyphic inscriptions found in Mellaart's estate are based on genuine documents. Most scholars will regard them as forgeries unless further evidence for their authenticity comes to light.

Once again, you might be the only person in the world who believes that the drawing of "Beyköy 2," as it was found in James Mellaart's office, is indeed based on a genuine Late Bronze Age document. Please tell me why you think so!

Well, it was, of course, a critical moment for me when you told me via video call that you had discovered proof of forgery in Mellaart's study. You had found the tool kit that Mellaart needed to compose the elaborate alleged translations. At this point, when it was clear that the so-called cuneiform texts were all forged, I had to decide whether I continue to believe that "Beyköy 2" is indeed genuine.

We jointly published two papers in which I merely provided the background information and alleged research history of the drawings of Luwian hieroglyphic inscriptions from Mellaart's estate, whereas you furnished the linguistic analysis. You concluded that the documents are authentic. What makes you think that?

First of all, the text of "Beyköy 2" is exceedingly long. One must be very creative to invent such a long text. As we now know, James Mellaart was indeed very creative, but his knowledge of Luwian hieroglyphic was rather pedestrian. I do not believe that he could make up such a long text using only his imagination. From my perspective, this is not possible. I also found that, based on the drawing, I recognized phrases, where Mellaart did not even understand the text. Among the documents you received is a superficial translation that only proves that nobody understood the contents of the Luwian hieroglyphic text.

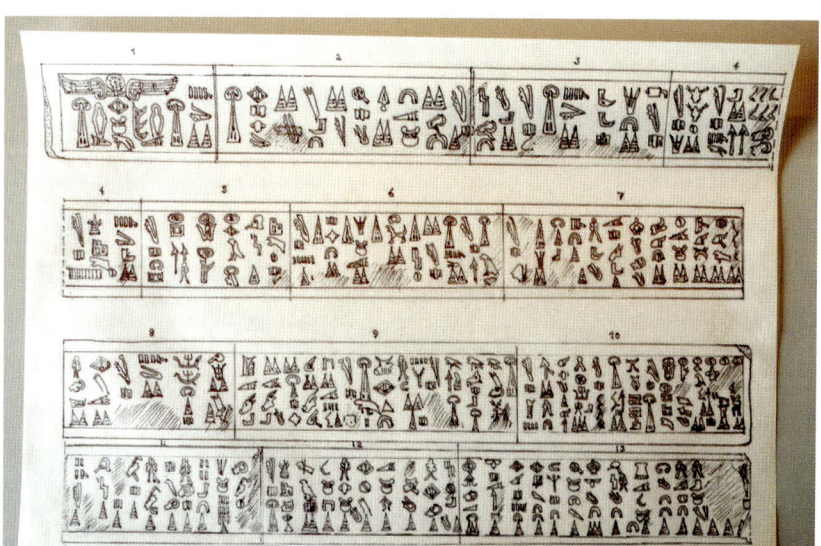

One out of four A4 sheets with felt tip pen drawings traced from an initial pencil drawing (both produced by James Mellaart) providing the Luwian hieroglyphic "Beyköy 2" inscription.

Secondly, Mellaart and perhaps even other people working on the document did not realize the proper order of the blocks to begin with. It took them four attempts until they had figured out the correct sequence.

What if Mellaart even faked his ignorance?
That would add an extra layer of deceit. If he pretended ignorance in one place, he must have had much more expertise in Luwian hieroglyphic somewhere else to be able to create such an elaborate document. There are no indications anywhere that James Mellaart had the knowledge that would have been needed to produce this text.

What if somebody else created the document – and then fooled Mellaart?
That is an interesting idea! From the paperwork you received we know that, in 1989, Mellaart had sent the drawing of "Beyköy 2" to two leading experts on Luwian hieroglyphic to request their assessment. Annelies Kammenhuber replied that she thinks it's a forgery, perhaps produced by one of Helmuth Bossert's students. But even then, the text is still very long. It just goes on and on. The forger would have had to make up all

those place-names, there are hundreds of them in it, and then in between there is distinct grammar which fits the use of Luwian hieroglyphic during the Late Bronze Age period neatly. Few people were acquainted with Luwian hieroglyphic, but virtually nobody knew how it was written in the Late Bronze Age …

… because few documents were predating the Early Iron Age.
The only existing longer text from the imperial period were the four altar stones from Emirgazi. And that was not well understood 30 years ago at all. Südburg was found later – and Yalburt was found later.

Yalburt was discovered in 1970.
It was not published until 1993 – and the "Beyköy 2" drawing was first presented in 1989. So it would not have been possible to use Yalburt as a source. Photographs of Yalburt had appeared in an initial report just before "Beyköy 2" was shown (in 1989), but these photos were impossible to work with. I tried it, and it did not work out.

It would have been possible if one knew the Yalburt inscription after it had been discovered but before it was published, so between 1970 and 1993. Because of Mellaart's good connections, and maybe even his source's connections, there may have been informal access to better depictions of the Yalburt inscription.
But you did not find anything like that in the study?

No, not at all! You know, of course, that his father-in-law possessed a spacious wooden summerhouse on the Bosporus and that it burned to the ground in 1976. James Mellaart had maintained an extensive study in that building and, of course, lost all his notes and manuscripts to the fire. Interestingly, he himself spread the rumor that the fire may have been caused by arson, even though the family knew very well that the negligence of a housekeeper indeed triggered it.
It is obvious, from Mellaart's notes, that he made up stories in numerous variations. For instance, when he spoke about Georges Perrot, whom he first claimed to have visited and worked at Beyköy and of whom Mellaart said that he had drawn "Beyköy 2"; but Perrot did not mention this important document in any of his publications, whereas he did mention the short hieroglyphic text of Beyköy 1.

As things stand today, we cannot say anything about the provenance of the inscription, when and where it was found. If it actually exists, it is probably hidden away in a private or governmental collection. Evidently, the only way to make any more progress in this pursuit would be by finding the original.

Yes, of course, but the chances may be low.

If, as a thought experiment, we assume that the document is indeed authentic, what would we gain from it?

"Beyköy 2" indeed contains a combination of the Old and the New Reading which exactly fits my Adjusted Old Reading, to boot, because sometimes sign *376 is used as *zi* or *za* and other times as *i*. *Mizra* is clearly Egypt and there it must be read as *z*, and we had the case of the place-name *Ikuwana* for Konya; there it must be *i*.

And in terms of its contents, "Beyköy 2" would help us understand the end of the Bronze Age.

Well, it is essentially a historical text: we hear of Muksas going to Askalon, which we hear about in Greek texts as well. So the document gives

Mr. James Mellaart in his study in North London.

us a unique window to see what was happening during this troubled period of the upheavals of the Sea Peoples.

In addition to the drawing of the large "Beyköy 2" inscription, the estate contained three other shorter hieroglyphic inscriptions and four fragments. Of course, any one of these would be easier to forge because of their smaller size. However, if we consider them authentic, they provide valuable information on the location of the country Seha. The document called "Edremit" lists 43 place-names beginning with towns on the island of Lesbos. From this document it is clear that Seha must be situated in the Kaïkos valley.

And this makes sense from today's perspective, but it did not make sense as far as James Mellaart's view of political geography is concerned.
Right! Indeed, it was David Hawkins who situated Seha in the Kaïkos! At the time, he did not yet have really strong arguments. And now these short texts from Mellaart's estate would verify this idea.

Does the style or the genre of "Beyköy 2" make any sense to you?
It is certainly a style because I don't know of any Luwian hieroglyphic text with so many enumerations of place-names. It can perhaps be compared to some Egyptian texts providing lists of places connected with captives. Those are the closest parallels I have seen.

This brings us back to Mellaart's resume because he had actually studied Egyptology. – Yet, you mentioned at some point that you have seen a similar enumeration of place-names in a document from Iron Age Mesopotamia.
Yes, I found an example in Elamite from precisely the same period which struck me as similar.

Despite the many place-names, "Beyköy 2" contains 50 complete phrases including verbs.
Yes, there is very detailed grammar, so one would have to be an outstanding Luwologist to make this up! Thirty years ago, it would have been challenging to forge something like that, and as far as Mellaart is concerned, I think it is out of the question that he produced it.

What I find interesting is that Mellaart created the so-called cuneiform "Beyköy texts" and while doing so went overboard. Counting different versions and copies, we had found about a thousand pages of his notes on the subject. The manuscript itself comprised maybe 120 pages. Anyway, while his imagination went wild regarding the supposedly cuneiform documents, he never touched the hieroglyphic texts. He did not change one letter in the translation. All his fantasies went into the work on the alleged translations of the cuneiform text.

The manuscripts on the cuneiform, which we now know never existed, was a blown-up version of what the hieroglyphic texts relate. It was his muse.

He did not touch the translation of the Luwian hieroglyphic texts. It appears as if he treated them like a gift from God, sacred and not to be touched. He left it exactly the same.

The complete "Beyköy 2" inscription as retrieved from James Mellaart's study combined in one picture. The illustration shows Mellaart's original artwork, only the yellow background has been added.

If I work on a Luwian hieroglyphic text, I tend to see new things every time I look at it. Consequently, you'll find several different hierarchical layers of understanding in my notes. In Mellaart's notes on the hieroglyphic, there is no hierarchy of investigations – except for the sequence of the blocks. Everything else is taken for granted.

This would make it quite likely that Mellaart had received the drawings and the translations as we found them in his estate.
That is my opinion.

Maybe he thought that the hieroglyphic text will eventually be unveiled and then he could come forward with his elaborate interpretation of an imaginative cuneiform equivalent.
And everybody would take it seriously! Perhaps he was so angry that the experts said in 1989 that this Luwian hieroglyphic text is a fake. So he thought, I will show them what a genuine fake looks like!

I perfectly understand colleagues who consider it too risky to enter a discussion on the subject, because Mellaart was evidently capable of producing fake texts – at an industrial scale! Now many scholars believe that much of what he presented may have been forged. I believe that the hieroglyphic inscriptions are genuine, but I understand other people's reservations. Mellaart is fully discredited.

Yet More Inscriptions Appear

Let us move on then! There are two Luwian hieroglyphic inscriptions that are somehow related to "Beyköy 2" since they were both found after the drawing was publicly shown ...
... and both to some extent confirm what is reflected in the drawing. "Beyköy 2" contains a sign for "great prince" – and this sign was not known when the drawing was first publicly presented at an international conference in Ghent in 1989. Actually, the appearance of such a sign was considered to be an indication of forgery. And then, in 2001, the Latmos inscription in the hinterland of Miletus was discovered, engraved in bedrock – and it contains the very same sign for "great prince." That is a stunning connection – it simply invalidated the argument that this sign indicates forgery.

And in 2019, another inscription was found in the Konya Plain. It is called Türkmen-Karahöyük after a tell site in the vicinity, and it also contains idiosyncrasies which are thus far only known from "Beyköy 2." Are these three inscriptions, "Beyköy 2," Latmos and Türkmen-Karahöyük, somehow related to each other? Not really, they are quite different in many regards. The style of the signs in "Beyköy 2" and Latmos is very different; the two inscriptions were certainly not made by the same person.

Rock inscription for the title of "great prince" Kupaä at Latmos (Peschlow-Bindokat/Herbordt 2001, 373, Fig. 7a) and the same expression as used in "Beyköy 2."

What about Türkmen-Karahöyük, then? Let me recapitulate briefly how the inscription was found and what it looks like. The stone is about one meter long and it was not found in a stratified context. It was simply dumped into a trench and could have come from anywhere. The find was not reported to the authorities, even though Turkish citizens usually receive a financial reward for such a find. The farmer who pointed out the stone to the archaeologists doing fieldwork insisted on remaining anonymous. The sequence – dumping the stone, then pointing it out to archaeologists, then demanding to stay anonymous – is peculiar. The material is soapstone – and there are simply no examples for Luwian hieroglyphic inscriptions on soapstone, since the scribes used limestone or basalt. Turkish craftsmen producing tourist souvenirs, however, use soapstone because it is so easy to work. A part of the inscription is in high relief, and part is not. It is the only inscription ever found like that. The former surface has a varnish from weathering and lichen and is thus dark, while the worked bits are much brighter, because the scribe's chisel removed the patina. Usually one would expect that the varnish, after three thousand years, covers the entire surface. Still, there is no sign of weathering on the worked bits, even though an erosional process must have occurred in one form or another, whether the stone was exposed, buried or remained under water.

It is a little bit of a strange inscription, because it starts with the signs worked in relief and then it goes on as engravings. So it comes across somehow as an unfinished object, but there is no reason to think it might be a forgery, this time on stone rather than merely in the form of a drawing. I don't think so! I see no reason to doubt the authenticity of this inscription. If the object is a fake, the falsifier in my opinion based it on a real text. And this document again contains features that were previously known only from "Beyköy 2." The sign *82 ta_6 in the form of a leg is usually only used for the roots of verbs and not for the ending, but in Türkmen-Karahöyük it is used for the ending, expressing the third person of the past tense – and in "Beyköy 2" (§§ 46, 48) it is also used as an ending. Again, in the discussion on the authenticity of "Beyköy 2," this particular feature was used as an argument favoring its falsification. So that is a fascinating observation, because Türkmen-Karahöyük as a find is totally unrelated to "Beyköy 2." There is no connection to James Mellaart. It provides – much like Latmos – an element that Mellaart could not predict and the inscription was found and published by an international team of archaeologists.

In retrospect these parallels justify having published "Beyköy 2," because if it would have continued to rest in a desk drawer, as it had done for almost 30 years, scholars would not be able to recognize such analogies. I think it is very important that this inscription is out there! I sincerely believe in its authenticity – and over 4000 people who checked it out on academia.edu indicate that there is quite some general interest in a highly specific subject.

Coming back to Türkmen-Karahöyük – what do you make of it?
The scholars who published it argue in favor of a late date for the production of the inscription – they place it in the eighth century. They are putting forward a number of arguments which I don't agree with. For example, the name of the well-known king Hartapus is written in the form "Kartapus." They interpret this as a late variant dating to the ninth or eighth century. For instance, in the Karabel inscription, the name of the ruler, Tarkuwa, is derived from Tarhunt, with the *h* being turned into a *k*. So we have already in the Late Bronze Age an example of *h* becoming a *k*.

The Türkmen-Karahöyük inscription that was found in the summer of 2019 in the Konya Plain.

So you think that the inscription dates to the Late Bronze Age?
I think it dates to the twelfth century. – Another argument the authors put forward in favor of a late date is a case of rhotacism (sound change), affecting the letter *t* in the script. Originally it is pronounced as *d*, but through rhotacism it becomes an *r*. The authors argue that rhotacism is first attested in the ninth century, but this is not true. There are various Late Bronze Age inscriptions that exhibit rhotacism in the endings.

Do you see any more indications arguing in favor of a date at the transition between Late Bronze Age and Early Iron Age?
The aedicula topped by the winged sun disk is a Bronze Age scribal tradition and as such not known from an Iron Age text. Therefore, Hartapus must have been a Bronze Age ruler. The winged sun disk still occurs later, but the aedicula in this form is not known from the Iron Age.

Hartapus belongs to the transitional period between the Bronze Age and the Early Iron Age. The mentioning of *mu-sà-ka^{UTNA}*, the "land of the Muski," as an ethnic designation of the Phrygians, makes sense in this context. There were already Muski or Phrygians in Anatolia during the twelfth century, they penetrated as far as the border with Assyria c. 1165. Apparently its people were causing king Hartapus some problems at the same time.

There are more inscriptions in the general area in which Hartapus is mentioned. They would, of course, all belong to the same time period.

Yes, of course! If you down-date Türkmen-Karahöyük to the eighth century, it means the other inscriptions in the region also need to be down-dated. Up until now these have been dated to the twelfth century. There is only one problem, since one of the texts is connected with an Assyrian-style depiction of the king. The question is whether the inscription and the late-style engraving are contemporary – or was the picture of the king added at a later time? There has been a discussion about this. As of now, David Hawkins dates Hartapus into the twelfth century.[18]

The Phrygians are also mentioned in the inscription at Topada, composed under the great king of Cappadocia, Wasusarma. In it, the Phrygians are not referred to as Muski or *ma-sà-ka-na*, instead they are called Parwíta, which is a reflex of "Phrygian" – in Luwian the voiced velar *$\acute{g}^h$ is regularly lost. And this is an eighth-century inscription, because we have the name of Wasusarma and his vassals in Assyrian texts.

So the name of the Phrygians has changed over the centuries from Muski to Parwíta?
Well, I only want to remark that the Phrygians were called Muski in the twelfth century and Parwíta, as used in the eighth century, reflects Phrygian.

Let's assume that the inscription found in 2019 near Türkmen-Karahöyük was actually produced during the twelfth century, as you argue. What would this tell us about the political situation in central Anatolia at that time?
There was a Luwian king ruling over a realm in the former province of Tarhuntassa who had to deal with Phrygians. This is what one would expect, by the way, because the Assyrians also had problems with the Phrygians in this period. I don't see any objections to an early date at all.

It must be said that there are also some Early Iron Age elements in this inscription, I agree with that, but my point is that these mark the text as transitional.

This would be another thing that Türkmen-Karahöyük has in common with "Beyköy 2."
I would date "Beyköy 2" a bit earlier than Türkmen-Karahöyük, but yes, they are certainly both transitional. But if you compare the signs, the tradition of writing in Tarhuntassa is more similar to that of Syria than

Fred Woudhuizen appeared to always be in a good mood.

western Anatolia. So Türkmen-Karahöyük looks different from what we know about Late Bronze Age writing traditions in western Anatolia, not because it was composed much later, but because it was produced much further east. This is how you could explain it.

Interviews conducted on July 10 and 24, 2020.

Byblos Needs Its Own Script

What was it like in 1700? Why Byblos wanted its own script. Previous attempts at decipherment. Jan Best and Fred Woudhuizen have a discord. Best deserves the credit! Colleagues regard the decipherment as speculative.

Let's go back in time to the year 1700! What did the political geography around the eastern Mediterranean look like?
First, we must decide which chronology we are using for the Middle Bronze Age. I prefer the so-called Middle Chronology favored by most conventional textbooks. It puts the reign of Hammurabi at 1792–1750 and the sack of Babylon by the Hittite great king Mursili I at 1595. We do have a triple coincidence confirming this chronology: a connection between Zimrilim of Mari, Yantin-'Ammu of Byblos and pharaoh Neferhotep I of Egypt, they all ruled concurrently during about the middle of the eighteenth century. Also important for the chronology is Alalakh Level VII, from which a few hundred cuneiform tablets were retrieved. This level dates to the time between 1720 and 1650 – at which point Hattusili I conquered the city. We need to use this Middle Chronology, because if we were to apply the Low Chronology, there would not be enough time to accommodate all the Hittite kings.

What did Anatolia look like at the time?
The Kültepe-Kanesh period had concluded 1717. The Hittite rulership did not officially begin until 1650, when Hattusili I formed the Old Kingdom. But he was actually preceded by Labarnas I in 1680 or so – and we even know of a Hittite royal named Huzziya from the time before this. So there is almost a continuity between the time of Kültepe-Kanesh and the beginning of the Hittite rule in central Anatolia. But in general the years from about 1720 to 1680 were indeed an interlude. Maps won't depict the political geography for this particular period, and it is hard to get an overview of what happened.

What was the situation in Mesopotamia like?
Hammurabi had passed away in 1750, and since then Babylon's strength had waned. Beginning around 1730, a significant change took place. Coming from the Caucasus, Mitanni rulers with Indo-Aryan names dashed into the Levant with chariot forces. Nobody could withstand these raids, and as a consequence, the new way of warfare disrupted the balance of power. Anatolia didn't possess strong rulership when Mesopotamia was weakened, and Egypt had also suffered a progressive decline of power during the preceding thirteenth dynasty. Consequently, the raiders could push all the way forward into the Nile delta, where they settled as the so-called Hyksos, who for an entire century and a half established foreign rulership over Lower Egypt.

This happened when exactly?
The earliest evidence we have for the presence of Hyksos is a horse skeleton with bit wear from Buhen in southern Egypt, which dates to 1675; but maybe the Hyksos had come already a bit earlier, perhaps around 1700. Before that, there was no horse in Egypt and even no wheel!

In other words, the Hyksos brought a major transformation!
Yes, they brought a big difference. The leading echelons of Egyptian society had to change their lifestyle completely. If they wanted to push the Hyksos out of Egypt again, Egyptian pharaohs had to establish their own chariot contingents to match the intruders' military force. Hence, the Egyptian army needed horses, horse trainers, chariots, charioteers and so forth to get into a position to challenge the intruders. It took over a century to accumulate this kind of strength.

The Byblos Script

Our topic of conversation is, of course, Byblos and the Byblos script, whose use you place at around 1700. What was going on in Byblos at the time?
Byblos had been linked to Egypt for a very long time, as documented in Egyptian hieroglyphic inscriptions found in the port city and dating from 2500 onwards. So the chariot warfare separated Byblos from Egypt for the first time in almost a thousand years. Consequently, the

local Semitic scribes – in splendid isolation – went on to develop a new provincial style of writing Egyptian hieroglyphic. It was these newly invented signs which were then also adapted for the Byblos script. So the Byblos script was developed at the time when the connection between Byblos and Egypt had fallen into ruins and Byblos was on its own. Byblos script documents were written in a pure Semitic dialect closely related to Ugaritic. This language is well documented from thousands of clay tablets, dating to the fourteenth to twelfth century, and inscribed with a consonant alphabet in a cuneiform script. This Semitic dialect was evidently the language spoken in Byblos around 1700.

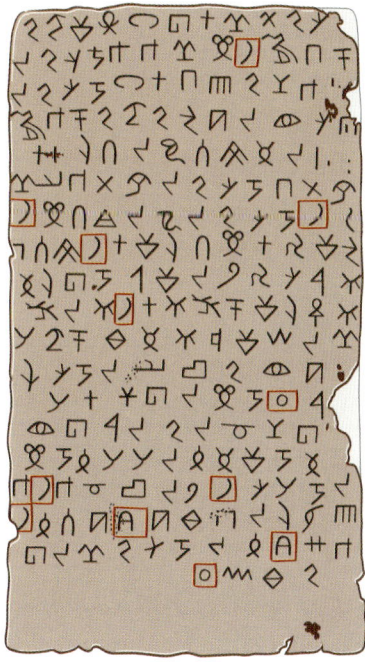

Byblos script (tablet d) in a photograph as well as in an illustration to highlight the punctuation marks with red squares.

Byblos was a crucial connection for Egypt to supply the timber needed to make ships and build large constructions.
Yes, of course. The wood came from Byblos and no doubt other valuable commodities originating from Mesopotamia and beyond arrived in Byblos, from where they were shipped to Egypt. The Egyptians considered Byblos their vassal. The earliest Egyptian hieroglyphic documents found in Byblos are royal dedications by Egyptian pharaohs to the gods in the local temples. The city was important, yet it is difficult to say how the political interdependencies actually worked. We don't know whether Egypt determined the politics in Byblos, but they certainly considered it to be within their sphere of influence.

The *corpus* of documents in Byblos script is small – and has been known for some time.
There are no more than 15 documents, among them two bronze tablets with substantial undamaged texts, of which the larger one is approximately the size of a hand. Also, a few inscribed bronze spatulas and some carefully worked carved stones with inscriptions have been found, mostly between 1928 and 1932, during the excavations under the direction of Maurice Dunand.

And the Byblos script was written from right to left?
Yes, it goes from right to left. If you look at the tablet, you will see some obvious line indentions on the left side, so it is clear that the lines begin on the right margin.

How were the signs written onto the bronze plates?
The signs are incised, most likely with a sharp tool and perhaps at a time when the metal was hot and malleable. They were certainly not stamped with a chisel or so.

You said that two documents are outstanding – what do they tell us?
Yes, tablet c and tablet d – those are the most important pieces. They say that during the reign of 'Egel of Byblos, the ruler of Aleppo, Yarimlim, and Ammitaku of Alalakh have brought gifts to the temple of Byblos. A prominent gift was a *bīt ḫilāni*, a portico house form that is typical for this period, but there were also other gifts, and the text goes on and on to describe what was brought as gifts and who was responsible for each

item. The documents are very detailed in this respect; for instance, they even state which two people handed over the gifts: one of them was the brother of Yarimlim of Aleppo, Kelidu, the other was one of the overseers of the people's assembly of Aleppo, Tisadal.

Tablet d devotes more attention to the mayor of Aleppo and the members of his board. It explains that the board is responsible for this and that. Otherwise, the same names occur as in tablet c. From what I can tell, all the documents we possess today date to the same time and maybe even to the same year. The spatulas were also dedicated to the temple at this event. The script was certainly used over longer time, but what has been transmitted represents a glimpse at a specific moment.

Of course, you provide the full translation in your publication in *Ugarit-Forschungen*.

Yes, for tablet c and tablet d as well as for one of the spatulas. Not all inscriptions are well preserved and complete. If an inscription is broken, I don't use it, because one can make anything out of an incomplete text. As far as linguistics is concerned, there are only two phrases with a verb, and the rest are prepositional phrases, ruled by the prepositions and without a verb. I found out that there are labels in Ugaritic consisting of such prepositional phrases. It turns out to be the typical bookkeeper's language in the region during the fourteenth and thirteenth centuries. And Ugaritic is, of course, the very same Semitic language in which the documents of the Byblos script were written.

What the Documents Say

What do we learn from the documents themselves?

We learn a lot about an otherwise dark period. Byblos had non-Egyptian scribes who wrote in this provincial Egyptian hieroglyphic style. One of the scribes, by the name of Kukun, was actually Lycian. The fact that the large tablets were made for Yarimlim of Aleppo indicates that Byblos had come under the influence of Aleppo, and this is an entirely new insight. We always knew that Aleppo was important until Hattusili I defeated it, but that it ruled over Byblos is something new. This Yarimlim was seconded by Ammitaku of Alalakh, evidently a vassal state of Aleppo at the time. However, the problem is that Aleppo had at least three different rulers named Yarimlim – and Alalakh had two named Ammitaku. To determine when the documents were composed, we need to establish which of these rulers are being described. The situation is thus a bit complicated.

Jan Best and Lia Rietveld had worked on the Byblos script and concluded that the ruler mentioned in the text is Yarimlim III. But this king ruled only briefly, and I think it might be more reasonable to assume Yarimlim II was meant, because he reigned for about 40 years, from c. 1720 to 1680. Yarimlim II was a contemporary of Ammitaku I of Alalakh. So I argue that rather than dating to the time around 1650, the documents were more likely composed around 1690. Additional arguments are supporting this date. The king of Byblos is also mentioned in the documents – and his name is 'Egel. We know that a king by this name ruled from about 1690 to 1670 – and so he was a contemporary of Yarimlim II.

But the documents are religious dedications ...
... which, of course, have some political significance.

The Road to Decipherment

Inevitably, many scholars attempted to decipher the script; among the first was Bedřich Hrozný, the famous decipherer of Hittite cuneiform.
Yes! Some of the signs in the Byblos script resemble the Phoenician alphabet, and the initial attempts all rested on exploiting those relationships. There are only a few parallels between the two scripts, and the connection is not working out. An alphabet typically consists of 20 to 30 signs, whereas the syllabic scripts consist of 50 to more than 100 signs. With around 114 different signs – including punctuation marks and numbers – the Byblos script is clearly a syllabary, while the Phoenician alphabet is based on 22 consonant letters. Besides, the alphabet only gained relevance at Byblos at a later stage.

There was no alphabet in 1700?
The alphabet is a consonant script and originally derived from Egyptian hieroglyphic; its use spread from Egypt into the Levant after 2000. So the alphabet may have been known by the time when the Byblos script documents were written. The Proto-Sinaitic inscriptions, retrieved by

Flinders Petrie during excavations on Sinai, are alphabetic and those date approximately to the time of the Byblos script; but Proto-Sinaitic was not common back then.

To work only with comparisons of signs is anyway tricky. Comparing one script with other script forms means exploiting external evidence. To decipher a script, however, some internal evidence is also needed. Part of internal evidence are doublets, triplets and quadruplets – in the case of the Byblos script, we even have a quadruplet! We spoke about this when we discussed the principle approach in decipherments: in doublets and triplets the last sign has the same consonant but varying vowels. I mentioned the example of *me-di-**cu**(s), me-di-**ci**, me-di-**co*** in Latin – in a syllabary, this would entail *-cu, -ci, -co*. Based on this principle it is possible to make predictions about the sound value of the signs. These predictions can then be compared with external evidence. For example, if the signs for *la* and *li* from the comparative scripts occur in the form of doublets and triplets, this confirms the chosen approach. We need to combine both methods, internal and external evidence, to achieve the most promising results.

And in the 1980s the first scholar to employ this approach to the Byblos script was Jan Best?
That's right. He made a breakthrough by comparing part of the signs with Egyptian hieroglyphic and part with Linear A. If a sign can be correlated to one known from another script, it makes sense to also transfer the sound value from the known to the unknown script – and proceeding in this way the text will ultimately become readable.

How many signs in the Byblos script are related to Egyptian hieroglyphs and how many to Linear A?
About half is Egyptian, the other half is identical to Linear A. This approach, of course, requires that one understands Linear A, which was indeed Jan Best's big advantage. The first Linear A documents occur around the same time as the Byblos script, and yet it is obvious that the Byblos script was conceived first. It has no signs which originated from Luwian hieroglyphic, but these do occur in Cretan Linear A. Therefore, the direction of movement must have been from east to west, because if it had been the other way around, we would expect to find a Luwian hieroglyphic component in the Byblos script.

In other words, when the Byblos script was created, half of the signs were taken over from Egyptian hieroglyphs which were then linearized. But from where did the scribes get the ideas for the other half of the signs?

I don't know where they got the other signs from. One component could have been Akkadian cuneiform, but I am only aware of one syllable that was derived from cuneiform, namely the sign for *pa*. I cannot be more specific on how this second component of the script was developed.

The work on the Byblos script ultimately led to the division between you and Jan Best. How did this come about?

You have to ask him! I agreed with his approach and also with his initial results, but I felt that he had not finished the job. Of course, the most important part in deciphering is the initial phase, to get a breach into the script – and this was entirely Jan Best's achievement. He was the first to pay attention to internal evidence and was able to read Yarimlim, Ammitaku and a lot of other words correctly. Very importantly, he also found out which signs were used for punctuation and numbers. There are indeed signs without a syllabic value that are used as a comma or a period to separate the elements of the text. It is crucial to recognize these elements.

Jan Best may have identified around 40 signs correctly, but there were 19 cases in which I disagreed with his transcription. That's a lot of signs! By filling in the wrong sound values, one will inevitably end up with a wrong translation. Like Jan Best, I used Egyptian hieroglyphic and Linear A to determine the sound values of the signs in the Byblos script. However, I was able to read the entire large documents whereas Jan Best worked mostly with personal names. He thought that Greek personal names occur in the Byblos script, something that is not very likely during this period, to be honest. As we have said before, personal names are a low category of linguistics and not confirmatory to the principle approach. Using the sound values which I propose for these 19 disputed signs results in entire sentences, including the verb – and that is a higher level of linguistic evidence. The verb mentioned twice is *yá$_2$-ta-wa* /yatanwa/, known from Ugaritic as *ytn* /yatenu/, and it is the dual of *ytn* for "to give." So the phrase says that the two men, Kelidu and Tisadal, actually *gave* – or donated – the *bīt ḫilāni* etc.

I want to emphasize that my work constitutes only the last step in the decipherment; Jan Best indeed devised the principle approach.

Could you perhaps give an example for a sign that is well known from Egyptian hieroglyphs and occurs in the Byblos script?
The bee sign, for instance, is typically Egyptian. One other sign, the sign for *pa*, certainly originates from Akkadian cuneiform, but it does not have the heads of the cunei anymore, so it has been linearized. It was then also taken over in Linear A. Another typical sign originates from the double axe; both, the double axe as an object and the sign of a double axe, were quite important in Minoan Crete. The sign stands for the letter *a* in the Byblos script as well as in Linear A.

Your article on the Byblos script appeared in 2007. Have there been any reactions?
Well, some people criticized it, so that is some sort of reaction. Juan-Pablo Vita and José Ángel Zamora said in an article in 2018 that I presented a "highly speculative approach" which from a philological and historical perspective "results in unacceptable translations" – without elaborating their judgement any further. I submitted a detailed reply – which has not appeared yet – in which I illustrated how my translations are indeed linguistically and historically very likely.

You have no problems translating the documents and are happy with what you are getting out of them – there are no open questions?
From my point of view, the discussion is concluded. But it is up to the specialists in the field to decide what stands the test of verification and what not.

Interview conducted on August 21, 2020.

A Cypriot Admiral Calls for Help

Long well-preserved documents from Cyprus. What Cypro-Minoan really is. Administrators kept records of goods in transit. Hittite overlords demand taxes. Nothing beats good bookkeeping. Trade routes are revealed. About the value of the acrophonic principle. The Enkomi clay tablet 1687 is a call for help. The Sea Peoples are coming – from Troy!

If you were asked to provide an executive summary of what we know about the Cypro-Minoan script, what would you say?

Cypro-Minoan is not so difficult, because we have Linear A as a related script, and we have the Cypriot syllabary as a continuation of the script used during the classical period. Many of the signs between those scripts are identical, so that the sound values can be transferred from one script to another. There are two variants, Cypro-Minoan 1 (CM1), representing the script *sensu stricto,* and Cypro-Minoan 2 (CM2), a locally used version only known from Enkomi. In any case, I prefer calling the two scripts Linear C and Linear D, respectively. From each of these variants we have long, well-preserved documents. For Linear C there are some cylinder seals from Kalavassos and Enkomi, and a tablet found in Ugarit, each bearing long texts reflecting the same kind of information. These are bills of lading and thus yielding information about the commodities brought by ships into the ports. These documents were written in a bookkeeping language, clearly indicating supplier, recipient, number of products and type of product, though most of the time, the product's name is abbreviated. Verbs occur only occasionally in the form of transaction terms. Structurally speaking, the documents are simple. It is, of course, crucial to identify the punctuation marks to distinguish the categories. All these documents reflect regular trade during peaceful times. Since they consist only of lists of items, places and people, the texts don't bear much language to speak of. Only the transaction terms reflect the

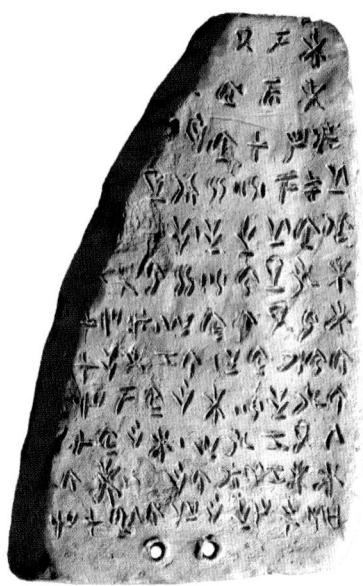

Terracotta tablet with Cypro-syllabic inscription.

language: it is Luwian. The recipient is often indicated in the dative ending using the syllable *-ti*, which can also be linked to a Luwian dialect.

From Linear D, the script employed locally at Enkomi, only one longer text is known. It dates to a few years after the cylinder seals were produced and it is completely different in nature. This is a letter by an admiral on a mission during the time of the Sea Peoples' upheavals, and so it gives us a glimpse into the events going on in the Aegean at a time of maritime warfare, c. 1190. The naval officer's most important enemy is a certain Akamas from Ilion.

Different Approaches

Your summary of what is known about Cypro-Minoan is probably unique around the globe. If I asked some other scholars, they would probably tell me that the script has been known since 1900 from findings originally made by Arthur Evans. Judging from the archaeological context, the script must have been in use from around 1500 to about 1190; and by today more than 1300 items bearing signs have been found, most of them dating to the thirteenth and late twelfth centuries. Above all, just about everybody else would say that the Cypro-Minoan script is undeciphered and that it is anybody's guess what these documents may say.

Silvia Ferrara put together the most recent *corpus*, and she says about the approach in dealing with undeciphered scripts: "One cannot in principle assume that identity in sign-shape presupposes, or is directly dependent on, phonetic identity, especially if the shapes in questions are hardly diagnostic."[19]

She thinks that the Cyprian script is an *ex novo* creation. Well, I don't agree! Because most of the time, scripts are very conservative. There are some exceptions; for instance, an American Indian has made up a script all for himself, but the effect of this is that nobody else can read it! Most of the time, scripts are very conservative with signs going on and on, rendering the same value.

Silvia Ferrara continues by saying: "The debate on whether it is legitimate to transfer the phonetic values of Linear B onto Linear A when two signs are identical may prove a case in point."

It is just the opposite: most of the signs of Linear B have the same value in Linear A. There is only a little change in the sense that we do not have the value *o* in Linear A, and at this point *o* is introduced in Linear B; but for the rest of the signs the value stays the same.

Deciphering attempts have been made by changing all values of the signs, even in the alphabet. We will see an example of this when we talk about Carian. And I say: okay, it's an alphabet! You have to read the signs as they are! The Greek alphabet, for instance, maintains all the Phoenician values. There is only one change regarding the Phoenician *kāp*, which is secondarily used for the related value *chi* and later for the unrelated value *psi*. Sound values can indeed change! There are signs which get a value that is unrelated to its original one. This can happen! But it will only happen in very few instances.

Silvia Ferrara also says in a footnote: "It goes without saying that the acrophonic principle does not lead one far in any decipherment methodology."[20]

Oh yes! I'm a fan of the acrophonic principle – in Luwian it works out perfectly. For almost 20 percent of the signs we can reconstruct an acrophonic value. So, they have logographic and acrophonic syllabic value.

That does not sound like a whole lot.

Well, we have more than 500 different signs, some of which are doubles though. Therefore, in more than 80 cases or so I obtain an acrophonic value.

The approach that you are pursuing in your work has been employed by some prominent scholars including Arthur Evans, Michael Ventris, John Chadwick, Piero Meriggi, Emilia Masson, Cyrus Gordon and Stefan Hiller. How can a fairly junior scholar be so negative about a methodology that numerous famous epigraphists have successfully employed for over a century?

Fred Woudhuizen looks up something in Eberhard Zangger's book "The Luwian Civilization."

Ferrara's objective was, first of all, to get the signs right to put together a *corpus*. So that is her focus. She does not want to know what the texts actually say. That was not her objective. She has a different point of departure in her research. I would say that the majority of the researchers working on Linear C and Linear D believe that the Aegean and Cypriot Bronze Age scripts are in some way related.[21] Of course, there are discussions about whether a particular sign is indeed identical to another sign in a different script. Does it really have the same sound value? Different authors have presented a spectrum of results. I think most people working on the Cypriot scripts are using pretty much the same approach and would agree that the main task consists of finding out the right genealogical connections for the signs. Emilia Masson has also

A CYPRIOT ADMIRAL CALLS FOR HELP • 119

acknowledged the connection with Linear A and departed from the hypothesis that Linear A and Linear C are related. She has read the word *pi-ni* as Semitic *bn* for "son," not as an offspring, but rather as a deputy official.[22] The same term occurs in Ugaritic in the form of *bn.lky*, the representative of the Lycians. Such parallels between different languages and scripts are quite common.

Michael Ventris used in his decipherment of Linear B the connection with the Cypriot syllabary of the classical period for the signs *ti* and *to*. They are identical, so he filled in their values for Linear B. Then he saw that on his grid *ti* and *to* are on the same level, so it was correct.

Silvia Ferrara benefited in her work from the advice of some leading scholars, thus I would assume that they share the same thinking.

Yes, but this thinking leads nowhere. If you want to know what the text is about, if you want to decipher it, you need clues as to the sound values of the signs and you must leverage the connection with Linear A for that. Otherwise, you will not be able to make any progress. There's no other way! You cannot decipher a script from nothing.

From what I can tell, it seems like there's much agreement on how to approach Cypro-Minoan and what to make out of it. And then, in the

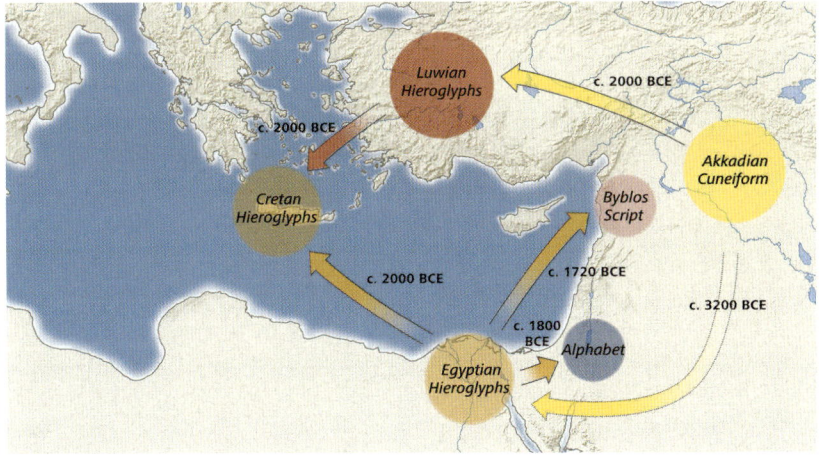

The Byblos script had an impact on the development of Linear A on Crete, and the latter impacted Linear C and D on Cyprus.

1980s, Jan Best laid the groundwork for your future research. In your book on Linear C and Linear D you are saying that he identified 45 signs correctly. So once again, you are following in Jan Best's footsteps.
Yes, certainly, he started it in 1988.

Why has Best's work not gotten any attention if he used a well-established approach?
I don't know! I cannot speak for other people; I have no idea why they think it's unconvincing. From my point of view, it was very promising and the way to go. Of course, a pioneer is bound to make some mistakes and every wrongly identified value may lead off in the wrong direction. One thus has to be careful in going forward, but it is the only route to success.

Would it be helpful if people were to acknowledge that yet another script has been deciphered, no matter whether its documents consist of dull inventories or international correspondence?
Yes, of course, with every decipherment we get information on periods that are otherwise pretty dark. We very much need this information to reconstruct the history.

As a natural scientist I am a bit puzzled about the lack of consistent terminology in a field that is 120 years old. The scholars involved in it could not even decide on how to call the script.
Yes, the terminology is indeed baffling; but it's a small discipline, we do not have many inscriptions, there are only a few people working on it, and everybody is making his or her own contribution. As the leading scholar in this field, Emilia Masson proposed dividing the script into three parts: CM1, CM2 and CM3. Jan Best and I opted to follow up on a suggestion already made by Fritz Schachermeyr and thus called it Linear C and Linear D. We subdivide the *corpus* into only two units. Emilia Masson considers CM3 consisting of some Late Bronze Age inscriptions from Ugarit, just like Linear C. It is not necessary to distinguish them in another category.

Linear C, by the way, is curvier, whereas Linear D tends to look more like cuneiform. It is also more economical, there are fewer signs in Linear D – and it only occurs in Enkomi.

All about Business

Linear C and Linear D as scripts were for the most part derived from Linear A, and both reflect Luwian language …
Basically, but some signs are also from Linear B. We cannot completely exclude Linear B. There are also some Semitic loanwords. But indeed, the documents reflect the Luwian language of the Late Bronze Age. In Cyprus there are no documents from that time in Greek. After the end of the Bronze Age, the Cypriot script was adapted to express what we now call Eteocypriot as well as the Greek language. And I consider Eteocypriot to be Luwian. So there is a continuity in terms of the script and language from the Late Bronze Age to the classical period. A bilingual inscription from Amathus bears an Eteocyprian and a Greek text, whose contents are not identical, although they were written by the same person as is indicated in both versions. Greeks moved to Cyprus shortly after the time of the Sea Peoples' invasions, and we see how the purely Luwian Linear C and Linear D evolved after the Late Bronze Age to express both Luwian, that is, Eteocypriot, as well as Greek in the form of a new script which we today call Cypriot syllabary. This script continued to be in use for almost an entire millennium until about the second century BCE. When the Anatolian alphabets came into use, signs from the Cypriot syllabary were integrated into it.

When Arthur Evans published the first objects with Bronze Age Cypriot scripts, all he had were a few clay balls with incised signs.
As it turns out, these clay balls are connected with economic registration. Somehow, people wrote personal names and abbreviations of products onto clay balls. These were part of the same accounting system as the bills of lading on the cylinder seals. The clay balls may have been some kind of receipt or so to complete a certain transaction.

The most important documents are the cylinder seal from Enkomi,[23] the cylinder seal from Kalavassos[24] and a tablet from Ugarit.[25] All these reflect the same kind of text: economic registrations and bills of lading, listing incoming products and commodities which were reshipped to continue on their route to the ultimate recipient.

Above: Cylinder seal (Enkomi 1610) with Linear C inscription providing lists of lading. Below: Drawing of script on clay cylinder 1610.

Which is not all that surprising, considering that this information is similar to that transmitted in Linear B tablets.

Yes, but the interesting thing is that these documents all stem from the period shortly before the Sea Peoples' invasions, a time of Hittite occupation of Cyprus. The Hittite overlords were anxious to charge taxes, but to do so, representatives on Cyprus had to record every transaction. The cylinder seals reflect this economic registration. Information on them is given in continuous writing, making use of punctuation marks, but it is still possible to turn it into a chart, and so I did. It looks much like a modern spreadsheet. The first column indicates the suppliant, the second names the recipient, often using the dative to indicate that the merchandise went "to" this particular person. The third column yields a number and the final column contains an abbreviation of the product's name.

The system used for economic registration is the same that we already know from lead strips with a Luwian hieroglyphic inscription that was found in Kayseri-Kululu in central Anatolia. It provides the same categories: deliverer, recipient, number of products. This evidently was the Hittite system of economic registration used throughout the kingdom, and vassals were apparently required to also use it. It is pretty much identical to the system that is still customary in accounting today.

How many people's names did you find in this document?

Quite a few, perhaps three dozen or so. Interestingly, the use of the system is that the scribe refers to himself with the first person singular pronoun *emu*, the Lycian expression for "I," which is equivalent to Luwian *amu*. For example, one of the scribes says: "I am the Lycian [named] Pihas," which is a common Luwian name. Anyhow, there was evidently a Lycian involved in administrating the trade on Cyprus. The Kalavassos seal was written by Sanemas, who belongs to the ethnic tribe of the Shekelesh. Both Lycians and Shekelesh were of course units involved in the Sea Peoples' invasions. The Shekelesh are also referred to as Shikala in an Ugaritic letter in which Suppiluliuma II requests information on these people who "live on boats." I think that they were at home in Sicily, which would mean that people from the central Mediterranean not only knew the route of long-distance trade across the Mediterranean but were also actively taking part in its administration. Furthermore, the future enemy Akamas of Ilion features in the texts of the Enkomi cylinder seal and the tablet from Ugarit as a recipient and representative of the town of Ephesus.

On Sardinia copper ingots from Cyprus were found bearing Linear A signs.
Absolutely! So the connection is evident. – The clay tablet from Ugarit says the commodities are going from there to the Hittite port town of Lamiya on the Lamos river in Cilicia. Since these goods are crossing the border, taxes were charged, and that's why a record was required. Not far from Lamiya is the town of Tarsus, and the text mentions two functionaries there, Apamu(wa)s and Masanawalas. I found those names on sealings from Tarsus, so these officials were stamping commodities coming from Lamiya to Tarsus on route into central Anatolia going all the way to Hattusa.

In Ugarit the text also mentions *i-si$_1$-pa-li*, a shorthand form of Sipatba'al, and *i-li-ma-li-ki* (= alphabetic *Ilmlk*), which are indeed names of functionaries already known from the reign of Ammurapi II and his mother Sharelli. Sipatba'al was the harbormaster, the most important governmental official in charge of the port. And he is mentioned in the text! So we know these people already from other Ugaritic texts, written in cuneiform and alphabetic. The date is also clear, since Ammurapi II was the last king of Ugarit. This Sipatba'al even had a seal in Egyptian hieroglyphic for his trade with Egypt.

To get back to Pihas, why do you think it is remarkable that a Lycian was working as an official in a port in Cyprus?
The Lycians are often described as adversaries of the Hittites. Tudhaliya IV conducted a campaign in Lycia as recorded in the Yalburt inscription. Suppiluliuma II led a campaign against Lycia which is mentioned in the Südburg text. So the Lycians were a bit troublesome. Maybe it was part of the Cypriot officials' tactics to involve Lycians in the trade to make sure that they were aligned with official politics and prevent them from attacking cities on Cyprus every summer. It may have been a way to allow them to earn money legally. However, this only concerns one individual and may not mean much; many of the others may still have been pirates.

The former water basin on the meadow called Yalburt with its 22 limestone blocks bearing a Luwian hieroglyphic inscription on their inward-facing sides.

If the names of the recipients are indicated in the records, can you reconstruct the trade routes?

Yes, indeed! The commodities are coming from northwestern Anatolia, most likely from the region around Troy, but Ephesus is also mentioned. From there they were shipped via Cyprus to Ugarit. We know from the tablets that the goods then went on to Lamiya in Cilicia and further to Hattusa. To transport goods from the Troad to Hattusa, the sea route was preferred, because it was easier and quicker. Some of the commodities for which Sanemas was responsible also came from Crete.

This kind of bookkeeping texts is discontinued completely when the Sea Peoples' invasions begin. At that time, the Hittite hegemony had collapsed and there was no need to keep track of transactions anymore.

Hittite Ambitions

How do you see the political geography and the international relations based on what you have found out through the reading of the documents and in combination with what is already known?

Before the end of the Bronze Age towards the end of the reign of Tudhaliya IV, the Hittites conquer Cyprus a first time and then again a second time under his son Suppiluliuma II, who then brags about it in the Nişantaş inscription at Hattusa. The Hittite rulers demanded that the local Cypriot population record products and merchandise. Since they could not require them to learn a new script for this purpose, they might use their own script and language. Hence, the economic records were taken following a Hittite accounting system but using a local Cypriot script as well as a local Luwian dialect. The same happened in Byblos and Ugarit, where letters were translated into local scripts and dialects.

And the motivation to conquer Cyprus was to get hold of the copper resources?

Yes, I think so, to get copper, for sure. In particular after the loss of the mines at Ergani Maden in the province of Isuwa to the Assyrians late in the reign of Tudhaliya IV.

But you did not find copper mentioned in the documents.

No, they only talk about the woven fabric, which was also important because people made a lot of money by trading clothes, as is evident from the records in Kültepe-Kanesh. Many of the records from there speak about tissues, but also about copper. In Linear C a product is abbreviated as *pa*, which may stand for PAD, the cuneiform term for metal ingots. But that is not really robust evidence.

It could of course be that metal was traded from a different port.

Yes, or using a different tax system, so metal may not be recorded on cylinder seals.

How do you see Cyprus as a political unit before the Hittites annexed it? Was it independent or who was in charge?

The Hittites considered themselves to rule over Cyprus already under Tudhaliya II and Arnuwanda I, and they considered the king of Cyprus to be their vassal. On the other hand, the Amarna letters reveal that Cyprus is quite independent – its king communicated more or less on eye level with presumably Akhenaten. The king of Cyprus says he would be willing to trade with the pharaoh, but he is also lamenting that pirates from Lycia are taking a city from his coast every summer.

And Cyprus acquired such a high standing because the island was so rich thanks to its copper resources.

Yes, already in the Middle Bronze Age copper went from Cyprus to the Levant. There are documents in Mari mentioning Alashiya, which was at the time the name for Cyprus. And Cyprus was also crucial in maritime trade, since ships on many routes were passing by. So when the Hittites occupied the island, they also annexed the ports of call and perhaps even some trade routes. The trade with the Aegean went on, but now the Hittites had some say in it. On the other hand, we also have letters from Ugarit indicating that the Hittite king declared how much copper had to be delivered from Ugarit to the Ahhiyawans, that is: Greeks, stationed in Lycia. The relevant letters speak of men of *hiyawa* rather than Ahhiyawa, the first A is omitted, as customary in Luwian, because people along the entire west and south coast of Anatolia, including Cyprus, were speaking Luwian at the time.

A Spectacular Discovery

We still need to speak about the Linear D document from the time when the regular trade contacts were already disrupted and maritime fighting was going on.

Things had changed dramatically. This is when the upheavals were caused by the Sea Peoples, when the merchant ships were not safe anymore. Once the trade was disrupted, we do not find any of the documents recording economic transactions anymore.

The Linear D text is a letter written by a Cypriot nauarch,[26] an admiral, writing from Limyra, in eastern Lycia, to inform his king in Cyprus about what had been going on in the southern Aegean. The admiral had been to Rhodes to seize the port city of Kameiros, and he argues that he had a right to do so, because Hattusili III and Halpazitis, the king of Aleppo, already maintained a stronghold there. So there was a territorial claim

Document Enkomi 1687 – a call for help from a Cypriot nauarch. The artist`s reconstruction on the book cover illustrates the scene when this document was composed.

from earlier times which he says was still valid. From there he went on to Samos, where he got beaten by the forces of Akamas of Ilion. Thus Trojan ships had advanced way south. Consequently, the admiral retreated his forces back to his first base Limyra in eastern Lycia.

This is the same kind of document that we know from the last days of Ugarit, but this time we get an eyewitness account from someone in an advanced position way over west.

Those documents from Ugarit are only pointing in the direction of Lycia, saying that there is much trouble there, but with this letter we get first-hand information from someone who actually saw what was going on.

The nauarch clearly states that the Hittite king should send a fleet and additional forces to his support, exactly as we know it from the documents in Ugarit. The last king of Ugarit says that his ships are supporting the fleet of Suppiluliuma II in a maritime battle in the waters of Lycia. Evidently, the admiral's call for help was indeed received and followed through. Unfortunately for the Hittites, this maritime battle against the Sea Peoples was lost.

This particular document provides inside information about a thus far dark period during the initial phase of the Sea Peoples' invasions. And this artifact actually exists and is exhibited in the Cyprus Museum in Nikosia. Photographs of it have been published as early as 1971.

You are the first to have been able to read this letter and published the translation in 2017. The contents have clear parallels to the "Beyköy 2" drawing of a Luwian hieroglyphic text which was first shown publicly in 1989.

We learned from "Beyköy 2" that Muksas, the ruler of the Troad, was commanding the navy of Kupantakurunta III of Arzawa, and that his fleet pushed forward all the way to Ashkelon in southern Palestine. They must have first conquered certain ports of call on Samos, Rhodes, Cyprus – otherwise they could not have proceeded all the way to the Egyptian border. "Beyköy 2" mentions Ialysos on Rhodes, a Luwian stronghold, and the Linear D letter refers to Kameiros on Rhodes as a Hittite stronghold. Consequently these two documents provide complementary information. Different kingdoms maintained separate ports of call on the islands.

Simply put, in the earlier document the Trojans were the good guys, producing textiles and interacting properly in the long-distance trade, whereas in the later document they were the bad guys, emitting pirates and raiding port cities in many places around the eastern Mediterranean.

To conclude this discussion from your point of view, if you were to continue the research on Linear C and Linear D, what would you do? It's a little bit over for me since I have worked on the well-preserved longer texts. Of course, one could begin to read every clay ball and every graffiti on cups or pottery pieces, but those will not yield an actual story.

The documents (in Linear C) from Cyprus and Ugarit help determining the trade routes (red) from Troy to Hattusa. The Cypriot nauarch's course is shown with yellow arrows.

The clay balls are connected with the bills of lading, but there's not much one can do with the graffiti. I have done what I could, I translated the text of the most important documents, and it is now up to other people to decide whether they think it is correct or not.

If one were to scrutinize the merit of your translation, where do you think there would be room for different interpretations?
You quoted Silvia Ferrara, who has used an entirely different approach. Her way of dealing with material is so fundamentally different from mine that she would not even address my work. There is no match here. She will say what I did is not possible and simply nonsense. This is indeed a little bit reminiscent of what Alice Kober said about Michael Ventris's efforts to decipher Linear B. Kober considered what Ventris was doing a waste of time. At this point, there's not even room for discussion.

I can see that, but let's imagine someone who agrees with your principle approach and method, but does not entirely agree with your results.
That's of course possible. If one changes the value of a sign or two, it will inevitably lead to a different reading. So one may end up reading different names, for instance. At this point, nothing is carved in stone and the results are up for discussion, but nobody is discussing it yet.

Of course, one has to be careful not to get carried away. Yet interpretations do gain extra weight if they fit well into what we know was going on during a particular period – if everything adds up, it may very well be correct.

Interview conducted on August 28, 2020.

Origin and Motives of the Sea Peoples

The political situation after 1250. Cyprus is annexed by the Hittites. The Hittites mainly collected taxes. Everybody saw the Lukka as troublemakers. At least nine tribes join forces. Several Sea Peoples come from western Asia Minor. Was the central Mediterranean involved? Fred presents his reconstruction; Eberhard sees it differently.

Our conversation today will not focus on the decipherment of a script or language; instead, we now aim to exploit the surviving textual sources to develop scenarios for the cause and sequence of events at the end of the Bronze Age, shortly after 1200. Internal strife, upheavals, raids and migrations caused a sudden end to the golden heroic age and led to a deep cultural incision that resulted in many areas in a Dark Age. The Hittite hegemony over central Anatolia collapsed and in Greece the knowledge of writing was lost for 400 years.

The cultural collapse coincided with and was to some extent induced by the raids of the so-called Sea Peoples, marauding pirates who attacked the shores of the eastern Mediterranean using advanced ships and highly effective tactics. No agreement has been reached about where the individual tribes that made up the Sea Peoples came from; neither do we know what their motive was. Your 2006 PhD dissertation aimed at identifying *The Ethnicity of the Sea Peoples* according to its title.[27] Since I also wrote a book on this subject that came out in 1994,[28] I may actively contribute to today's discussion.

How the Situation Evolved

Before we discuss in more detail what happened during those battles, let's have a flashback to the preceding times. The last major battle had taken place at Kadesh in 1274. The largest Egyptian army to date, led by Ramesses II, clashed with 37 000 soldiers under the command of the Hittite great king Muwatallis II. A number of the names of peoples and kingdoms which later appear in the Sea Peoples' inscriptions also occur in the accounts describing the battle of Kadesh, including Carchemish, Ugarit (Amurru), Kizzuwatna, Lukka and Arzawa. Despite its unprecedented scale, this fight was strictly an Anatolian/Syrian affair from what we can tell.

Following the battle of Kadesh, a peace treaty was signed between Egypt and Hatti in 1259. It affected the interactions across the eastern Mediterranean countries for the next 50 years or so, until the Hittite kingdom had vanished. Thanks to this treaty, fighting between the two countries ceased and the common frontier through the Levant remained fixed. Assyria then ranked as the main aggressor, taking over Mitanni and advancing further to the northwest. Late in the reign of Tudhaliya IV, the great Hittite king's battalions were defeated at Nihriya, and Hatti lost the important copper mines of Ergani Maden in eastern Anatolia. To compensate for this loss, Tudhaliya IV decided to annex Cyprus.

Can you say something about the Hittites' business model during peaceful times? How were they making money?

Well, the Hittites didn't produce much of anything that we know of. The Mycenaeans were famous for their fine ceramics and olive oil, Cyprus had copper, Lebanon had cedar trees, Egypt had gold from Nubia and the Trojans were famous for their fabrics. We know the commodities, for instance, from the shipwreck at Uluburun, containing 10 tons of copper and one ton of tin as well as a broad portfolio of luxury products. – Frankly, I do not know what the economic basis of the Hittite kingdom was. Chances are that they were simply collecting taxes from their vassals. And north Syria was also important for them since the trade routes between Mesopotamia and the eastern Mediterranean passed through Carchemish and Aleppo. This region was ruled by a vice-regal family member of the royal family in Hattusa and thus the most reliable vassal of the Hittite kingdom. As for Cyprus, there the Hittites caused maritime trade with western Anatolia and the Aegean or even the central Mediterranean to be meticulously registered in the local Linear C script for purposes of extracting taxes.

There are basically two phases of strife in which Egyptian sources record a coalition of tribes that we summarize under the term Sea Peoples. The first time we hear about the Sea Peoples is connected with a battle which pharaoh Merenptah fought in 1208 against Libyan forces in the desert west of Egypt. Some of the tribes which were later listed among the Sea Peoples were then mercenaries in the Libyan army. Ramesses II had previously ordered the construction of fortresses along the Egyptian coast to defend his country from attacks. So the Libyan leaders, knowing the desert well, circumvented these bastions and marched across the Sahara towards the oasis of Faiyum. The Egyptian and the Libyan armies clashed in Perire, on the west side of the apex of the Nile delta.

Merenptah says that the Libyan forces were supported by Lukka, Ekwesh, Teresh, Sherden and Shekelesh. According to your analysis, these allies would have come from Lycia, Greece, western Anatolia, Sardinia and Sicily. Wouldn't the attack have been disproportionate with forces coming from all over the Mediterranean to fight alongside Libyan warriors in a relatively minor skirmish on the edge of the Sahara?
We do not know how many mercenaries the Libyan leaders had hired. The forces did not have to be very big; it could have been several hundred legionnaires. As far as the registration of the dead is concerned, the Ekwesh were most numerous, with more than 2000 casualties.

Famines in Anatolia

Towards the end of the heroic era, Hatti experienced multiple famines. Indeed; when the Hittites wrote that it is a matter of life and death, however, the kingdom was still functioning at large, so it is difficult to determine how serious the situation really was. When Hatti suffered famine, pharaoh Merenptah arranged a shipment of grain. However, the carriers of the relevant shipment were attacked by Libyans and their allies, among them were again the Lukka from southwestern Anatolia, who officially ranked as vassals of the Hittites at that time. This was an infringement of the peace treaty between Egypt and Hatti, therefore the pharaoh complained about it. Obviously, the Lukka were disloyal and acting against the Hittite great king's interests. This was most likely the reason why Suppiluliuma II then ordered a military campaign against some kingdoms in western Anatolia, including Masa and Lukka.

Hattusa Chamber 2 was built and decorated in the time of Suppiluliuma I and contains a Luwian hieroglyphic inscription (called Südburg). The inscription is 4 meters wide and 1.8 meters tall.

The Nişantaş inscription in Hattusa was produced early in the reign of Suppiluliuma II, because in it the king still refers to his father to legitimize his own rule. The latest 3D scanning of this inscription brought to light a mentioning of Lukka. The nearby Südburg inscription also mentions Lukka, but it was composed late in the reign of Suppiluliuma I, for the great king did not need to spell out a genealogy anymore. This inscription is unfinished in the sense that the last details of the signs were not made out. It might very well be the last monumental inscription produced under a great king of Hatti. Both inscriptions reveal that the Lukka were causing troubles.

This is where the Linear D letter from Enkomi enters the picture.
Indeed the letter in Linear D from a Cypriot admiral, which we discussed previously, produces evidence that Hittite naval forces had left Cyprus to check the situation regarding the Lukka in Lycia. From its base at Limyra in eastern Lycia, this convoy could still navigate freely off the coast of Lycia. Its commander could indeed claim access to the port of Kameiros on Rhodes. Still, he could not proceed much further north, because a navy consisting of Trojan contingents under the command of Akamas defeated the Cypriot admiral's forces off of Samos. The Hittite officer then navigated his fleet back into the port of Limyra, from where he sent the letter to Enkomi to demand backup forces. It is not clear whether the Lukka, in general, were still hostile towards the Hittites at that time, or whether they had already succumbed to the Hittite army during Suppiluliuma II's military actions against them. However, in any case, there still was a haven loyal to the great king in this region.

From all we know, the Hittite admiral actually received the reinforcement he requested.
In the famous letter RS 20.238 from Ammurapi, the king of Ugarit, to the king of Carchemish, Ammurapi says that "all the troops of my father's overlord are stationed in Hatti" and "all my ships are stationed in Lukka." Evidently, in order to impede the Trojan forces from advancing any further east, Ugarit and most likely other Hittite allies had sent their ships westward to the tip of southwestern Anatolia …

… where they were patently defeated.
They were never heard of again. The next thing we know is that Cyprus was released from Hittite oppression. The Trojan general Akamas fought victoriously whatever naval battles there were. He made it to Cyprus where in the end even a mountain was named after him: Akamantion.

From Cyprus it was a small step to Ugarit, the city was annihilated. Documents found in the destruction layer vividly describe the imminent threat. After that, we have to rely on Egyptian sources to find out what happened next. Accordingly the "Sea Peoples," actually a modern umbrella term to embrace the united forces of the attackers, established a camp in Amurru in southern Syria.

The Sea Peoples' invasions as related and depicted on the walls of the mortuary temple of Ramesses III in Medinet Habu relate how the

The reliefs on Ramesses III's mortuary temple in Medinet Habu show Sea Peoples' warriors wearing feather headdresses as captives of the Egyptian forces.

attackers proceeded from the Levant and eventually reached Egypt. The final battle occurred on the east side of the Nile in Migdol, near a lagoon that is now silted up. The invaders advanced from the sea to the lagoon and proceeded from there attempting to capture this Egyptian fortress on the east side of the Nile near the coast but inland.[29] Archaeologists found and excavated a fortress 4 kilometers west of Migdol and discovered evidence for destruction at the right time.[30]

Where Was Haunebut?

We shall talk more about the inscriptions in Medinet Habu – and their infidelities – later on. Let's first discuss who the Sea Peoples actually may have been. The Egyptians used the name *Haunebut* for the attackers. What does it mean and where does it occur elsewhere?
We find different expressions for the homeland of the Sea Peoples in the Egyptian accounts. They are said to be "of the sea" or "from the Great Green" or, as you said, from *Haunebut*. I found this word in Egyptian

hieroglyphs on a carved Middle Bronze Age scarab from Crete. It is quite possible that this scarab was locally made, providing one of the Egyptian names for the island – alongside *Keftiu*. Another scarab from Crete bears the term *w3d wr*, which refers to the "Great Green" and is also a reference to Crete, situated in the middle of the Great Green, the Mediterranean. Later on, during the historical period, *Haunebut* was the Egyptian term for mainland Greece. In short, the Aegean as the principal homeland of the Sea Peoples has always been quite obvious. There is no question where the Lukka were at home – in the southwest Anatolian region called Lycia from antiquity until today. The Lukka feature prominently in many accounts: those dating to the time of Merenptah, as well as the documents from Hattusa, Cyprus and Ugarit, but not in that of Medinet Habu.

In the illustrations of the sea battles in Medinet Habu, most attackers are depicted wearing feather-crown headdresses ...
They are named Tjeker and have been identified with the Teukroi of Greek literary tradition as early as the nineteenth century. The Teukroi were at home in the Troad – which thus fits well with the Enkomi letter relating how a Trojan navy was advancing south.

Artist's reconstruction of a feather-crown warrior.

Are there any more hints pointing at western Asia Minor?
Another Sea Peoples' tribe is called Teresh. In the literature, these are often associated with the Etruscans, also known as Tyrsenoi in classical Greek texts. In my opinion, at 1200, the Tyrsenoi were still at home in the Aegean and had not migrated to central Italy, since the Etruscan colonization only took place in the Early Iron Age at around 700.

The Peleset are another important unit of the Sea Peoples and they most likely came from the Aegean including Crete. Linguistically the only connection I can see for the Peleset is with the Pelasgians, the Indo-European migrants who had come to the Aegean as early as 3000. Pelasgians were still known even in classical times to have lived along the west coast of Anatolia and Crete. Jean-François Champollion was the first to argue that the Philistines can be identified with the Peleset.[31] He saw the mentioning of Caphtor in the Bible as the homeland of the Philistines and identified it as a reference to Crete. Crete is called *Keftiu* in Egyptian and *Kaptara* in Akkadian cuneiform. And if it is written in the Bible, then it must be true (*chuckles*)!

The Philistine pottery types and their decorations point to Crete and Mycenae. In particular, the bird looking backwards is a design that is known from Crete. But this type of pottery was also copied all around the Aegean.

What about the western side of the Aegean – were any people from Greece amongst the Sea Peoples?
The account of the Egyptian war against the Libyans lists Ekwesh among the tribes fighting against the forces of Merenptah. This, in my opinion, is a term for Mycenaean Greeks or Achaeans. The name does not occur in the Sea Peoples' inscriptions provided by Ramesses III, but perhaps the Denyen were listed in their place. This ethnic term can be derived from Danaos, the legendary forefather of the Greeks, which is also related

The bird looking backward on Philistine pottery is a design also known from Crete.

to *Tanayu*, the Egyptian name for the Greek mainland. However, these Greek soldiers may have only been involved in the fighting as mercenaries with some warriors acting on their own behalf.

Weshesh, Sherden, Shekelesh – and All the Rest of It

The entire Aegean is thus well represented among the Sea Peoples: Trojans from the northeast, Pelasgians and people from Arzawa and Lukka from the east and southeast Aegean, people from Crete in the southern Aegean and some Greeks from its western shores. Were there also tribes involved from outside the Aegean?

We have not discussed three more Sea Peoples' tribes: the Weshesh, the Sherden and the Shekelesh. In my opinion, these came from the central Mediterranean. For the Weshesh, Wassos in Caria (Anatolia) has been proposed as a possible home city, or alternatively Waksos in Crete. Still, I think the Weshesh were the Ausones, an Italic people who originated from the Urnfield culture across the Alps and who invaded Italy at the end of the Bronze Age, thereby displacing indigenous people in Italy. I consider this even the prime trigger of the whole movement. So the upheavals began in the central Mediterranean and from there moved forward to the east.

The Sherden are a remarkable group! At the beginning of Ramesses II, Sherden are already said to have attacked Egypt with "warships" – a new term in the Egyptian vocabulary. These new ships were much better adjusted for fighting at sea, giving the attackers an advantage over the Egyptians. The ships, true galleys, had brailed sails and decks which could be used by archers and warriors – in this form they are also depicted in Medinet Habu. After their defeat, these Sherden were employed as mercenaries in the battle of Kadesh. When fighting on land, the Sherden used Naue-Type-II swords, another innovation of Urnfield antecedents and much more effective than the earlier swords. The Sherden also had round shields which permitted them to attack in a phalanx. All these weapons combined gave them an advantage in the fighting in the Levant and Orient.

A detail from the sea battle scene on the northern wall of the mortuary temple of Ramesses III shows Sea Peoples wearing feather headdresses and helmets with horns.

Linguistically I think the Sherden can be traced back to Sardinia. Yet the old Indo-European root *sard-* is found in a number of places throughout the entire region. The meaning of the root is not clear, but it goes back a long time. The city of Sofia in Bulgaria was also initially called Sardica. Also, the name of the Lydian capital Sardis goes back to the same root as Sardinia.

In my opinion, the technological innovations and sophisticated weapons of the Sherden argue against Sardinia, since people on the island have never been very innovative or influential. Much of the island was mostly used for husbandry for thousands of years.

You're a little bit prejudiced here. There are many fortresses, called nuraghi, and there is even one perfectly built well though …

… the nuraghic well of Santa Cristina in Paulilatino!

So there must have been a rich man who had something built out of precisely hewn ashlar basalt stones according to the latest standards to produce a lunar observatory.

This device is truly mind-boggling, but it is a genuine exception. Apart from this, Sardinia has always been rather rural. When Romans settled there, they stayed on the coast and did not venture far inland.

And yet Sardinia could have brought forward mercenaries, much like the Greeks in later times engaged the Thracians as *peltastai* in their armies, and the Carthaginians employed Celtic mercenaries.

I am quite willing to accept the possibility that mercenaries may have come from Sardinia, but they would not be in a position to develop sophisticated warships. Sardinia has many copper ores, but the people were not able to process it; instead, they had to get copper from Cyprus. Please note that Shelley Wachsmann has identified the Gurob ship model from Egypt in 2013 as a penteconter and associated it with the Sherden or Weshesh living there at the time. And yes, it is a little bit strange that Cyprian copper has been found on Sardinia; it is like carrying sand into the desert. – What convinced me of a central Mediterranean home of some of the Sea Peoples' tribes is the fact that the Sherden are not the only ones who can be placed there. They are accompanied by the Shekelesh, whom I identify with the Sicilians. Again the idea has been put forward that the Shekelesh may have come from western Anatolia, from Sagalassos in Pisidia in classical times, but I consider this to be based on weak evidence. Besides, we have the so-called Shikala letter written

Made of ashlar basalt stones, the construction of the sacred well of Santa Cristina near Paulilatino on Sardinia is assumed to date to the eleventh century.

in Ugaritic by Suppiluliuma II, in which he asks for information on the Shikala, who are said to "live on boats." So they cannot have been from Anatolia because the great king did not even know where they came from; it must have been so far away that to him they had to live on boats.

What Fred Thinks Happened

All things considered, what is your reconstruction of what happened at the time of the Sea Peoples' invasions?

In my model, this is a period of general disturbance when people were on the move. It may have all started north of the Alps in central Europe. There is archaeological evidence that Urnfield people were going across the Alps into Italy. They certainly disturbed indigenous Italic people who may have decided to move away. These then went to places where they knew the sea route from their long-distance trade, such as port cities in the Levant. Somehow Troy was also gaining importance at this time,

The nuraghe Santu Antine on Sardinia is an example for the monumental architecture that existed on the island during the second millennium.

since we have the Linear D letter from Enkomi mentioning the Trojan general Akamas who defeated Hittite vessels near Samos. Hence two different movements were taking place at the same time.

We also see a movement of people on the Balkan Peninsula. The Phrygians were facing troubles, possibly caused by the people of the Urnfield culture. So Phrygians were leaving their homeland and advancing towards Anatolia. This movement on a lesser scale began already in the sixteenth century or, in the Troad, even earlier.

The Trojans, in the form of the Tjeker, are depicted in Medinet Habu wearing feather-crown headdresses. The origin of the feather headdress has been traced back to Italy, where the metal bands of the headdress, so-called *tutuli*, have been found and described by Reinhard Jung.[23] So the feather headdresses of the Trojans were no doubt an emulation, everybody wanted to wear the outfit of the people which were of importance at the time. We know that Sardinians wore helmets with horns, because there are statues of warriors from Sardinia with such elements. And the Sherden are depicted in Medinet Habu wearing helmets with horns. The Europeans had developed a new style of fighting without chariots that was totally new and very effective.

There is additional evidence for people from the central Mediterranean going east since we know of Urnfield cremation burials from this period near Hamath. Moreover, the pottery called handmade burnished ware is now divided into Sardinian type, Sicilian type and Italian type. It is a pottery of low quality and can be made on the spot, but it proves that people from the central Mediterranean made it all the way to the eastern Mediterranean. So there is more and more archaeological evidence for people from the central Mediterranean having been involved. Also the boat types of the Sea Peoples, with bird head devices at both stem and stern, are typically Urnfield antecedents.

If we look at the speakers of Indo-European languages, we see migrations causing difficulties at 3000, 2300 and in 1600. For the most part it is the same story: people from the steppes moving towards Europe and into the Mediterranean, causing problems for the people who lived there. Although it is not recorded, this may have happened c. 1200 as well.

After the fighting had come to an end, a number of tribes who had been involved in the Sea Peoples' invasions are said to have settled peacefully in the Levant. What do we know about these settlements?

The Tjeker settled in Dor and the Sherden are said to have settled at Akko. The biggest group of settlers in the Levant were the Philistines. They established themselves in the Pentapolis, the five cities of Ashkalon, Ashdod, Ekron, Gaza and Gath, but also in the Amuk Valley in Syria. They took over those places, and so they must have come in large numbers. Most of those settlements were already mentioned earlier in Egyptian and Ugaritic sources and their names actually stayed the same. Only Ekron is a new foundation and bearing a new name, one going back to the Indo-European root *aḱer-* for "height," which also occurs in "acropolis."

Artist's reconstruction of a Sherden warrior.

After the Philistines had settled on the coast in the Levant, they soon thereafter started to trade with the central Mediterranean. And we know about contacts between Cyprus and Sardinia during the Early Iron Age, because copper ingots from Cyprus were found on Sardinia. Only a little bit later, the Phoenicians took over these trade routes and then colonized Sardinia. So there is a continuity in contacts between the Levant and the islands in the central Mediterranean from the Bronze Age into the Early Iron Age. – For a short period of time, after Hittite forces had conquered Cyprus during the reign of Tudhaliya IV, the long-distance trade routes were indeed controlled by Hittites. These were then taken over by the Philistines to ultimately become the Phoenician trade routes.

So in the Levant the picture is completely different from what it was during the Bronze Age. In Anatolia we see that the Hittites abandoned their capital which intruders then took over. Gradually Phrygian immigrants take over the region around the Halys River.

How do you explain the fate of Troy?
I would place the Trojan War in 1280, during the reign of Muwatalli II, concurrent with the Alaksandus treaty. A clash between the Ahhiyawans and the Hittites in the region of Troy is also mentioned in the Tawagalawa letter. Further evidence of the same historical incident is provided by the Manapatarhunta letter. This, I would argue, was the Trojan War as famously described by Homer. In 1280 the Mycenaeans were still an important power, whose ruler is acknowledged by the Hittite great king as his peer, thus as another great king.

A second destruction of Troy (VIIa) occurred at the end of the Bronze Age, for sure, but I cannot see how the Greeks would have engaged in this fight as a united force led by a great king. For me, this could only be achieved at an earlier stage when the Mycenaean states were still more powerful. This late in the game, Pylos, for instance, was already destroyed.

Many classical Greek writers regard the Trojan War to mark the end of the heroic era and the beginning of the Dark Age – pretty much everybody agreed on that. If the Trojan War took place three generations earlier, this would not work.

How do you explain the destructions in Greece and the abandonment of 90 percent of the settlements?
Pylos was destroyed around 1200, but we cannot date it exactly to one decade. So it can have happened around 1190 too. We know from the tablets at Pylos that guards were watching the coast facing west toward Italy. I think that Pylos fell first; when the Sea Peoples advanced eastward from Italy, Sardinia and Sicily. We then get the battle in the waters of Lycia, the takeover of Cyprus and ultimately the destruction of Ugarit.

Some Discrepancies

Don't we have to be careful not to take the temple inscriptions in Medinet Habu too literally? In the account provided by Ramesses III in Medinet Habu, Arzawa, Hatti, Kizzuwatna, Cyprus and Carchemish were destroyed. This is simply inaccurate. How do you explain the discrepancy?
The culture in Carchemish continued basically uninterrupted, for we know the tradition of royal names is continuous: Kuzitesup, Aritesup and Initesup. We don't know exactly what happened, of course. Some of the Sea Peoples are said to have settled in the coastal region of Syria, and we see the name Philistine appear in the Alalakh region and in the Amuk Plain. It is quite conceivable that Carchemish was indeed facing problems somewhere within its kingdom, but certainly not in the capital. Cyprus was impacted because the Sea Peoples took it over. But the mentioning of Arzawa is puzzling, because we now have the "Beyköy 2" document in which Arzawa is evidently the aggressor.

Why was Kizzuwatna mentioned as a victim in the Medinet Habu inscription?
Even though at this point in time Kizzuwatna was not a vassal of Hatti anymore, the region was partly conquered by the followers of Muksus. While the Karatepe inscription dates 500 years later, the same royal house of Muksus is still referred to in this text. Asiatiwata is a regent of the king, and the king is from the house of Muksus. Muksus is said to have established all kinds of strongholds along his route into the Levant and he also founded the royal house in Adana – again a fact mentioned in the "Beyköy 2" text. And so port cities in Kizzuwatna were among them, even so.

Infidelities are to be expected since all Egyptian documents are propaganda. And yet they also reflect to some extent events that were really going on. There's a strange text from the period of Ramesses III, also from

Right page: A majority of the tribes making up the Sea Peoples appears to have come from western Anatolia and Thrace. Whether some contingents also came from Italy, Sardinia, Greece and Crete is a matter of debate.

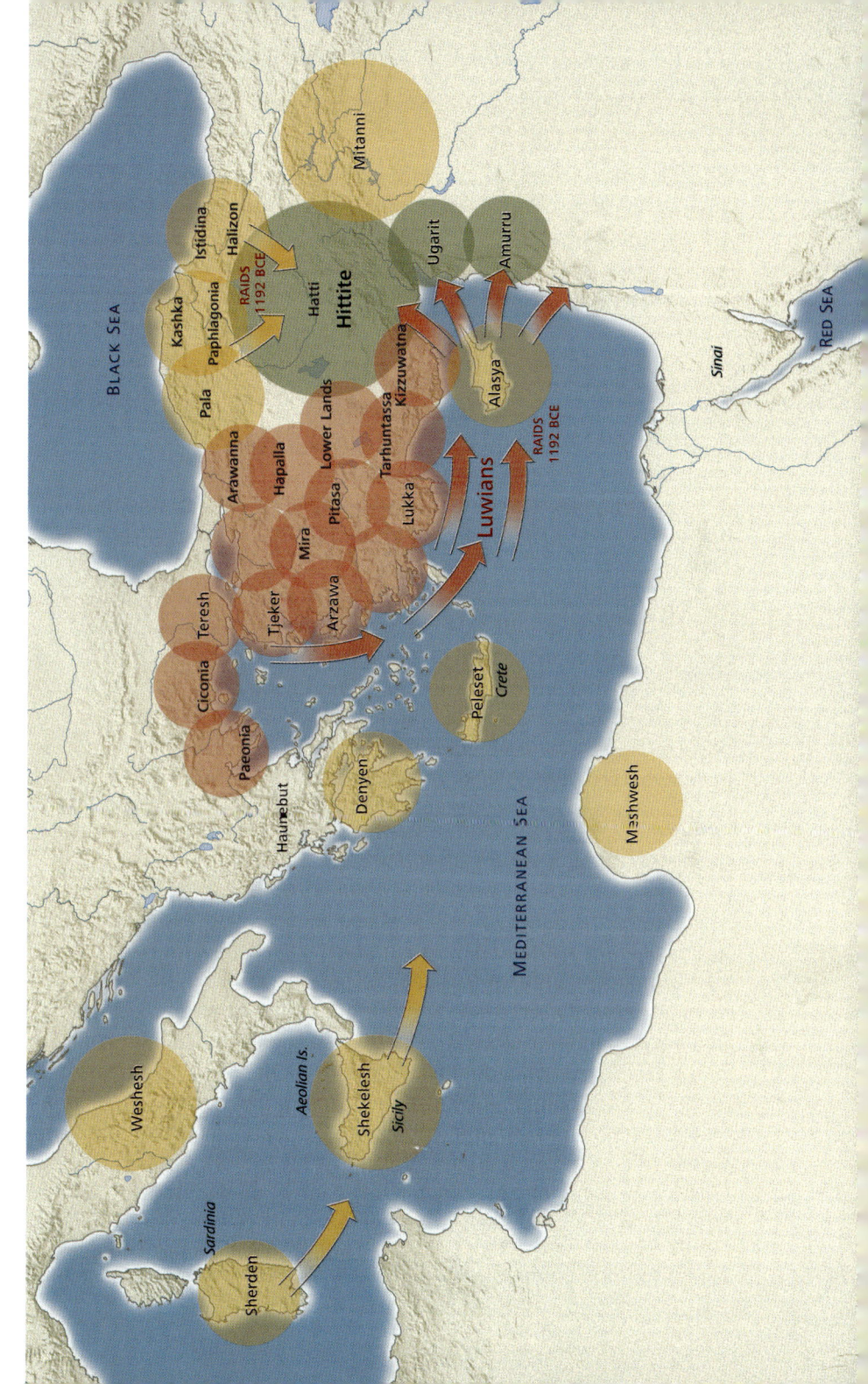

Medinet Habu, that specifically mentions places on Cyprus – and the identifications are indeed correct. The list is so accurate that some scholars have suggested the pharaoh himself had militarily invaded Cyprus, but this is of course nonsense since he had to fight the Sea Peoples, as we have seen above, at his own borders. Even if much of what has been said is propaganda, as historians we have to deflate the text to extract the real picture. And I do think this is indeed possible.

We know, for instance, that the drawings of the ships are quite accurate. At this very time warriors started fighting from decks. So there are some historical elements in the Sea Peoples' accounts and depictions. Whether there was only one fight, or whether a longer period of conflict has been telescoped into one battle in which the pharaoh was naturally victorious, is difficult to tell.

The Homeric sources talking about Agamemnon and Odysseus going to Egypt are in my opinion a reference to the movements after the Sea Peoples. These stories provide parallels for the Greeks among the Sea Peoples going to Egypt to plunder, and sometimes they even were settled there. Maybe some had been taken captive and were then stationed to live in a certain place.

The Sea Peoples' invasions differ from most other conflicts because no state or king appears to have masterminded the attacks. If we take, for instance, the battle of Kadesh, the situation is very clear: two empires clash and the rulers muster all available forces. If we consider the list of tribes involved in the Sea Peoples' invasions, the question still remains, was there perhaps a leader who orchestrated these attacks to increase political power?

The first conflict at the time of Merenptah was a clash between Egypt and Libya, that much we know. During the second phase, the actual invasions of the Sea Peoples, there was apparently no governing force, it was the individual tribes themselves who were attacking Ugarit and Hatti. They proceeded on their own behalf in a somewhat anarchistic fashion all the way to Egypt.

In that case it is difficult to explain how there could have been mercenaries, since those would want to be paid, and for that you need someone who is in charge and has a keen interest to engage additional soldiers.

– Let me put it differently, if the Sea Peoples had a leader, who would have been the most likely candidate?
That is difficult to tell because all we know is that the groups fought together but they settled separately.

What Eberhard Thinks Happened

In my opinion, the inscriptions in Medinet Habu were produced about 20 years after the events had occurred. The pharaoh, as usual, wanted to brag about his achievements, which also explains the discrepancies, such as that Carchemish and Arzawa were counted amongst the victims. Looking back 20 years from Ramesses III's perspective, everybody had indeed severely suffered during the time of upheaval, but for different reasons and to a different extent, because there was a whole lot more going on, including what we now abridge under the term "Trojan War."

In my opinion, the two phases of conflict, the one with Merenptah and the one with Ramesses III, ought to be looked at separately, because they are quite different in character. The clash between Merenptah and the Libyans was clearly a political power struggle resulting from tension between Egypt and Libya. The king of Libya may have found some other people who were anxious to weaken the Egyptian kingdom. It would be worthwhile to look into this: who would have benefited from forming a coalition with Libyan forces against Egypt?
Basically, you are right, but it is a bit more complicated because there were also mercenaries involved.

Concerning the actual Sea Peoples' invasions around 1192, Egypt was so much on the periphery that its people may not even have understood who was actually leading those attacks. Somebody must have been orchestrating these invasions out of particular interest, and I think that research has thus far not paid enough attention to this issue. The inscriptions reflect the names of the individual tribes, and these are somewhat similar to the list of mercenaries in the battle of Kadesh, in which the supreme leader was Muwatalli II. With respect to the Sea Peoples' attacks, we only know who was fighting at the periphery; we do not know who was pulling the strings.

In my opinion, the mastermind must have been at home in western Anatolia. If we look at the regions around the eastern Mediterranean, we know much about how Egypt fought against Nubia in the south, Libya in the west, and Hatti in the north. We recognize the Hittite army as an important military force who at one point seized Babylon, fought the battle of Kadesh, and frequently engaged in skirmishes in western Anatolia. We know that Crete possessed a thalassocracy for some time, and the Mycenaeans seem to have loved warfare for its own sake. In the middle of all this lies western Anatolia, a region that never was a military power to speak of according to our current knowledge. And yet, the only war from this time that is still well-remembered today is the Trojan War, which, of course, took place smack bang in western Anatolia. I am not against this scenario at all; I too believe that western Anatolia is a very important factor during this period and played a major role in these conflicts. Tribes that I attribute to western Anatolia, such as the Lukka, Teresh and Tjeker, are prominently listed amongst the Sea Peoples. So they were clearly involved. But I believe that the Mycenaeans were also involved in the form of the Ekwesh, against Merenptah, and Denyen, against Ramesses III. The Denyen probably only participated in these battles with some warriors as mercenaries fighting on their own behalf.

I think that several kings from western Asia Minor were upset about the disturbance of the long-distance trade routes by the Hittite annexation of Cyprus. The Linear C documents which you deciphered indicate how the Hittite king subsequently collected taxes on goods in transit. Indications are that what comes across as an anarchistic and apparently aimless invasion of chaotic Sea Peoples was indeed a highly orchestrated military campaign that had taken several years to prepare. The plan had to be conceived, coalitions had to be formed, a fleet needed to be built, spies and couriers had to be stationed in the proper places, warriors had to be equipped with weapons, ships needed to be supplied with provisions; above all, potential allies who would be willing to change sides when the time is right had to be persuaded. All these preparations took place while the Luwian kings were waiting for a fortuitous moment of internal strife in the royal house of Hattusa that would provide an opportunity to strike.

When the sign was given, ships making up the fleet departed from several ports in Thrace, in the Troad and from the coasts of western Anatolia. All this was still taking place outside the field of view of Hatti. It took a naval mission into the Aegean by a Cypriot commander to see what was coming – the enemy ships became visible when they had left the Aegean and passed into the Mediterranean off the coast of Lycia. Even at this point their ultimate aim to overthrow the Hittite hegemony over central Anatolia may not have been apparent to the Hittite rulers and their allies in Cyprus, Ugarit and Carchemish.

As is well known, the attackers freed Cyprus from Hittite oppression and then continued further to Syria to beat the only remaining vassal of the Hittite great king. The invaders' ultimate success may to some extent be attributed to support from the Kaska who advanced south to capture the Hittite capital – another maneuver that must have been carefully orchestrated.

The Mycenaean petty kingdoms were not at all involved in any of this. Their kings, however, realized that they would be facing an almighty Luwian power controlling the land and sea routes from Macedonia all across Anatolia, Syria and Canaan. The Greek kings eventually agreed to copy the strategy of the Luwians: they formed a coalition, appointed a leader, built a fleet, equipped ships and armed their warriors. Much like the Luwian "Sea Peoples," they then used a surprise moment to attack port cities in western Asia Minor – without a declaration of war or even an apparent reason. These raids would account for the destructions in Arzawa which are mentioned in Medinet Habu. It was a fairly easy game for the Mycenaeans, because the Luwian forces were distributed and absorbed all across the eastern Mediterranean. In Homer's *Iliad* Achilleus is bragging how many cities he has captured in Asia Minor before his unit even got to Troy.[33]

In the end, both sides, the united Mycenaean forces and the Luwian kingdoms with their allies, gather at Troy to settle the dispute in one decisive battle. Even then the Greeks are considered the underdog, because the Luwians have support from states reaching from Macedonia, over Thrace, all along western and southern Anatolia and even including some peoples from the shores of the Black Sea – those who had already helped bring down the Hittites. The actual fighting at Troy was probably limited to a few weeks. The city was ultimately destroyed, and the Greeks were able to plunder it.

When the Mycenaean warriors with all their loot went home, they learnt that the victorious army would not be welcome in many places, because deputies had taken over their thrones and sometimes even their beds. According to ancient lore Agamemnon was stabbed to death by his wife's lover, and other kings heard about his fate and decided to not even aim for the home port. Greece became entangled in a civil war which I think is graphically illustrated in the *Odyssey*. Ninety percent of the surviving population left the Greek mainland and moved to the periphery: to Euboea, Rhodes, Cyprus, to Italy and Sicily and, above all, to Syria and Canaan – where the Egyptian pharaoh allowed them to settle (as "Philistines") in the most fertile plains, because the Greeks had after all overcome the Luwian aggressors.

So the sequence of destructions begins in the far east with Ugarit and then moves westwards over a few years, until Troy is captured. The wave of destruction then continues to go further west all across Greece until at the very end even Pylos and Ithaca fall. When the dust has settled, the Luwian states in western Asia Minor turn out to be in the most advantageous position after all, because they have plenty of mineral resources and still control the land and sea trade routes.

You are saying that the conflict was in principle a clash between Arzawa and Egypt, but I would argue that Kupantakurunta, the great king of Arzawa, used some mercenaries …

… allies, vassals and mercenaries make up the Trojan contingents as listed by Homer in the *Iliad*.

I don't want to play down the importance of western Anatolia. Ramesses III is not mentioning Kupantakurunta and not listing Arzawa as an enemy, but one of the leaders who is depicted in Medinet Habu as a captive is a *m-'- š3-3-k-n*, which in Luwian hieroglyphic is equivalent to *ma-sà-ka-na* or Muski – and as such an indication of a Phrygian name, thus pointing at the northern Aegean. I would argue that Muksus is also a Phrygian name, and Muksas is, of course, the most important protagonist in the "Beyköy 2" text, who is actually commanding an entire navy to proceed all the way from Troy to Ashkalon to establish a fortress there. Evidently, Ramesses III was indeed confronted by a Phrygian leader.

Nominally, Kupantakurunta may have been a great king, but the attack that he claims took place under his command may have been carried out for the most part by Phrygians.

Interview conducted on September 5, 2020, in Heiloo.

The Etruscans Came from Asia Minor

Etruscan could be read but not understood. Many attempts have failed. One sign comes from Lydia. There is a bilingual inscription – and it is in gold! A whole book in Etruscan. The Lemnos stele is not quite Etruscan. Etruscologists are anxious to establish European roots. Do some Swiss speak Etruscan? Etruscan is a colonial Luwian dialect.

Roman writers speak about the Early Iron Age Etruscan culture in central Italy and its literature, the people who can be regarded as the predecessors of the Roman culture and whose achievements have been known archaeologically at least since the seventeenth century. The Etruscans wrote using the alphabet, so the sound values of the syllables are known. Yet for over a century, scholars have tried in vain to decipher their language. If we were to look up the Wikipedia entry about Etruscan language, we would find that over 13,000 documents with Etruscan texts have been retrieved. You have probably never read what Wikipedia says about Etruscan.
No (*chuckles*)! Most of the many documents are short mentionings of personal names on cups or so. There are, however, a few important larger texts.

About a dozen different deciphering attempts are briefly described in Wikipedia, including yours. Even though scholars do not agree on how to read the script, the entry says they do have reached a consensus that the language was not Indo-European. How did they arrive at this conclusion?
They have identified some terms in the inscriptions, such as "father" or "mother," and concluded that these do not look Indo-European. One of their most important arguments concerns numerals. The famous Tuscany dice undoubtedly bears the names for the first six numerals. One

of them is *θu*, which has been read as "one"; then there is *zal*, which is read as "two" – and there is no relation between these two words and Indo-European. Of course, you could flip those numbers around; then *θu* stands for "two" and is suddenly very Indo-European; and *zal* or *esl-* resembles the Indo-European word *sem-* for "one"; the element *-l-* indicates ordinal numbers, so *zal* or *esl-* means "first."

What are other scholars' approaches to Etruscan and what are their arguments?
There have been many attempts at identifying Etruscan. Several scholars suggested that the language is Semitic or even Sanskrit. Etruscologists like Massimo Pallottino used a combinatory method, as they call it, in which, for example, grave inscriptions are employed to identify personal names. In a next step, connections between these personal names are sought and related to kinships and the kinship terms used to express these. This work seems to point out that the language is not Indo-European.

Are those identifications correct from your point of view?
No, in many ways I do not think they are correct! In my opinion, Etruscan can be derived from Indo-European Anatolian, which forms a special group within the Indo-European language tree. Before World War II, in the time of Paul Kretschmer, it was considered "Proto-Indo-European," a little bit Indo-European, but not quite the real thing – in contradistinction of the present use of Proto-Indo-European for an earlier stage of Indo-European. This view was very popular and hence Anatolian Indo-European was not really regarded as an Indo-European language for a long time.

The lead disc of Magliano dates to the fifth century and is only 7–8 centimeters in diameter. It contains one of the most important Etruscan inscriptions.

What can be said about the script?
The script is alphabetic and can be read without any problems. There is only one peculiarity and that has been recognized already by Ferdinand Sommer in the 1930s. For the letter *f* a new sign is introduced in the form of an 8 or as a horizontal stroke with two circles at each end. This is equivalent to the Lydian F sign – and this peculiarity by itself indicates that the Etruscan script was wholly derived from Lydian. Today, the Lydian F sign can even be traced back further to Phrygia thanks to inscriptions found after the 1930s. Whatever the extent of the latter observation, the idea that Etruscan is directly related to Lydian has been around for almost a century, but it has been suppressed by Etruscologists who prefer to maintain a Eurocentric view of their discipline.

Connections with Anatolian Languages

Some scholars say that the Etruscan alphabet is similar to that used on Euboea.
From my point of view, the F sign makes it clearly Lydian. Of course, alphabets are closely related. This Euboean interpretation is simply an expression of Eurocentric thinking.

The problem lies in identifying the words and the linguistic elements. We can read the text, but we don't understand it. Syncope is frequent, meaning that vowels are lost; all we see is a cluster of consonants. It is not always easy to find the right connections.

Is there any earlier work that you would want to highlight because you think it has been useful?
Yes, the Anatolian connection was recognized in 1929 by Bedřich Hrozný and subsequently underlined in the early 1960s by Vladimir Georgiev, a Bulgarian scholar. Emmanuel Laroche and Piero Meriggi also provided identifications; for example, you have *-hawa* or *-ha* "and" in Anatolian and it is a *-c* in Etruscan, the word for "and." It is enclitic "and," comparable also to Latin *-que*. Francisco Adrados, a Spanish scholar, has also argued in favor of an Anatolian connection. Erich Neu too saw some connections with Anatolian languages.

Which approach did you use in deciphering the Etruscan language?
I started out by learning as much as possible about the Etruscan culture, including what is known about the graves, plus the historic sources, with Herodotus, for example, and his difference of opinions with Dionysius of Halicarnassus.[34] I studied all that, but in the end, you need to know the language, so it remains a linguistic problem.

For me, the search began with the terms "Tarhunt" and "Tarquinia," which Gustav Herbig had already discussed both in 1914 in his work *Kleinasiatische Namensgleichungen* – and Jan Best actually spoke about this in his courses when I was a student. "Tarhunt" is reminiscent of the Luwian storm god Tarhunt, whose name is also at the root of the city and country name Tarhuntassa. In Etruscan, the city name Tarquinia is written as *Tarχna-*, with the *q* being spelt in Latin, thus bringing Etruscan even closer to Tarhunt. If such a prominent term was directly derived from Luwian, it made sense for me to look for more words that may be related to Luwian.

How could Gustav Herbig at the time identify the name "Tarhunt" in an Etruscan text?
The Hittite language had not been deciphered in 1914, but Lycian was already known, including the Hellenistic personal names of Luwian antecedents. Herbig discusses this issue prominently on four pages.[35] The presence of Tarhunt in Etruscan documents has been known and accepted by the established scholarship for more than a century. Since Tarhunt is a Luwian god, its mentioning points towards Asia Minor and possibly Luwian roots. It's a starting point, but one needs, of course, more than that.

The only problem with Etruscan is that Lydian and Lycian, which are closely related, belong to the fifth and fourth centuries. In contrast, Etruscan falls basically into the seventh century. Taking Luwian hieroglyphic into account helps in this case, since it was in use until about 700. Etruscan is in its use related to Luwian much like the sixteenth-century Dutch language is used in South Africa or the seventeenth-century German among the Amish in North America. All three languages were introduced at some point in the past and were then frozen in their development, while the languages in their core territories evolved further. Etruscan is basically a seventh-century Luwian, but from this period we have very little evidence as far as Luwian documents are concerned.

The Pyrgi Tablets

How did you then begin with the actual work on the decipherment?
The obvious place to start is a bilingual inscription, in the case of Etruscan the Pyrgi tablets on gold sheets bearing two texts in Etruscan, a longer and shorter one, and one in Phoenician. The Phoenician version is translated and undisputed. In the Etruscan versions, I simply replaced the individual Phoenician words with their equivalent Luwian roots and produced exactly the same text in Etruscan that is provided in the Phoenician version.

The Pyrgi tablets written in the Phoenician language (left) and the Etruscan language (center, right). In both cases, the text is written right to left.

Could you give an example for parallels?
Let's take the Etruscan word *masan* – it is equivalent to *masana*, the Luwian word for "god." Also, the personal name in the text is that of the functionary who is making the dedication: Thefarie (= Latin Tiberius). In Luwian this is Tiwata, a name that became rhotacized Tiwara in Luwian hieroglyphic, so the person was named after the sun god.

Of course, in a bilingual inscription the two texts are never exactly the same. At the very least, there are differences in expression between the Phoenician and Luwian, but the main text is the same. One Etruscan text is a bit longer than the Phoenician version, so we receive some extra information. The shorter Etruscan version gives a summary of the longer Etruscan and the Phoenician one.

And what does the text actually say?
From the Pyrgi tablets we learn about Etruscan history. A functionary named Thefarie Velianas saw that the goddess had favored him at sea and at land and thus he dedicated a holy place including two altars for the goddess Astarte (Athena). His victory took place on the day of the burial of the god in the month of the dances during "the praetorship of Artanès and the sultanate of Xerxes." Because of this dating formula, the text can be dated precisely to the year 484, when the Persian king Xerxes ruled together with his uncle Artanès – Herodotus hints at this.[36] All this happened during preparations for the battle which then took place at Salamis in 480. In 484 Xerxes was closing in on Greece from two sides. The Etruscan city-states had formed coalitions, and so did the Greek cities in southern Italy. Xerxes aimed to divide the Greek population of the mainland from that in Magna Graecia. He assembled troops in Anatolia and was also rallying in Magna Graecia in southern Italy to gain allies. The Phoenician version of the dedication may indicate that Xerxes conspired with Semitic Carthaginians who were responsible for the battle of Himera in 480, perhaps to reinforce his connections to the people in Italy.

When Thefarie Velianas spoke about the good fortune he had in conflicts, he was referring to a battle that took place in 484 with Greek forces stationed at Cumae near Naples, the most important Greek settlement in southern Italy. He had decided to attack Cumae on a particular religious holiday when his opponents would be least prepared. Textual sources relate how the people of Cumae had been in disarray since they were drunk – and that is why they lost the battle. A decade later, Greeks in Sicily came to the aid of Cumae and became the most important adversaries of the Etruscans.

The victory occurred in the month of the dances, on the day of the burial of the god. The dedication was dated to the first of the feast *cluvenia-* and is meant for an annex to the temple in the form of a libation and a fire altar, which could have been made in the same year as the victory.

Where were the gold plates with inscriptions actually placed?
They were attached with nails most likely to a wooden door of the newly built annex to the temple with the two altars. The Etruscan text speaks of altars in the plural: one used for fire and one used for libation. Not that the temple was newly founded, merely this annex to the temple. The temple was destroyed during an attack by Sicilian forces about a century after the inscription was produced. After the temple's destruction, the gold sheets bearing the inscriptions were intentionally buried in the ground together with some other religious objects.

The core region of the Etruscan culture in central Italy.

When did you publish your work on the Pyrgi tablets?
It first appeared in a book published in 1989.

The work on the tablets yielded access to the language, but it took you many years to complete the work on the subject.
Yes, if you have one text, it does not necessarily mean that you can read other texts as well because they can be dealing with different subjects. However, most of the texts are religious, so they contain names of deities or lists of offerings for the gods. The Tuscany dice with its numerals is a completely different subject. Then there is a large text from Capua providing a liturgical calendar; it took some more time to translate this. Another document is the so-called Cippus Perusinus, a decision by a judge about using a certain piece of land. As a juridical text, it differs from the other Etruscan documents. A longer text has also been found more recently at Cortona; it deals with the religious storage house, a so-called thesaurus.

The "Linen Book of Zagreb," or *Liber Linteus*, is the longest Etruscan text and the only extant linen book, later used for mummy wrappings in Ptolemaic Egypt.

A Whole Book: The Liber Linteus

Are there any open questions for you in Etruscan or can you now read the entire corpus?

Forgive me if this sounds a bit presumptuous, but I do indeed think I can read it all. The longest text we know of is the *Liber Linteus*, a book that is fragmentarily preserved. The text is written on linen, it is indeed the only extant linen book in Etruscan in the world. The tissue was cut into strips and used for wrapping up an Egyptian mummy. The book was written in the early second century BCE, and this serves as a *terminus post quem* for its use as mummy wrapping in Ptolemaic Egypt, which happened simply because the material came in handy. The Egyptian people who did this could evidently not read Etruscan. In 1848, the mummy was bought in Alexandria and since 1867, it and the manuscript are kept in Zagreb, Croatia.

Have you translated the whole thing?
Yes.

What does it say?
It is a manual for priests! It tells the priests when certain religious activities such as offerings are required. Topics are clustered by type and not strictly arranged according to the calendar. For instance, the text may mention a certain offering in June, and then in the same paragraph it says this offering should also be made in September.

Wikipedia says it is a list of prayers!
No, there are no prayers in it!

When you embark on a project like that, do you start from a certain assumption as to what you might be dealing with?
Well, there is, of course, literature. Much like the liturgical calendar from Capua the *Liber Linteus* also contains calendar dates, and these had been recognized before. Both the names of the months and the numerals had already been identified. It has thus been clearly shown by other researchers that the document is dealing with dates in some way or another.

Did you learn anything from being able to read the contents of the *Liber Linteus*?
We find a lot of information about the Etruscan religion and its festivals. At last, we possess written information on the mystery cult. The Etruscans employed the same mystery cult as the Greeks, using their own gods, of course, but they actually wrote about it and thus provided us an insight into how this religion worked. In Greek religion, priests mentioned the mysteries, but they never wrote about them, because it was forbidden.

An important event in the religious calendar, and as such a holiday, was the day of the burial of the god. The whole story reminds one of the books *The Dying God* by James George Frazer, also going back more than a century.[37] Basically, the secrets revealed in the *Liber Linteus* show that Frazer was right in saying that a god may die – a role Dionysus assumed in Greek religion. There was a particular burial ground for Dionysus in Delphi. Frazer had collected a lot of information on all this but was still lacking the necessary proof from surviving texts.

The myth of the dying god is, of course, also an ancient Anatolian custom.
Yes, we know the Hittite myth of Telipinu, the son of the weather god Tessup and of the sun goddess of Arinna. He disappears, thereby causing the death of vegetation. The Phrygians also celebrated a dying god.[38] The Phrygians took over the region formerly ruled by the Hittites, so they may have also adopted some religious customs. In the Etruscan variant, the god dies and, of course, becomes resurrected.

Can you say after how many days?
No!

How about 40?
Okay, then it coincides with the disappearance of the Pleiades. For now, we cannot be sure, because I have not found the term for the resurrection.

Forty days is a timespan that occurs in many customs and religions. Hesiod mentions it in *Works and Days*[39] and it still today marks the period between Easter and Ascension.
Yes, there are many parallels with Christianity. Christ, of course, also dies and then becomes resurrected.

The Enigmatic Lemnos Stele

May we now turn to the famous inscribed Lemnos stele, found by Italian archaeologists in 1884 in the village Kaminia on the island of Lemnos as a stone built into a church wall. Today it is in the National Museum in Athens …
… I've seen it – it's a very large slab!

What does it say?
Everybody makes a connection with Etruscan, because some words on the stele are known from Etruscan. So the connection between Lemnos and Etruria is not in doubt, the question is only how to explain it. Some Etruscologists claim that the Etruscans moved eastward to the north Aegean and thereby colonized Lemnos. Others say we have Tyrsenians in the north Aegean and Lemnos reflects a Tyrsenian settlement. This would prove that the Etruscans had their root in the north Aegean and at a later point migrated to central Italy.

The stele itself dates to the sixth century; the script is boustrophedon, like the ox ploughs – and everybody is focusing one's deciphering attempt on the picturesque front side. This is unfortunately inappropriate because the front side is a mess. An inscription on one of the lateral sides of the stone is much more helpful since it is more systematically arranged. It basically repeats two thirds of what is said on the front but consists of only three lines and so it is impossible to mix it up.

The Lemnos stele is today exhibited in the National Museum in Athens.

The stele turns out to be a tombstone bearing a dedication for a deceased person named Sivas. Sivas is said to have been a functionary during the kingship of Holaios over the Seronians and Myrinians – and Serona and Myrina are places in Aeolis on the coast of northwestern Anatolia. This implies that the island of Lemnos was part of the greater realm Aeolis and not independent.

What can be said about the language?
The language is closely related to Etruscan, but it is not identical; it has dialectal features. This is only logical considering that the Etruscans colonized Italy from 700 onwards. The Lemnos stele was produced one or two centuries later and during this period the language continued to develop in Anatolia, of course. The language in the colonized region was frozen to some extent and maintained archaic features.

The Dutch linguist Robert Beekes also worked on this subject ...
He thought the ancestors of the Etruscans were speakers of a non-Indo-European language who, at the end of the Bronze Age, came from Anatolia and settled in Italy. This is a quite different view, since he considers northwest Anatolia to have been inhabited by non-Indo-Europeans. Note that the non-Indo-European nature of the language in the Troad at the end of the Bronze Age is highly unlikely regarding the frequent Indo-European incursions in the region from c. 3000 onwards. This relates to the notion that Lydians from the region east of Troy (Bithynia) colonized Lydia after the end of the Bronze Age, whereas I argue that Lydians have

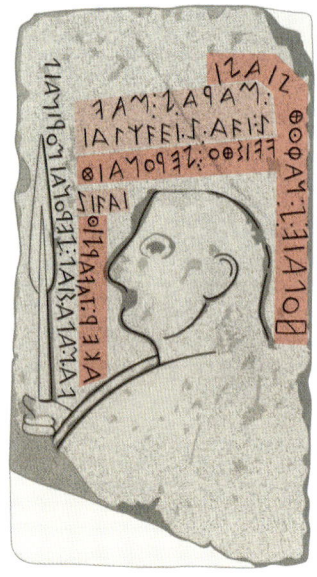

always lived in Lydia and basically represent the continuation of the Bronze Age Luwian culture.

In 2011 a new inscription was found on Lemnos.
Yes, I dealt with that in the digital update of my book which is available on academia.edu. The new inscription can be read and understood, but it is short, comprising only four words. It is a memorial inscription set up by someone who was victorious in a battle.

The inscription on the side of the Lemnos stele includes elements that also appear on the front.

Where Do We Go from Here?

Has your decipherment of Etruscan received any acceptance?
I cannot say that. I can only say that the review of my book about the *Liber Linteus* was rather defensive.

From your perspective, what would you say needs to be done next in this particular avenue of research?
I did what I could, and it is now up for others to decide whether this is of any value or not. In an ideal world, the people in the field would read my book, try to recapitulate the grammar and perhaps verify or disprove certain aspects of my work.

This would also imply that people begin to enter a conversation with peers who follow a different line of thinking, and as a result perhaps we even start thinking out of the box.
Yes, but I don't see this happening in the near future, to be honest, as far as Etruscologists are concerned. But specialists in the Indo-European

languages of Anatolia might well be interested. It is clear now that Etruscan is simply a Luwian dialect. There can be no doubt today that the language was wholly derived from Anatolian roots and that it was introduced to the Italic Peninsula by migration. This is where Herodotus comes in since he describes the roots of the Etruscan culture as a movement of Lydians from western Anatolia who went to the present-day Tuscany.[40]

The Etruscologists form a closely knit network and employ their own paradigmatic framework without alternative explanations. They argue that the Etruscan people lived in Italy already during the Neolithic and explained the Lemnos stele with Etruscans moving from west to east and settling in the northern Aegean, but they are wrong. Etruscans cannot have been the earliest inhabitants of Tuscany, because river names such as *Arno* and *Albula*, the ancient name of Tiber, are already Indo-European – Old Indo-European! The people who introduced those names came first and Etruscans came in much later. There is even an intermediate Umbrian layer, recorded in the river name Ombrone, in archaeological terms to be equated with the Proto-Villanovan and Villanova culture of European Urnfield background of the twelfth to eighth century. Hence, the Etruscans cannot have been in Italy since the Neolithic; this is a modern myth and completely wrong!

It is difficult to prove that a new population has immigrated into a certain region, since what we find in the archaeological record for the most part consists of continuity with some new elements. The question is how important these new elements are, and this is, of course, a judgment call. In the case of the Etruscan culture, however, I think the evidence is clear. Suddenly, at 700, chamber tombs under tumuli of Anatolian type occur. However, the very same tombs which we know from Lydia and Lycia are slightly younger than those preserved in Anatolia. Etruscan chamber tombs were carved in stone but imitating a wood construction – this is exactly the Anatolian style. If you would see a photograph of the Lydian graves from Mysia, you would inevitably think that these are Etruscan graves without a caption. The tomb walls of the Lycian graves bear colorful paintings, and similar paintings occur in the graves in Etruria. Southern Etruria has façade graves on vertical rock faces, just like they are characteristic of Lycia. It could hardly be clearer that the Etruscan funeral culture came from Anatolia.

Don't Forget the Rhaetians!

What did the later development of the Luwian dialect spoken in Etruria look like after the seventh century? Did remnants survive in certain regions?
The Etruscans colonized the Po Valley and spread further into the Alps. Etruscan is also much influenced by Italic languages such as Latin, Faliscan, Umbrian and Oscan. The colonists coming from Asia Minor soon married local women and, in this way, Anatolian and Italic roots of the languages became mixed from the very beginning of the colonization, but more than 95 percent of the grammar are impeccable Luwian.

The Rhaetian language spoken in the Swiss canton of Graubünden is said to contain remnants of Luwian. How is this possible?
The Rhaetic that survived in Switzerland still contains remnants of Etruscan but is also heavily influenced by the language substrate that pre-existed in the area. So the evidence is slight, because extant old inscriptions are short and only occasionally contain a verb. I think that the population consisted of people who formerly lived in the Po Valley and were forced out by Celts, and then went into the mountains for protection. They took with them some Etruscan vocabulary but acquired, of course, other components of the language spoken locally among the people living in the mountains, which would have been Celtic or Italic. And yet, for example, the ending of the verb in Rhaetian is the same as in Etruscan.

What Are the Consequences?

Let's assume that your decipherment of the Etruscan is correct. What would be the consequence for other open questions in archaeology?
It helps, for example, in reading Luwian hieroglyphic.

In other words, you can apply reverse engineering to illuminate the language from which Etruscan was – at least partially – derived?
Indeed! If we take, for instance, the ongoing discussion regarding the signs *376–377 for *i, ī* and *zi, za* in Luwian hieroglyphic, it was essentially

the understanding of the Etruscan language that made me become aware that the sign is polyphonic, so it can be read in both ways. I saw connections to Etruscan words and realized that some contained *i*, while others had *zi*. For instance, in the case of the Etruscan verb *ziχ(u)n-* "to write," which originates from Luwian hieroglyphic *376-ku-na-* "written

Fred Woudhuizen never used notes during the interviews.

account," *376 is *zi*, hence the Luwian word reads *zikuna*. On the other hand, in the case of the Etruscan deity name *Asia*, which is derived from the Luwian hieroglyphic verb *á-s(i)-*377-* "to (be) love(d)," *377 is *ī*, and the Luwian word reads *ás(i)ī-*.

First, I used the information at hand on Lydian, Lycian and Luwian hieroglyphic to understand Etruscan. But once I understood Etruscan, I could use it to understand the Anatolian languages, because Lydian is also poorly known since there are at most a hundred texts. Because so little evidence remained, we have to make use of everything that has been transmitted.

That is possible because Luwian hieroglyphic was still around when Etruscan began to form.

Yes, but the colonization occurred around 700, while the use of Luwian hieroglyphic came to an end at around the same time. Of course, the actual use of the language continued all the way into the first century, well into Roman times. In the early seventh century, Luwian hieroglyphic was still in use in eastern Anatolia and Syria, while the people in the west of Anatolia spoke Lydian, Carian and Lycian. Surviving documents in these languages date to a time a little after the colonization of the Italic Peninsula, but they are the closest dialects to Etruscan, because the people who migrated to the central Mediterranean obviously came for the most part from western Anatolia; only a few may have been from Syria and Cyprus. In the historical sources the settlers are called *Xenoi*, a term that is typical for people coming from the Aegean.

If I may recapitulate, the Etruscan language was derived from western Anatolia, but what has been transmitted in the form of Luwian documents from this period stems from far eastern Anatolia including Syria up until around 700. And then in the fifth century, we get Lydian, Lycian and Carian documents in western Anatolia. Luwian language developed further into Lydian, Carian and Lycian in western Anatolia, whereas it remained pretty much unchanged in Etruria.

According to my model, Lydian, Carian and Lycian are directly derived from Luwian. They have split up in the Early Iron Age, while Etruscan preserved the early phase in which Lydian, Carian and Lycian had not yet separated.

Interview conducted September 14, 2020.

Other Luwian Dialects, Such as Lydian, Lycian and Carian

The Hittites have vanished. Phrygians are migrating into Asia Minor. Most people still speak Luwian. Lycian is a Luwian dialect – and so are Lydian, Sidetic and Carian. Is Qλdãnś really Apollo? Minor changes in reading Luwian have a big effect. Sidetic consists half-half of Phoenician and Cypriot signs. Sidetic is closely related to Lycian B. Some questionable scholarship on Carian. Carian contains Cypro-Minoan characters. Scripts do mingle! Greek is overrated.

The dust has settled, the imperial period and even the entire Bronze Age have come to an end. How would you describe the situation in the twelfth century in Anatolia? What had happened to the Hittites?
Surviving members of the Hittite ruling class evidently moved to the south into the border region with north Syria. Neo-Hittite Luwian hieroglyphic texts from this region yield all sorts of Hittite royal names, including Suppiluliuma, Mursili and Muwatalli. We also see an increase in Hittite loanwords in Luwian hieroglyphic texts from this period. Thus, there clearly was an influence of Hittite culture in Syria, but I don't know how big it was, and whether it was only the upper echelons of society, I cannot say either. The capital of the Hittite kingdom was left vacant and the culture as such did not continue. There are no Hittite documents after the abandonment and destruction of the capital.

The Hittite ruling class had lost their capital as well as control over the entire kingdom. The surviving aristocrats went south towards Carchemish, because one of their family descendants was still in charge there. Central Anatolia was left to other tribes, Kaska perhaps to begin with …
The Kaska were cooperating with the Muski. We are getting some information from the border of Syria about these so-called Muski, a new population group that had entered Anatolia, and came to stay. There is an

Lydian, Carian, Lycian and Sidetic are Luwian dialects – written in alphabetic script.

ongoing discussion amongst scholars whether the Muski were Phrygians or not. I think that Muski is just another word for Phrygian, especially so as their great king Mita of Muski is none other than the Phrygian Midas.

The movement of the Phrygians, coming from the Balkan and entering Anatolia from the northwest, must be seen as part of the migrations taking place on a large scale during the Early Iron Age. We also see people from the Urnfield culture coming across the Alps into Italy, disturbing the people who lived there, of whom some left for the Levant. There is a general pattern of peoples on the move during this period.

Parts of western Anatolia were no longer under the powerful control typical of the Late Bronze Age – and the Phrygians moved in, perhaps they were interested in natural resources and trade connections?
I don't know, it's a dark period! We cannot say much about it, only that they came in large numbers and were there to stay. They spoke Phrygian, an Indo-European language that is close to Thracian and Greek.

Vowels		Consonants							
a	⌐	b	B	m	M	t	T	ñ	⌶
e	↑	d	Δ	n	N	τ	Ψ	?	M
i	E	g	Y	p	Γ	θ	X	?	◇
u	O	h	+	q	✳	χ	V	w	F
ẽ	Ψ	k	K	r	P	z	I		
ã	W	l	Λ	s	Ƨ	m̃	X		

List of Lycian signs (after Kolb 2018, 81).

The Luwian-speaking population continued to thrive, particularly in western and southern Anatolia, along the coast of the Aegean and the eastern Mediterranean.
Most of the population would have been Luwian speaking since this is the language that survives, in particular in the southwestern part running from Lydia all the way to Carchemish. Along this coastal stretch we find people who are speaking Lydian, Carian, Lycian and Sidetic.

Lycian Can Be Read and Understood

The Lycians are famous for their graves hewn into bedrock along the coast. What do we know about them?
Frank Kolb recently published a voluminous book about the Lycian culture covering also, of course, those famous graves.[41] Most of the material is from the fifth and fourth centuries; some earlier, it dates to the seventh and sixth centuries. During this earlier phase, the people built chamber tombs under tumuli. Kolb, however, is a little bit downplaying the earliest evidence. He predominantly works with surveys and not with excavations, which could unearth earlier layers, so I don't agree with everything he says …

As an ancient historian, he naturally focusses on the time from the sixth century onwards.

Turkish colleagues have, based on excavations, also pointed out earlier evidence that exists in Lycia, but unfortunately there is only little of it. We currently know that the Lycian culture belongs to the fifth and fourth centuries, which is undoubtedly reflected correctly by Frank Kolb.

What can we say about their script and their language? They basically used the Greek alphabet, right?

Let's say they used the alphabet, I would not call it Greek, though! The Lycians called themselves "Termmile." Their language was in the main a Luwian dialect; it can be directly derived from Luwian and is closely related to Luwian hieroglyphic. There are some 200 inscriptions, dating from the late seventh to fourth century. Already beginning in the 1950s, Emmanuel Laroche wrote four very important articles on Lycian, in which he showed that the language is indeed a Luwian dialect. And then in 1973, the Letoon trilingual was found bearing identical texts in Lycian, Greek and Aramaic. This is a religious text because something is ordained, or a political decision has been made to celebrate a cult. This kind of text provides one particular type of vocabulary. We know exactly how to read it because we have the Greek and the Aramaic version. So there can be no doubt about what the text says. The other Lycian documents are mostly grave inscriptions, saying something along the lines: "This is my grave and you put my wife on top and my son and daughter next to us – and if you don't do it, or if you demolish something, you'll get punished by the local authorities or by the god himself." Even today, it can still be difficult to understand these texts, because the vocabulary is different from that of the Letoon trilingual. – But there is no alternative explanation saying, for instance, that Lycian is closer to Hittite or Palaic. It is clearly a Luwian dialect, which may have some ancient features.

There are two Lycian dialects …

Yes, Lycian A and Lycian B, of which the latter reflects an older variant closer related to Luwian. Where Lycian B has an *s*, Lycian A will have an *h*, the later development of the *s*. If you have *ma-sa-na* for "god" in Luwian, it will be *masa-* in Lycian B and *maha-* in Lycian A.

What does your contribution to the study of Lycian consist of?

I made a list of connections between Luwian hieroglyphic, Lycian and Lydian. – Lycian is most closely related to Luwian hieroglyphic, which is clear from the grammatical paradigms. The nominative masculine/ feminine plural in *-i* relates to Luwian hieroglyphic and the genitive plural in *-āi* is an exact parallel between the two – three actually, if we take Lydian into account as well.

Three Signs in Lydian Should Be Corrected

Let's move on to Lydian then; how many documents do we have in Lydian? And how do you describe the Lydian kingdom?

Slightly over one hundred, so considerably less than there are for Lycian. Lydia was, of course, a large and powerful kingdom for a few centuries. It will be eternally remembered, partly because Herodotus, who came from Halicarnassus in Lydia, put an artfully crafted account of the deeds of the Lydian king Croesus at the beginning of his book *Histories*. Sardis, the capital of Lydia, was regarded by its Greek contemporaries as a city of unfathomable wealth. Indeed, still ongoing excavations reveal architectural remains of unique dimensions, certainly as far as western Anatolia is concerned. So there must have been a lot of writing, but very little is preserved.

In principle, the Lydian kingdom is the successor of the most powerful Late Bronze Age state in western Asia Minor: Arzawa. Cuneiform inscriptions, such as the songs of Istanuwa in Hapalla in northeastern Arzawa, reveal some information about the language spoken there. We also have a few Luwian hieroglyphic texts from western Anatolia; so, it is possible to compare Luwian as spoken in Arzawa with Lydian. And from what I can tell, it is the same language. Strabo mentions that around his time, the Lydian language was no longer spoken in Lydia proper but was still being spoken among the multicultural population of Cibyra (now Gölhisar) in southwestern Anatolia, by descendants of Lydians who had founded the city.[42]

Who is doing research on Lydian?

Roberto Gusmani did the most important research on Lydian during the twentieth century. He published a Lydian dictionary in several volumes and in a way monopolized the subject. Piero Meriggi had already identified Lydian as Luwian in the 1930s, because of the word *amu*, which means "I" or "me" in both languages. Then, in the 1960s, Onofrio Carruba presented pro and contra arguments for Lydian being either derived from Luwian or Hittite. He recognized both influences and thought that the connection to Hittite was clearer.

In the proceedings to the EAA session 2019, which we have mentioned before, Alwin Kloekhorst argues that the Lydians actually came from northwestern Anatolia.

This idea goes back to the Dutch scholar Robert Beekes. He thinks Lydian speakers originally came from Masa in northwestern Anatolia and have migrated south to the Sardis region where they chose to establish their capital. I don't quite see it that way. There may have been peoples, such as Muski or Kaska, moving into Lydia at the time of the Sea Peoples' invasions, because populations, in general, were on the move at the time, but the Arzawan language is the same as the Lydian language, and in my opinion there is no need at all for migration. Alwin Kloekhorst has described Lydian inscriptions from Daskyleion and considers this a verification of Beekes's model. But if you take into account that the father of the famous Lydian king Gyges was Daskylos, it is quite likely that he came from the city Daskyleion, which would therefore have been part of the Lydian kingdom. When in the seventh century the Milesians wanted to assume control of Abydos on the Dardanelles, they had to ask permission from Gyges, because Daskyleion lay in between Miletus and Abydos. The entire route to the Black Sea was basically under Lydian control at that time. Hence, there is no need for migration, since even northwestern Anatolia was part of the Lydian kingdom.

How did you contribute to the research on Lydian language?

In my opinion, three signs are currently read incorrectly. There is, for instance, the plus sign (+), which in the old days was considered to reflect the letter *p*, but nowadays is read as *q*. In my opinion, the Old Reading was correct, because a word such as *Pλdãnś* is currently read as *Qλdãnś*, which is less clearly "Apollo."

The second one is the Lydian *yod* sign, which is exactly like the Phoenician *yod* and must be read as the vowel i_1 in my opinion. Enno Littmann saw the parallels with the Phoenician sign already in 1916, but argued that it ought to be read as a secondary *nu*, to be distinguished from the regular sign for *n*, and transliterated by the Greek *ν*. Consequently, in translations we now find the Greek *v*, but people have indeed noticed that it is actually a *yod*.

The third sign is the upward arrow (↑); it is related to the Cypro-Minoan sign for *ti* and renders the acrophonic value t_1 as an alphabet letter. It often occurs before an *i*. – If you read those three signs correctly, you'll get exactly a Luwian dialect.

These are relatively minor changes, but they have a big effect!
Yes, because the *yod* sign frequently occurs in the endings, and if we don't translate it correctly, we simply do not get proper endings. For example, from Luwian hieroglyphic we know the word *tàśaī* for "stele" – in Lydian this becomes *taśẽi₁* – both nominative/accusative neuter singular. Also important in this connection are the endings of the nominative plural of the communal gender in -i_1 and genitive plural in -ai_1, which are paralleled for Luwian hieroglyphic in the Adjusted Old Reading and Lycian.

We know of one bilingual inscription, in Lydian and Aramaic.[43] It is a grave inscription and as such explains the parts of the grave and to whom it belongs etc. In it, we find the typical damnation formula: "Whoever (will bring damage) to this stele or this grave or these columns …"

But there are also texts such as Lydian no. 22 (LW 22), which deals with cult. Ilya Yakubovich provided a very good structural analysis of this text and made clear what the sentences are. He also identified the mentioning of the brotherhood of the Mermnads, or *Mλimnaś* in Lydian. This is the old royal family, which by the time the inscription was made was no longer providing the king, yet still influential. The inscription says they are making provisions for the altar of Artemis in order to support the practice of her cult. This text reflects a vocabulary different from the grave inscriptions.

Your work on the *yod* sign only came out recently, right?
Yes, but I started working on this subject in the early 1980s. The recent paper reflects material that I have collected over a time span of almost four decades.

In one of those recent papers you said: "With almost boring repetition, case after case points out that Lydian is, like Lycian, just an ordinary Luwian dialect."
And there's nothing I can add to this.

Sidetic Contains Signs from Cypriot Script

So we turn to Sidetic next. What's the story about Sidetic?
Sidetic is the easternmost Luwian dialect that is preserved from the fourth to the second century, and it was spoken primarily around the city of Side, near the modern town of Antalya. There are only about ten inscriptions and a few dozen legends on coins that we know of. The script consists of 21 signs written in an alphabet, just like Lydian and Lycian. Normally, people think that the alphabet was introduced into Anatolia coming from Greece, but concerning Sidetic, there is a problem. The alphabet that was used there consists of two components: signs from the Phoenician alphabet, which are alphabetic letters as we know them, and signs from the Cypro-Minoan syllabary, which are in this case also used with their acrophonic value reduced to alphabet letters.

What is the ratio between the two?
It is about fifty-fifty. The Cypro-Minoan component is thus very large, more so than in any of the other Anatolian alphabets. From the Phoenician component of Anatolian alphabets, we know sign variants that are not related to any Greek inscriptions, such as the *yod* sign in Lydian, which is evidently Phoenician. To this comes the arrow sign, which is Cypro-Minoan. Neither one is known from Greece! The only conclusion can be that the alphabet in Anatolia is a totally independent innovation and that it was introduced without input from Greece …

… and the Anatolian alphabets are, of course, in terms of geography and chronology much closer to Cyprus and Phoenicia than Archaic Greece was. Does this also imply that the Greek alphabet may have been derived from the Anatolian alphabet?
Not necessarily, because we find a very late form of the Phoenician alphabet in Greece, one that clearly dates to the eighth century. It is surely a possibility, but there's also the possibility that it came directly from Phoenicia or from some middle zone, like north Syria and its trade city al-Mina. As a typology, the Anatolian alphabets have earlier features. In any case, the Anatolian elements are not part of the Greek alphabet. Some of the sign variants in the Anatolian alphabets are very old, so they may have been introduced there earlier than in Greece. However, as far

as surviving inscriptions are concerned, the alphabet is documented in Greece and Phrygia from the eighth century onwards, and in Lydia, Caria and Lycia from the seventh century onwards. Thus, the alphabet appears a little later in western Anatolia than it does in Greece.

What is your contribution to the study of Sidetic? You wrote about Sidetic already in the early 1980s!
Yes, indeed! The people working primarily on Sidetic are Christian Zinko and Michaela Zinko, but their translation attempts came to a halt on the level of personal names which they think they can read. They consider the inscriptions to be basically enumerations of personal names. My approach is to trace the origin of the signs. If I find Phoenician alphabet letters, I attribute the alphabet values accordingly. If I can trace the sign back to the Cypro-Minoan syllabary, I'll give it the value that it has there, not the syllabic value, but the alphabet value according to the acrophonic principle. Thus, *ti* becomes t_1, and mi becomes m_1. Using this approach, I get the right values and can thus read the text. It is as simple as that. If you fill in the right values in the longest inscriptions, you'll see that Sidetic is a Luwian language that is closely related to Lycian B. There are entire sentences with verbs, subjects, objects and all kinds of other linguistic features.

And so what do these inscriptions say?
Well, you know the usual thing: "This memorial is for Artemon. He has founded the thank-offering …" etc. However, the longer inscriptions deal with dedications to the god or goddess. The benefactor provides complicated and detailed accounts of who is dedicating what to the deities and from whose inheritance it came and so forth.

This is quite sophisticated information, so you are even able to read between the lines.
Yes, it is very detailed with verbs and endings. – Most of these Sidetic inscriptions date to the third and second centuries. Thus, it is the latest writing in which Luwian as a living language is transmitted to us from Anatolia. Luwian personal names continue to be used in Greek inscriptions until the first century BCE. So in Roman times, people could still have Luwian names.

Carian Has Not Been Deciphered Correctly

And with this we turn to Carian, which is even more exciting, because there we have the biggest spectrum of interpretations, right?

There are a lot of inscriptions in Carian, something like 200. Part of them were found in Egypt and part of them in southwestern Asia Minor. Caria is basically a region within the Lydian realm. Still, at the time, Carian mercenaries were fighting on behalf of Egypt, so these forces were based in Egypt. They could be understood as political and military support from Lydia to Egypt on account of an agreement between the Lydian king Gyges and the Egyptian pharaoh Psammetichus.

Carians are characterized in historic sources as people who speak a strange language. Herodotus says they were the first to attach feathers to their helmets.[44] He also writes that during the era of Minos, so in the Late Bronze Age, some say that Carians had lived on the Cycladic islands. They had to row the ships of the Cretan king.

What do we know from the archaeological record about the Carians?

The archaeological evidence for Carians is older than that for Lycians, for instance. Some Carian graves near Iasos date to the tenth century. Miletus was part of the Carian region and Halicarnassus, today's Bodrum, with its famous mausoleum that became one of the Seven Wonders of the Ancient World.

The Carian script is considered to be deciphered, right?

The current theory, which everyone adheres to, claims that Carian has indeed been deciphered using the Ray-Adiego-Schürr system. The British scholar John D. Ray did some work on Carian which in my opinion was very good. For instance, there is a sign (F) that looks like the Phoenician *wāw*, but its value is an *r*, because the strokes of the *wāw* used to be connected, thereby reproducing the Phoenician *r*. Another sign that John Ray identified is the *s* in the form of a circle with a vertical or horizontal stroke through it.

Ray did some good work in my opinion – and as it turns out, he does not agree with Ignacio Adiego and Diether Schürr! Even though it is called the Ray-Adiego-Schürr system, the former does not support what the latter did after him.

What did they do?
They wrote each letter on a small piece of cardboard, put those into a vessel; they shook the vessel thoroughly, and then they took out the first card and said: "This is letter A." The second card: "This is letter B," and so on … (*laughs*). There is no relationship between the so-called decipherment of Carian and the Phoenician alphabet as far as the values of the letters are concerned! If it existed in this form, it would be the only alphabet in the world with values like this, something that I consider very unlikely. To me, this is substandard scholarship.

And John Ray sees it the same way?
I can only say that he did not agree with what came after his work. – As we have said before, the alphabet is a mnemonic device, children learn it in a certain order – and this order has remained the same for the past 3000 years all across the world. The order of the signs has to be fixed, otherwise you would get a problem. There are, of course, signs which have been used for secondary values that are not necessarily related to the original value. For example, in Greek, the sign *psi* (*Ψ*) was originally *chi* (later *X*), and this is a form of the Phoenician *kāp*. The *psi* has a totally different value, so something must have happened to get attributed to this secondary value. But these things only occur in very few instances. It is not normally the case for the alphabet. What is normal is that A = A, B = B, C = C – and this continues throughout the use of the alphabet until the present day!

Besides, alphabetic letters can also be used for numbers, for instance, in Greek and in Latin – so the C indicates one hundred, and M is one thousand. This too implies that the values were fixed.

From what I know, the Ray-Adiego-Schürr system was picked up, for instance, by Peter Frei and Christian Marek.
Yes, that is right. They argued that the system must be correct, because there are names in the Greek text of the Kaunos bilingual inscription[45] which they think can be found in the Carian version of the text using the current reading. This is true to some extent, but it can be a fluke, an accidental coincidence. In reality, the Carian decipherment does not recognize any complete sentences, since there is no phrase with a verb or a subject. So far they have only identified personal names, and personal names are the lowest category in linguistics. An entire sentence

ἔδοξε Καυν[ί]οις, ἐπὶ δημιο-
ργοῦ Ἱπποσθένους· Νικοκ-
λέα Λυσικλέους Ἀθηναῖο[ν]
καὶ Λυσικλέα Λυσικράτ[ους]
[Ἀ]θηναῖον προξένους ε[ἶναι κ]-
[α]ὶ εὐεργέτας Καυνίω[ν αὐτο]-
ὺς καὶ ἐκγόνους καὶ [ὑπάρχει]-
ν αὐτοῖς ε[ἴσπλουν καὶ ἔκπλουν]

"It seemed good to the Kaunians, under
the demiorgos Hipposthenes: Nicocles,
son of Lysicles, Athenian,
and Lysicles, son of Lysicrates,
Athenian, shall be proxenoi
and benefactors of the Carian people,
both themselves and their descendants
and [...]."

OTHER LUWIAN DIALECTS • 185

Image Enlargement

Transcription

va-cś | cordś | ctor-
ovo | cénś | dnẽdéa
murnoruoś | nẽoś
aéduśé

Comments

Expression	Related to	Meaning
va-	Luwian	Introductory particle wa-
-cś	Etruscan	Enclitic demonstrative pronoun -c(a)- "this"
cords	Lycian	Noun ϑurtta- "brotherhood"
ctorovo	Greek	Showing the same root as the Greek Ἕκτωρ
cénś	Greek	Noun γένος "gens"
dnẽdéa	Greek	Ethnic group Δαναΐδαι or Danaans
murnoruoś	Lycian/Luwian	First element corresponds to Lycian Murñna- Second element to Luwian hieroglyphic Ruwa-
nẽoś	Greek	Kinship term for "son," corresponding to νέος "young"
aéduśé	Greek	Greek ἔϑυσε "he has sacrificed" in Carian transcription

English Translation

"On behalf of this brotherhood, Hector-
ovos, the gens Danaidae,
son of Murnoruos,
has sacrificed."

Fred Woudhuizen transcribed and translated four lines of the Carian text on the famous Kaunos bilingue for the purpose of this book to illustrate his approach.

including a verb and the right endings would be required to justify the claim that the script has been deciphered.

For our conversation today I transcribed the famous Kaunos bilingual inscription consisting of a Carian text on top and a Greek one below. Even though they are both damaged, we can reconstruct the Greek version of the text, because that is just easy to do. It is a proxeny decree in which the Kaunians, during the magistracy of Hipposthenes, honor the Athenians Nicocles and Lysicles as public guests and benefactors. On the other hand, the Carian text is more difficult and only lines 15–18 are well preserved. Employing the transcription method I propose, the text becomes readable as a normal phrase of someone who is making an offering. The worshipper turns out to have a Luwian-type of name that does not occur in the Greek text. Actually, the two texts are totally unrelated, so the Greek version must be a later addition. The Luwian man belongs to the clan of Danaïds, a tribe known from the time of the Sea Peoples' raids and sometimes associated with Greece. So there may have been an earlier Greek connection, which could have been why a Greek inscription was later added.

I would argue differently, namely that this is a good indication that the Danaïds were indeed a Luwian tribe from western Anatolia. – Anyhow, is it still a bilingual text even if the two texts are completely different?
Yes, "bilingual" only means "two languages" – it doesn't mean that the same information is repeated in both inscriptions.

And is anybody else aware that the two texts are different?
No, they think the Carian text is repeated in the Greek version.

What is your approach to interpreting Carian? How does it differ from what Ignacio Adiego and Diether Schürr did?
In deciphering ancient languages, the challenge always lies in finding the right values for the letters. There are some 28 signs altogether, most of them are Phoenician, but there is also a substantial component of Cypro-Minoan characters. For instance, the *m* in Carian is derived from Cypro-Minoan *mi*, and some scholars have indeed recognized this connection early on. An influence of the Cypro-Minoan script on the Anatolian alphabet was mentioned in the scholarly literature a long time ago, but these parallels are not part of current paradigms. Today, linguists

are convinced that scripts cannot mingle. Apparently, some authorities maintained this view and now everybody believes it. The truth is: scripts do mingle! In the Cretan context, the hieroglyphic script is basically of Luwian type but supplemented by Egyptian hieroglyphic. By taking the Phoenician letters and attributing the Phoenician values to them, and then identifying the Cypro-Minoan letters and giving them their Cypro-Minoan value reduced to alphabet letters according to the acrophonic principle, one inevitably gets entire sentences with verbs, subjects and objects.

The opinion according to which scripts cannot mingle might be part of the problem, but I could imagine that another part of the problem is that many scholars don't know Cypro-Minoan very well, since it is officially considered to be undeciphered.

Yes, that is quite possible. Indeed Cypro-Minoan was quite important and in use from at least the sixteenth until, in the form of its successor, the Cypriot syllabary, the third century. Inscriptions on Cyprus were written in Greek language using Cypro-Minoan characters until that time. Most importantly, Cypro-Minoan was continuously known throughout this timespan. During the Dark Age, we have no records, but afterwards, the signs continue in the same syllabary. So there must have been a continuous script tradition throughout the Dark Age.

When I read your analysis of the Kaunos bilingual inscription, I was amazed about the spectrum of connections you are making – between the Carian text, on the one hand, and Etruscan, Lycian and Greek on the other.

Well, Carian, Etruscan and Lycian are all Luwian dialects! And the influence of Greek is to be expected because the Carians lived in cohabitation with the Greeks from the Late Bronze Age onwards.

Yes, but still, one needs to be acquainted with these different languages to recognize parallels. I believe this is your unique selling proposition as a scholar. Basically, what you're doing is a plea for employing a generalist's scope to be able to see such interrelations. Linguists benefit in deciphering a script if they look beyond a well-defined subject.

To find the origins of the signs we do have to be very open-minded. When we trace the origin of the signs, we're able to understand their use by the scribe. The whole purpose of writing is an agreement to adhere to a certain standard, otherwise people would not understand each other. Thus scribes cannot just make up signs or new ways of using them. A has to be A, and B has to be B – otherwise we'll run into problems understanding a text. If you fill in the right value, however, you are able to pronounce the words, and by comparing them to known vocabularies, you'll become able to understand them. – Basically, almost all my work takes place within the Luwian language sphere and not outside of it. Etruscan is indeed very closely related to the Carian language, and both are ultimately derived from Luwian hieroglyphic.

We have already said that those ancient Anatolian languages are called *Trümmersprachen*, because we possess only fragmentary evidence for their existence. But you take these inscriptions as jigsaw puzzle pieces which you combine to reconstruct a much bigger picture. And you find a coherent and consistent use of one language, Luwian, which took place over a long period of time, more than a thousand years, and across a very large region, from Italy to Greece, across the Aegean and almost all of Anatolia, all the way to Syria and Canaan.

From what I understand, you are not really prepared to talk about Greek, even though it is an important component on the map of ancient languages in the eastern Mediterranean.

Well, Greek is overrated!

As far as the influence on the Anatolian region is concerned, Greek is indeed overrated. There was influence of Greek speakers on Anatolia, because they had settled there, but this would have worked in both directions. The Greeks are influencing the Luwians, and the Luwians are, of course, influencing the Greeks. This applies to western Anatolia, Greece and Italy, where there were Greek, Anatolian and Phoenician migrants. The picture is more complicated than most people are willing to admit.

Willemijn Waal recently wrote a paper about the early alphabet which I found very interesting.[46] She also speaks about Luwian hieroglyphic in western Anatolia and argues that most of the documents were written on perishable material. Of course, we do find some Luwian inscriptions on stone (seals) that are still preserved from this period – and we also have correspondence in which the sender speaks about previous letters going back and forth. So writing was clearly used in this period, but most of it apparently took place on perishable materials such as wax, wood, lead, leather, clay or papyrus. Willemijn then continues by saying that this may also have been the case regarding the earlier use of the Greek alphabet. According to her, the Greek alphabet may have been used on perishable materials as early as the eleventh century. From Byblos we know the story of Wenamun, who came there and claimed to get trees for free as this had been the traditional custom. To this the local king, Zakar-Baal, replies: "My records actually tell me that you paid last year and the year before that!" Hence, there must have been all kinds of economic records, and these were most likely written in the Phoenician alphabet. But for the eleventh century they have not been found yet. It is thus quite likely that these records were written on perishable materials.

In the same general area, the Levant, we find arrowheads with Phoenician alphabetic inscriptions already in the eleventh century. Hence, from the larger region around Byblos there is evidence for the use of script. Applying this argument to Greece, however, is tricky, because the additional evidence, such as signs on arrowheads or in whatever other form, is lacking. There is not a single scratch on a vase or so during a period of over 300 years. That is a long time! I think that Willemijn's argument is correct for Anatolia, but for Greece it is more problematic.

If we recapitulate what has been said today about those Luwian dialects, what would be your conclusions?
The alphabet is genuinely Anatolian, and it consists of two components: first, the Phoenician alphabet, which can have very ancient sign variants; and secondly, signs from the Cypro-Minoan syllabary were used as alphabet letters. If we use the right values of these signs, we will inevitably end up with clearly Luwian texts that are most closely related to the Luwian hieroglyphic language. And this applies to all four languages we talked about: Lycian, Lydian, Carian and Sidetic. These languages are distinct from each other, but they have principles in common.

Interview conducted on July 24, 2020.

Southwest Iberian Is Celtic

Southwest Iberian is older than the alphabets in Greece and Anatolia. A need to become semi-syllabic. Influences from Cyprus. The language is Celtic, but the transcription needs fixing. A tin master appears. The Phoenicians established ports in southern Spain, where people spoke Celtic.

So far, we have spoken about cultures in the eastern and central Mediterranean. In this section today we will move to the west – all the way to the Iberian Peninsula. What are the principal issues to be considered when discussing Early Iron Age scripts from Portugal and Spain? The language in question bears various names, I prefer calling it Southwest Iberian, others are calling it, for instance, Tartessian. One thing is clear, the Southwest Iberian script was derived from the Phoenician alphabet. A so-called abecedarium, a list of the alphabet letters in the right order, was found, in Espanca. It contains thirteen letters that originated from Phoenician signs and occur in the same position as they do in the alphabet. Most extant documents of Southwest Iberian date to the sixth to fourth century, but the script was most likely introduced as early as the ninth century.

How do you know that it was adopted in the ninth century?
One inscription from Huelva, ancient Tartessos, clearly dates to the ninth century. It consists only of one sign but is well dated. Besides, in the Phoenician alphabet the sign for *mēm* was originally tilted by 90 degrees. Then around 750 it was turned into its still current horizontal position. So, this yields a *terminus ante quem* for the introduction of the script on the Iberian Peninsula. There are no such early alphabetic texts from Greece and Anatolia. The Southwest Iberian alphabetic script was evidently in use before any of the surviving documents we know from Greece and Anatolia took shape.

Another interesting aspect of the script is that it contains vowel signs. The scholarly community maintains a modern myth by claiming that vowels were a Greek invention. In Iberia we find a completely independent case of making vowels – and the result is a ninth-century alphabet with vowels that cannot be derived from any Greek alphabet.

Because we have no evidence for any use of the Greek alphabet that early in time?
No! Because two Iberian signs for vowels differ completely from Greek. So we know for sure that the Greeks have nothing to do with this vowel development.

The Alphabet Becomes Semi-Syllabic

Are there any other peculiarities?
Yes, indeed! The script on the Iberian Peninsula was partly turned into a syllabary. Three consonants were developed into a series of syllables – each with its own sign. There are signs for *k*, depending on the combination with different vowels, so it becomes *ka, ke, ki, ko, ku*; and *p* becomes *pa, pe, pi, po, pu*; and *t* becomes *ta, te, ti, to, tu*. All of these syllables are written using different signs. That's how the script got 36 signs.

How do you explain the semi-syllabic character?
Evidently this reflects a secondary development. Initially there was only an alphabet and thus a consonant script. People then added vowels and for some reason three consonants were made into a syllabary. This is peculiar, yet similar developments have occurred elsewhere – for example, in the Latin alphabet. There, the letter *k* is used before *a, ka*; *c* before *e* and *i, ce* and *ci*; and *q* before *u, qu*. Evidently a bit of syllabic thinking was applied to the Latin alphabet too; syllables are also written as an exercise in a seventh-century Etruscan inscription on an ink bottle from Caere with an abecedarium – and in Iberia a similar development occurred.

This effected only those three characters.
Yes, the rest remained alphabetic; there is only one *m* and one *l* etc. The vowels are also alphabetic. In the literature some scholars ponder about the idea that the script may have been derived from Linear A or something

along those lines, because that is also a syllabary, but Linear A has nothing to do with Iberian scripts. There may be some influence from the Cypriot syllabary, though, which, as we have seen, is directly derived from Linear C and D and continuously in use during the earliest phase of the Early Iron Age. Two syllabic signs, the one for *tì* and the one for *ku*, can be shown to originate from a Cypriot syllabic counterpart [see below].

They Spoke Celtic, What Else!

Where do we stand in terms of understanding the language?
That's the other thing to be considered, one is the script, the other the language. For a long time, it was an open question which language is reflected in Southwest Iberian. The Welsh linguist John T. Koch suggested a few years ago that it is Celtic. He used the values of the signs of the Celtiberian script that was common from the third to the first century, a few centuries after the acme of Southwest Iberian. Manuel Goméz Moreno deciphered the Celtiberian script in 1925.

I agree with Koch that the language is Celtic, but I think that the original Phoenician value of the signs should be used in several cases. For example, the Phoenician sign for *mēm* appears vertically in Southwest Iberian, whereas in later versions of the Phoenician alphabet it is turned over and thus becomes horizontal. This vertical *mēm* in the Iberian is read in the later Celtiberian as *pa* or *ba*. So if Koch transfers these values to the earlier Southwest Iberian script, he ends up with totally different sound values. On the other hand, I consider *mēm* to have had the original sound value of *m* – and in this way I get identifications that make sense.

How did you get interested in the subject?
Every undeciphered script finds my interest! There has been a lot of discussions whether Southwest Iberian might be related to Minoan, Iberian or Basque, or whether it might be a pre-Mediterranean language that is not Indo-European and was maintained by a rest group like Basque. Such discussions arise every time we come across an undeciphered language. But if you have deciphered it, it turns out to be an Indo-European language!

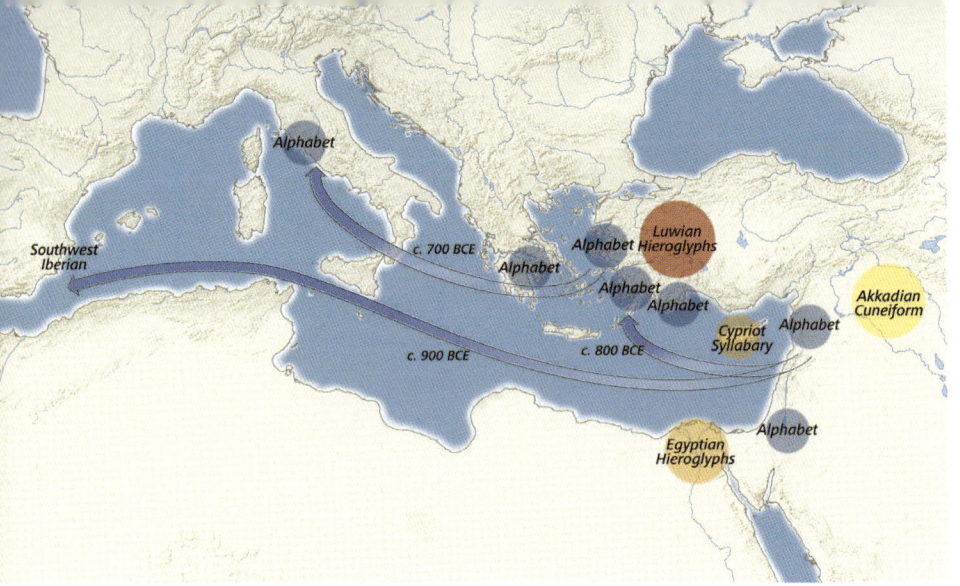

The use of the alphabet spread with Phoenician trade between 900 and 700. One of the first areas where it was commonly used was the Iberian Peninsula at the far western end of the Mediterranean.

In the beginning, however, it ought to be considered that any of such ideas might indeed be correct.

When you start, you know nothing. Of course, one has to take all possible ideas into account. But if you look closer at the language, study it and end up having an Indo-European language that can be read and understood, then all those earlier ideas fade into insignificance. I began to work on Celtiberian in the late 1990s. My approach rested on applying the original Phoenician alphabet to the Southwest Iberian script. By doing this, I was soon able to read Celtic words. We first have to study the signs and then the language. If it turns out that the sound values lead to readings closely related to Celtiberian and Gaulish, this will verify the initial assumption about how the signs must be read.

I must say, though, that my first attempt was not entirely successful, so I corrected it in later publications.

Where were the mistakes?

There is a very important word, namely the honorific title "tin-master": *casidanos*. In Southwest Iberian it is written *ka-a-ś-e-ta-a-n-a*. I had initially interpreted this as a personal name. Koch read this correctly.

The King Is Named after the Silver

There is much research on Southwest Iberian, I assume partly because historiographers including Herodotus and Plutarch mention the language. Herodotus writes about a man by the name of Kolaeus who comes from the coastal region of western Anatolia and is connected with various ports there, including Phokaia and Samos.[47] His ship got into a storm, so the story goes, and he claims to have been blown all the way through the Straits of Gibraltar to the port of Tartessos, a little-known trade port back then. He established good relations with king Arganthonios, a name derived from the same Indo-European root as Latin *argentum* for "silver," which is indeed Celtic, to boot. Arganthonios was anxious to become friends with Greek people and wanted them to stay and establish a colony. Kolaeus says that he got so much silver from this king that he could make a magnificent dedication in the temple of Hera on Samos. So he went back to western Anatolia and lived as a rich man, thanks to this incident. This happened during the late seventh century, whereas the Phoenicians had already been in western Iberia in the area since the ninth century.

Basically the Phoenicians established a port in southern Iberia and brought the script with them.
They established a number of settlements in southern Spain and all across the Mediterranean. Tartessos lies just outside the Pillars of Hercules, whereas the Phoenician coastal settlements were inside the Pillars of Hercules. Phoenicians ventured to Iberia for tin, they had even gone all the way to Brittany and Cornwall to reach tin sources there. The whole sea route outside the Mediterranean was established for tin trade. We can be sure about this because an ingot from southern England was found at Falmouth. Even though the Bronze Age had come to an end, there was still much demand for copper and tin to produce bronze. The Phoenicians kept their sea routes secret and if pirates or competitors pursued them, they were prepared to sink their own ships so that nobody else could find out about the ultimate destination of their routes.

Are there any indications that this route was already used during the Bronze Age?

As far as I know, ships did not venture outside the Pillars of Hercules during the Bronze Age. Iberia was anyway somewhat outside the picture at that time. The tin mines in Cornwall were used from about 2300 onwards – and an active trade connection with Cornwall existed, but this was an inland route all across today's France along the valley of the Rhône to the Seine river.

Phoenician Port Towns Were Not Harmed

After the Bronze Age collapse the coastal cities in northern Syria had been destroyed by the Sea Peoples ...
... but the Phoenician ports in Lebanon were not attacked. The Sea Peoples raided the region north of Lebanon, including Amurru, where they established a camp according to the inscriptions in Medinet Habu. Then they went past the Phoenician cities further south to Canaan, where they also captured places.

Northern Syria was a loyal ally to the Hittite great king, whereas the Phoenician port cities may not have been harmed; perhaps they were on amicable terms with the Sea Peoples.
Maybe. I think that the Philistines, who were, of course, one of the Sea Peoples' tribes, knew the route to the west and that the Phoenicians took over those routes later. It appears as if there was some kind of connection between the Sea Peoples and the Phoenicians. Having not suffered any destructions, the rulers in the Phoenician trade cities were in an advantageous position after the crisis years. They were handed control over long-distance trade routes on a silver platter. We know from the Uluburun shipwreck that the vessel itself and its crew came from Lebanon. At that time ships and crews were hired on behalf of suppliers or customers. When those markets collapsed, the ship owners could conduct the trade on their own behalf – and they had a monopoly to boot.

Where did they establish the first ports of call?
They aimed for Iberia and preferred to take the southern route near Africa. By owning and operating the ships used for long-distance trade, Phoenician merchants got to know the entire Mediterranean and its most lucrative production centers, including the tin sources in Iberia. In order

Phoenician trade routes extended across the whole Mediterranean.

to travel such long distances, it was crucial to establish havens along the route, where they could stash food and obtain fresh water. Consequently, Phoenician traders established colonies in Africa, Crete, Sicily, Sardinia and even at Pithecussae near Naples in Italy from as early as the eleventh century up to the eighth century. At first the new settlers only cared about their seaports; later on, they also aimed to conquer the hinterland.

During the ninth century, the Phoenician merchants bring their alphabetic script to Iberia, where it undergoes a separate development, is equipped with vowels and becomes partially syllabic. This development continues for several centuries.

There's an interlude of Greek presence in Iberia in the seventh and sixth centuries, as reflected in the script by the use of the Greek *san* in form of our present M for *ś*; and, of course, Etruscan vessels also went west for trading. Their Lydian ancestors may have even preceded the latter, as the vowel *i* in Southwest Iberian is expressed by the Lydian variant of the Phoenician *yod* sign.

The Celts Enter Iberia

So much about the script – let us now talk about the language. You say it is Celtic.
Celtic-speaking people had migrated into Iberia after the end of the Bronze Age, between 1200 and 800. This movement coincided with the spreading of the Urnfield culture all over western Europe. Italic-speaking

people were then crossing the Alps and entering Italy. From 1200 onwards stones with engraved chariots appear in Spain, in my opinion reflecting Celtic immigration. There are also places with the typical Celtic name endings *briga*, a term with the same linguistic route as the German *Burg*, a fortress on a height. Scholars have mapped the distribution of these *briga* names and found them in southern Iberia too. When Phoenician ships reached the shores of southern Iberia, the Phoenician people met with an essentially Celtic local population. To express their language in writing, these people adopted the alphabet that the Phoenicians had brought with them.

Based on the *briga* names, some scholars suggested distinguishing two linguistic regions: Indo-Europeans in the west of the Iberian Peninsula and Basque-related non-Indo-European speakers in the east. They call this second language group Iberian, East Iberian, some even think that Southwest Iberian is part of it. But this whole idea is absolute nonsense since Old Indo-European speakers had already reached the peninsula from 3000 onwards.

Some Spanish scholars have recently published an investigation of ancient Iberian river names, and they found no trace of a Basque-related language in them. As far as we can tell, all the old river names are Indo-European. Even the Los Millares culture in the east was Old Indo-European as is evident from tholos graves of Indo-European type, which are also found at Pai Maho in the Lisbon region of Portugal to the west. Then after 1200 another wave of Indo-European migrants arrived in Iberia and scattered all over the peninsula.

What then is East Iberian?
We don't know. There are indeed some documents in Iberia whose contents we cannot read yet. Instead of interpreting them as being non-Indo-European, it is also possible that there is some aberrant development of the sign values, but I cannot read those texts either. They occur in the northeast in the region near France as well as in that of southeast Spain.

How did the Basque language get into Spain?
I don't know, but Basque is only becoming important in the Middle Ages. As far as I know, there are no sources for Basque dating back to antiquity, though the Basques as a people are mentioned in Roman sources. I assume that the people were quite ancient, they may even be traced

The languages spoken on the Iberian Peninsula during the Early Iron Age belong to the Celtic branch.

back to Neolithic farmers. But the assumption that their language was once spoken in the entire Mediterranean is the result of dubious linguistic identifications.

When I prepared today's conversation, it soon became obvious that the Southwest Iberian script had to be Celtic. Why is there such a debate about it?
As long as one cannot read the script, one can interpret all sorts of things, including that it is a non-Indo-European language. Basically, people see what they want to find.

Iberia as a Sideshow

There's quite a bit of scholarship on the subject. How do your views differ from these studies?
Well, Iberia is a little bit of a sideshow, not many people are studying it; most of the scholars are Spanish. Also, there is John T. Koch, of course,

and the work of Jürgen Untermann, who died a few years ago. He had produced a *corpus* which is crucial to have. Koch uses the sound values as established for Celtiberian of the second century BCE and disregards the idea that some of the values might have originally been different in Phoenician and the Cypriot syllabary. I disagree with him about 6 of the total of 36 signs. During a timespan covering some four centuries, of course, some development may have occurred.

But didn't you tell me during our previous conversations that sound values do not change?

In the main! I also said, for example, that the Phoenician *kāp* later on changes from *chi* to *psi* in the Greek alphabet. So there can be developments in which a sign takes on a secondary value regardless of its original one. This happened only in a few cases, but those do make a difference! Besides, the texts were written in *scriptio continua*, which means without punctuation marks. As a consequence, Koch's and my transliterations may also vary with respect to word boundaries. Taking all this into account, the difference between his and my reading is considerable.

Cyprian Syllabic		Southwest Iberian		Phoenician Alphabet	
ku	✻	ku	✻		
ti	↑	ti	↑		
		m	≷	m	≷
		m₁	⋀	m	⋁

Table showing how some Southwest Iberian signs relate to Cyprian syllabic whereas others relate to Phoenician.

In 2019 Koch published a book listing every identification that he and I agree about. The script consists of 36 signs, and as I said, I disagree with the reading of 6 of them – enough to result in major discrepancies in our interpretations. Thus far, only my reading leads to endings, nominative, accusative etc. and also verbal endings which are of patent Celtiberian or Gaulish nature. Koch is not mentioning this. He does, however, suggest that the introduction of syllables in the Southwest Iberian script might be connected to an influence from the Cypriot syllabary. The use of the two signs coincides; one of them was in continuous use from the Late Bronze Age to the Early Iron Age. Thus, I had recognized the arrow sign for the expression of the value *ti* and attributed the sound value *ti* accordingly. But I did not realize that there is one more case! Koch now says

	k-	p-	t-	b	l	m	n	r	ś	s
a	A	∧		X	9	1	⌇	Y	⟨	M	⚹
e	O	⟩∣	⟩	⧗			⋀				
i	⩫⋔	⥉	⟩	⥉			⋁				
i	⪽⪾		↑	⦾	⦽						
i				↑							
o	⚹	⋈	□	⩓	D						
u	4	⋇		⩓			·				
sol	✵	⌣		⧗							

The Southwest Iberian sign list reveals how the script was partly turned into a syllabary. Depending on the combination with different vowels, *k* becomes *ka, ke, ki, ko, ku* – and each syllable is written using a different sign. The same applies for *p* and *t*.

that the sign for *ko* is also directly derived from Cypriot syllabic, but this identification is flawed. On the other hand, the one for *ku* can be shown to originate from Cypriot syllabic *ku*. I had attributed the right sound value, but only now I realize that it can be derived from the Cyprian script. Koch's recent work thus reinforces my *k* reading, whereas other scholars have been reading it as *bu*.

What are the implications of that?
Why did these Celtiberians make the script a partial syllabary? Their knowledge of a syllabic script might have induced it. Phoenicians and Cypriots were, of course, in close contact early on – exploiting copper mines on Cyprus as well as tin mines in southern Iberia.

A Dedication to Reinforce a Bilateral Treaty

What do the inscriptions say?
That's an interesting point! Koch thinks they are all grave inscriptions, which is, of course, possible. The way I read them, however, indicates a wider variety in contents. There are indeed a few grave inscriptions, but we also find dedications. The two most important dedications involve

bilateral relations. From Alcalá del Río in the land of Tartessos, one of them is between the Meseta region, where Madrid is located, and the Guadalquivir river region in the south, which was called the Baitis in ancient time. In Southwest Iberian inscription it occurs in the form of Dedunbaitis. The people from southern Iberia had made some kind of arrangement with their contemporaries in northern Iberia.

There is another such bilateral agreement between the Celts in southwest Iberia – they actually call themselves Celts – and the "Libyans," namely in the text of the inscription from Mesas do Castelinho. Those were not people from North Africa, instead they lived near Zaragoza along the Ebro river. The Celts had a Drynemeton as a sanctuary, which is basically an open field, but it could have graves or even monuments in it. On this holy ground international treaties were agreed upon. As part of the ceremony, the two parties may have jointly made a dedication to a certain god. We only find the dedication, but there was obviously a treaty connected with it.

Hence we have different genres for the documents: funeral inscriptions, dedications to a certain deity and bilateral dedications. One nice aspect of these documents is that the grammar is clearly represented, it includes the right endings and verbs – all in Celtic. The language is very close to Celtiberian and to Gaulish.

There are about 95 inscriptions altogether – how many of those did you look at more closely?
I worked on 10 inscriptions.

And I assume that you picked out the ones that looked most interesting for your inquiries.
Yes, as always, the text has to be complete, because if it is not, then one can easily make anything out of it.

Interviews conducted on September 18 and 21, 2020.

SOUTHWESTERN IBERIAN IS CELTIC • 203

The Southwest Iberian inscription Herdade da Abobada from Almodôvar. The text says: "Numat(os), on behalf of the Altusielna people, has dedicated to the coastal (goddess of) regeneration."

Etymology or No Etymology – That Is the Question

There are no old-school approaches in linguistics. Using etymology is standard practice in Indo-European studies. Languages are distinct from each other, but they also affect each other. Luwian had a lasting impact after the end of the Bronze Age. How everything was interconnected: an overview of the script developments during the second millennium. What are the open questions? The value of historiographic sources. Centum and satem languages. The significance of making mistakes. Where Fred's interpretations have already been confirmed. How much of European archaeology is Eurocentric? Where to go from here?

We have reached the final session of our conversations and now ought to tie up the sack with all the elements we have touched upon. Let us perhaps start by discussing once again your approach, one that is based on etymology, a methodology that was fashionable and quite successful for a long time, but somehow seems to have gotten out of favor. Would it be correct to say that you are maintaining an old-school approach?
I don't know whether one can distinguish between old-school and new-school approaches. There are indeed people who are against the etymological method. In my opinion, it depends on the context in which it is used. If a language is certainly Indo-European or Semitic, one has to make etymological identifications, otherwise the text can simply not be interpreted.

Your critics have pointed out that you see connections to all kinds of languages.
Well, that is not correct. A language is a language; there may be some loanwords; for instance, considering the diplomatic correspondence during the Late Bronze Age, it is crucial to realize that the Semitic language

was influential. Accordingly, Semitic loanwords may occur. Nevertheless, there is always a matrix language and its grammar has to be of one and the same language, otherwise you have a problem.

If we look at the famous Kaunos bilingual inscription in Carian, for instance, you've made connections to four different languages: Luwian, Lycian, Etruscan and Greek.

The main associations are with Luwian, because Carian is basically a Luwian dialect – and so are Lycian, Lydian and Etruscan. And Luwian hieroglyphic is, of course, Luwian *sensu stricto*. Carian is indeed unusual because its language shows a strong Greek influence. That is indeed another language, and there you are correct: in this case, I'm using material from another language. This becomes understandable when we take into account that Carian is actually close to Greece. Since the Late Bronze Age, Greek-speaking people had settled in the Carian region, so there have been hundreds of years of ties between Carian and Greek. In every border region one is likely to see how two languages affect each other; this is completely normal. Come on! You live in Switzerland, where German, French and Italian are all official languages.

And there are many French loanwords in Swiss German – for example, here a scooter is called Trottinett!

Of course, this is exactly how languages in border regions affect each other. – With respect to Carian, the connections are basically all Luwian, plus many adstrate influences from Greek.

Are there other scholars today who are using an approach similar to the one you favor?

With respect to the investigation of Indo-European languages the etymological approach is common, because within the Indo-European language family it is possible to compare languages with each other – from Tocharian to Celtic. *The Oxford Introduction to Proto-Indo-European and the Proto-Indo-European World* that James Patrick Mallory and Douglas Adams edited provides an entire volume full of etymological roots. Nobody is complaining about the etymological approach in Indo-European studies. First, you have to ask: what is the nature of the language? Then you can use etymological connections. These are two distinct steps.

In other words, you are basically using the standard approach in Indo-European studies. Let's leave it there and move on to another subject. Would it be possible to summarize in a few sentences how scripts evolved during the second millennium across the Mediterranean territories?
It started in 3200 with two scripts, Akkadian cuneiform and Egyptian hieroglyphs. This situation remained the same for an entire millennium. Around 2000 an evolution began, and this was essentially triggered by contacts between the different regions around the eastern Mediterranean. Incited by the use of scripts in Mesopotamia and Egypt, people in other regions began to develop their own scripts for essentially similar purposes, but local use.

Circa 2000 the Luwian hieroglyphic script was conceived in Anatolia. We find symbols on seals to mark owners, but more elaborate documents may have existed on perishable materials. Almost immediately the script was also introduced to Crete where it went through a specific development and incorporated more elements from Egyptian hieroglyphic. And that script became Cretan hieroglyphic.

Luwian hieroglyphic was invented from scratch, except for one or two signs that also occur in Egyptian hieroglyphic, is that right?
The sun between wings is clearly Egyptian and the ankh sign is close to Egyptian hieroglyphic, so there may have been some influence, but basically the Luwian writing system is closer to Akkadian cuneiform. The Anatolians use similar determinatives, logographic writing, a combination with syllabic – this latter feature is not related to Egyptian. Luwian hieroglyphic is basically a pictographic script whose system is related to cuneiform. It has syllables – and Egyptian hieroglyphic is a consonant script.

What happened after Luwian hieroglyphic and Cretan hieroglyphic had come into use?
The Byblos script was invented at the end of the eighteenth century, c. 1720. With the intrusion of Indo-European chariot gangs, Byblos became separated from Egypt and some people there decided to develop a script for local use. The Byblos script was then also transmitted to Crete where it led to the development of Linear A. So Cretan hieroglyphic was linearized and came under considerable influence from Byblos to form Linear A.

Why would people linearize a script?
Because it's simpler! In comparison to having to draw hieroglyphs, using linearized signs is much easier; so the writing process is more economic. On Cyprus there had been some use of Luwian hieroglyphic with a local touch as early as the eighteenth century. Then during the sixteenth century, people on the island chose the simpler linearized script that had become customary in Crete. Linear A was implemented in Cyprus around 1600, and then adapted to become Linear C, with a local variant at Enkomi that I call Linear D. The script then evolved further into the Cypriot syllabary which remained in use until the classical period.

Crete itself came under Greek influence during the fifteenth century, and therefore Linear A needed to be adapted to accommodate the needs of the Greek language.
If the language changes, inevitably the syllabary needs to be adapted. For the most part, the language recorded in Linear A was Semitic, so the script did not include the vowel *o* that occurs in the Greek language. After c. 1450, when Greek became the predominant language on the island, the script needed to be modified – and hence became what we now consider Linear B.

Parallel to these developments the incipient development of the alphabet took place.
The alphabet originally formed around 2000 from Egyptian hieroglyphic and was then used to express Semitic language. During the eighteenth century it developed into Proto-Sinaitic, but did not get into common use, because other scripts, such as Akkadian cuneiform, were more popular. From what we can tell, the alphabet was initially only used in the Levant and only for very few documents. But it continued to be used, and then during the twelfth century it ultimately became more important.

Why did the alphabet become so successful?
The Phoenicians had started to write using the alphabet, and they distributed it all over the Mediterranean. The alphabet came into use along the coast of southern Anatolia, and it was transmitted to the Iberian Peninsula early on. In Greece people began writing in the alphabet, and around 750, it was also introduced to the Italic Peninsula. By the sixth

century the alphabet had become the most important script in the Mediterranean – at the expense of the other scripts.

As far as the big picture is concerned, you're the only one who is providing such a broad and comprehensive panorama from what I can tell. Am I correct?
There are, of course, not many people who study the ancient Near East and include western Anatolia and Crete in the picture. Scripts tend to be very international, though, and mainstream archaeological research is perhaps less so.

Are there any open questions from your perspective as far as this general development is concerned?
I think the outline is clear. Open are questions such as what came first, the Anatolian or the Greek alphabet? Inscriptions in Greece occur from c. 800, but they use a developed type of the Phoenician alphabet, whereas in Anatolia, inscriptions were found dating to a little later – into the course of the eighth century. But the Anatolian alphabets contained ancient forms of Phoenician signs that are quite remarkable. They also use signs from the Cypro-Minoan script or the Cypriot syllabary that are not known from Greece. At the very least, one can say that the Anatolian alphabets are an independent development, and I would not be surprised if they had gotten into use earlier than the alphabet in Greece, because of these early sign variants.

Are you the only scholar in the field who sees things this way or are there people who agree with you?
The discussion of the alphabet is a little bit Eurocentric (*chuckles*), in the sense that things are always seen from a Greek perspective. Everybody is talking about the Greek alphabet. I'm actually one of the few who would use the Iberian evidence in this framework. When people talk about the transmission of the Phoenician alphabet, they hardly ever mention the

---

Next pages: This table illustrates how some signs, including their sound values, became incorporated into other scripts. The scripts on a green background are deciphered, those in red are (according to Wikipedia) considered to be undeciphered. If the sound values are known, however, the words can be read – and thus translated using a dictionary for the relevant language.

Meaning	Egyptian Hieroglyphs			Luwian Hieroglyphs			Cretan Hieroglyphs		
vessel	W9		$ḫnm$	346		ki	E47		ki
tablet with stylus	Y3		$mnhd$	326		$TUPA, tu_4$	E31		
symbol of life	S34		$ʿnḫ$	369		$vita, WÁSU, wa_{12}$			$ankh$
cat	E13		miu				E74-5		ma
wine	M43		irp				E116		$WAINU$
supporting pole	O30		$šnt$				E60		sa
door	O31		$ʿ3$				E44		ya
bee	L2		$bity$				CHICO21, E85-6		$pì$
loaf of bread	X8		di				E18		$pí$
functionary	A21		sr				E27		$SARU$
harp	Y7		$bint$				E29		
djed column	R11		$ḏd$						
balance	U38		$mḫ3t$						
negation	D35		n						
star				186, 445		$*lukka-, lu$	E9, E91, E112		lu
arrow				499		ti_8	MA6		ti_7
house				247		$PARNA, pa_5$	E46		pa_3
eye				191		$TIWATA, ti_6$	E5		ti_6
tree				151		$TELIPINU$	E97		te
				15		mi_4	PD06		mi
bull				107		mu	E62		mu
bird of prey				130-3		ARA, ar, ra	E79-80		ra
sword				312		$ZITI, zí$	E15		zi
helmet with cheekpiece				329, 1		$HWÁ, ḫù$			
spoked wheel				292		$HARSANTAN, ḫa+r$			
double axe							E36		a

Byblos Script			Linear A			Linear B			Linear C/D		
E10	⍱	ki	L103		ki	B67		ki	70		ki
			L93		du				115		tu
			L23		za	B17		za			
A21		ma	L95		ma	B80		ma	53/107		ma
D3		wa	L75, L82		wa, WAINU	B54		wa	95		wa
B11	Y	sa	L31	Y	sa	B31		sa	57/82	Y	sa
D5		ya₃	L32		ya	B57		ja	73		ya
A6		pi	L56		pi	B39		pi			
		di							51		pi
			L100a		i	B28		i	101/104		i
			L34		pu₂	B29		pu₂			
B3		tu	L39		tū	B5		to	8b		tu
			L85		TALENTUM, qa	B118		TALENT			
			L114		nwa	B48		nwa			
G7, G17	†	lu	L22	+	lu	B2	+	lu	5	+	lu
G13		ti	L78		ti	B37		ti	21		ti
			L1		pa₃	B56		pa₃	74		pe
			L101		zu	B79		zu	116		ti₁
			L92		te	B4		te	7		te
			L76		mi	B73		mi	87/91		mi
			L27		mu	B23		mu			
			L53		ra	B60		ra			
			L36		zi						
			L45		kū	B70		ko	117		ku
			L29	⊕	ka	B77	⊕	ka	25		ka
B12/E1		a	L52		a	B8		a	102/103		a
E17		pa	L2		pa	B3		pa	6		pa
F6	△	ke₁	L24		ke	B44		ke	26		ke

occurrence of an alphabetic script in Iberia this early on – dating to the ninth century and onwards! As we have said earlier, the development of the vowels is so distinctly different from that in Greece that it clearly denotes an independent evolution.

Some scholars argue that the Anatolian alphabets may have occurred earlier and this discussion revolves around the date for the destruction of Gordion. Certain Phrygian inscriptions antedate the destruction layer that has traditionally been dated to 700 to coincide with the Kimmerian invasion. On the basis of dendrochronologically calibrated dates one school of thought argues that the destruction must have occurred around 800. If this date is correct, the Phrygian documents belong in the ninth century. Thus, an Anatolian alphabet would have gotten into use earlier than expected and predated any evidence we have for its use in Greece. – I have my doubts about this 800 date for the destruction; I still think that the Kimmerians destroyed Gordion, and that Midas committed suicide by drinking bull's blood as Strabo (1.3.21) tells us. So in this particular case I am indeed a bit old-fashioned.

Thank you for mentioning Strabo because that is also characteristic of your approach, namely that you frequently consider ancient historiographic sources.
Yes, I do, because they were 2000 to 3000 years closer to the subject of our inquiry than we are. Many sources available at that time have been lost. For the most part, those people knew what they were talking about, certainly better than we do today.

Only 2 percent of the historiographic accounts have survived until today, 98 percent were lost.
Yes, for sure.

Of course, there can always be inaccuracies in those accounts.
Absolutely! Herodotus, for example, didn't know everything; even though he travelled a lot. His account of the people in the steppe is more difficult since he did not get to that area. When he says that the source of the Danube lies in the Pyrenees, this is wrong; because he didn't travel so far west, the information provided is inaccurate. Even if Herodotus did not get everything right, we should take into account what ancient authors wrote. If the information is put into an interdisciplinary context

including the archaeological record and surviving documents, certain statements might be verified or disproven.

You don't even shy away from considering peoples and places that very well may have been fictitious, including Scheria, the Phaeacians and even Atlantis.

Interestingly, in the Cretan documents we find the name Saharwa, which looks like Scheria. If one looks up the sources describing Scheria, it is possible that the references were based on a location in Crete – which in the second step of transmission perhaps became a fairytale place. And that is naturally making things more difficult.

Early on in our conversations, you said that you are a bit of a loner, but my impression is that you have never really felt ostracized and that you accepted the role that you were assigned.

I really don't care! I do what I like, and I like what I am doing – it is up to other people to decide whether this has any value or not. For me, my method is a fruitful way of approaching open questions. I try to argue and clarify to others why I think this method is effective, but if others don't accept these arguments, then that is entirely their decision. I write what I think is valuable and try to verify it as much as possible using the sources at hand. Scholars don't necessarily write for today's use; many write for tomorrow's researchers. In 50 years additional evidence will be available and, who knows, some people may say then: "Hey, this Woudhuizen got something right after all!"

From what I can tell, I have never seen you considering what may be politically correct or not, or whether something you write might be either beneficial or harmful. You just say what you think needs to be said whether people like to hear it or not.

Yes.

If you follow such an unfettered approach, you're bound to make mistakes. What is the area in which mistakes are most likely to occur?

We all make mistakes. I don't think that other people don't make mistakes. One can also learn from those mistakes. I've written articles which contained mistakes. Was it still worthwhile to produce them? Absolutely! Research and thinking, in general, involves a hierarchy of incremental progress. Initial tentative steps are imperative to be able to reach new ground in a second or third step of even deeper involvement in a certain subject. Making mistakes is part of the job, and if one is too worried about making mistakes, the likelihood is that this person will not get anywhere.

I made mistakes in details but I never changed the principle approach in any of my inquiries. For example, in Etruscan, I have always argued from the beginning that it reflects Luwian language – and I never had to reconsider this. The basic line of approach has always stayed the same in all my investigations. Actual mistakes, however, can be made in reading signs wrongly or arguing in favor of wrong etymological connections. That is all quite possible.

Was there a point in time where you had accumulated so much knowledge and realized so many interconnections that since then mistakes have become less frequent or unlikely?
This might be different for every topic, but in general, most mistakes are, of course, made at the beginning. In a 1988 publication on the Enkomi cylinder seal I was wrong in certain aspects of interpretation; something I was able to fix later on. On the other hand, my 1989 interpretation of the Pyrgi tablets was correct. In this case I was able to make only a few improvements later on. It is part of the learning process to try to eliminate mistakes in order to get further.

Your work has never really become the standard, but many arguments that you have put forward were later incorporated into standard research. Could you perhaps give a few examples of those cases where your work has been verified?
Already in the 1990s, I interpreted the word *tíwaná* to represent the "enemy" in the Late Bronze Age Luwian hieroglyphic inscriptions from Yalburt and Südburg. For the interpretation of the text, this is a crucial word, because it occurs frequently in both documents – and consequently we're able to understand the text much better if the word for "enemy" is recognized. Then, in 2008, Ilya Yakubovich wrote an article for *Kadmos* in which he referred to precisely this word as designating "the Luwian enemy."

Surely Ilya Yakubovich referred to your earlier work.
No, he did not quote me.

According to academic standards, researchers ought to consider all publications relevant to the subject in question.
Maybe he did not know. Perhaps he had arrived at this conclusion independently.

Of course, when we are considering which sources to include in our papers, a number of requirements need to be considered and the first among them concerns credibility. From what I can tell, most of your work was published in peer-reviewed journals. Hence the credibility is warranted and one runs the risk of being blamed of sloppy scholarship if your work is not properly quoted.
Indeed this happens a lot. For example, also regarding Luwian hieroglyphic, I was the only scholar who had maintained Piero Meriggi's identification of *ma-sà-ka-na* as "Phrygians" in Kızıldağ 4 that he had presented as early as 1964. Now the word "Muski" turns up in the Türkmen-Karahöyük inscription and Petra Goedegebuure and Theo van den Hout argue that this proves that Kızıldağ 4 also has "Phrygian" in it. But they don't cite my work. I was really the only one who had maintained this.

Do you have more examples like that?
When we spoke about Etruscan, we said that the numerals on the Tuscany dice are used to argue that Etruscan is not an Indo-European language, because the terms for numerals are closely related across all Indo-European languages. On the dice, *θu* has been read as "one" and *zal* is read as "two"; whereas I argue that these should be flipped, so that *θu* stands for "two" and is thus quite Indo-European. – Subsequently, John Ray wrote an article about this issue and ended up doing exactly the same thing that I had published years before!

Another example: Forty years ago, I learned from Jan Best that the coming of the Greeks should be placed around 1600 – and ever since then have argued along those lines. Now Robert Drews basically confirms this late date. But this is still a minority view, since most of our peers think that Greek speakers arrived in Greece between 2300 and 2000.

At some point you have argued that Luwian hieroglyphic is a centum language. Is that not a terminology that has become outdated?
Early Indo-European languages are all centum. In that sense, Luwian has to be centum, and there is evidence that this is so. Craig Melchert

took over this argument in a paper from 2012 – and he did refer to my work! But, you know, the development of satem can happen in every language. For example, in French the word *cent* ("hundred") with its s-sound is also satem. Luwian started as a centum language, and then, in Anatolia, it secondarily developed satem qualities. It is not entirely clear what the course of this may have been, but it is a very common linguistic development and can happen independently anywhere. Indo-Aryan is very fundamentally satem, though. Every *k* which developed from palatal *k* became a sibilant.

Another idea that you have been advocating is that Luwian hieroglyphic came into use as early as 2000 …
… and Willemijn Waal recently published a paper saying that there are Middle Bronze Age Luwian inscriptions. Yet, most scholars interpret this early use of signs as individual symbols that cannot be linguistically interpreted. They argue that the earliest readable inscriptions occur in the fourteenth century, so quite late. They take the name of the wife of Tudhaliya III as the first word that is syllabically readable.

You also argued that some of the Sea Peoples tribes came from regions in the central Mediterranean …
Yes; I don't disagree with you because western Anatolia was an important home of the Sea Peoples. For me, this is not a question of either/or, but it is as well as/and. The central Mediterranean, in my opinion, played a certain role in this period, and we can trace three groups amongst the Sea Peoples back to this region. Other people suggested this long before me, and I provided the relevant references in my dissertation. Shelley Wachsmann and Reinhard Jung have produced archaeological evidence proving influence from the central Mediterranean on the coastal regions of the eastern Mediterranean at the end of the Bronze Age.

You've also argued in favor of a close relationship between Phrygian and Greek …
… and again, others have said the same. Bartomeu Obrador-Cursach wrote about this fairly recently. I think the relationship is clear – I provided an overview and used the work of other scholars who have argued along the same lines.

Eberhard Zangger and Fred Woudhuizen during their conversation in Heiloo on September 5, 2020.

And if we look at your identification of Southwest Iberian as Celtic, when did you publish this?
My first publication on the subject appeared in the late 1990s. At that time, a Spanish scholar, José Antonio Correa, had already used Celtic identifications mostly for personal names. The work of John Koch came only later. Since Iberia has been considered to consist of an Indo-European part and a non-Indo-European part, the identification with Celtic was not as obvious as it now appears. But I think that this initial reconstruction is flawed and Indo-European spread all across the peninsula from c. 3000 or 2800 onwards.

Let's move on to another subject. Suppose I look back on almost four decades of my own collaboration with archaeologists on topics regarding Bronze Age eastern Mediterranean cultures. I got the impression that the more Eurocentric scholars in Turkey were, the higher they have risen. If you look back at your career and your experiences, what do you think is the effect of directing one's research interest towards early Anatolian cultures?

Well, I don't have a career to begin with, so that I don't need to care much about what other people think. As I said already during the discussion of the alphabet, Eurocentric scholarship usually prevails. Often people neither consider the east nor the west. In my opinion, it is not fruitful to always repeat the same paradigms. It's just not working! In publications on the Mycenaean culture, you're not likely to find a mentioning of Anatolia. And in publications about Anatolia, not much will be said about Mycenaean Greece. The Aegean Sea is considered a divide rather than a link. The field of Aegean prehistory was, after all, largely conceived by Arthur Evans – and he was clearly Eurocentric. Of course, a hundred years ago not much was known about western Anatolia.

It was also the time of the war between Greece and Turkey.
Yes, of course. There has been some kind of frontier between the subjects ever since they were conceived as research fields.

And the rigidity of this frontier depends on current politics. Today's division in the politics of Europe and Turkey does not make it easier for archaeologists to develop an overall reconstruction of what happened during the Bronze Age.
It is indeed difficult to talk about the possibility of non-European roots for the Mycenaean society. If the people came from the Orient, we would get a completely different story from the one told in today's textbooks.

Much has been written about the Persian War considering the setting-free of Europe. As far as I am concerned, the positive effect for Greece to not have been included in the Persian Empire escapes me. The Persians simply paid Sparta to fight the Athenians to the death, and then the story was over in Greece anyway. So what was the big achievement? The Persians played it very well from their perspective.

My feeling is that it takes some time to overcome the Eurocentric thinking.
Yes, of course! I became specialized in Luwian early on and therefore grew up with a different perspective. Since Luwian is an Indo-European language, one can argue that I'm still tracing back our roots, but the subjects of my inquiries lie in Anatolia, so this is by itself providing a different viewpoint.

How can archaeological studies in the future be less biased and more productive?

In my opinion, it is a prerequisite to use an interdisciplinary approach and to combine all the sources about ancient cultures that we can possibly put our hands on. We also need to cross boundaries and look at the influence Anatolia has had on Crete, for example, but also on Greece. The impact of the Levant on Crete is also highly relevant. It is pretty much the same story for the Iron Age: the Phoenicians go all the way to Spain and impact everything between Lebanon and Iberia. Basically, we ought to do everything at once: consider the archaeological record, the linguistic evidence, as well as the historical sources.

The interpretation of the past was impacted by the prevailing political and ideological concepts of the eighteenth, nineteenth and twentieth centuries. People have been projecting today's political map 3000 years back in time. Directing research interest into particular geographic regions, such as Mycenaean Greece in favor of Luwian Anatolia, has created a lasting effect, so we are now facing an imbalance of knowledge. Yes, but it doesn't work that way in the Bronze Age. Europe may have been the source of tin and amber, but otherwise it was not really important. Back then, the action was in the Orient, in the Near East and in Anatolia, that's where technological innovations occurred. The *ex oriente lux* approach is still valid. However, it should be realized that, for example, Celtic druids studied for 20 years and purposely avoided putting their learning in writing as they considered learning from memory of a higher order. So we will never know what exactly it entailed.

If you were able to say what our field should be like 30 years from now, what would you wish for?
I would say that people should be able to cross boundaries. If we exclude valuable material from our investigations, it will never be possible to come up with proper results.

In my opinion, experts tend to have a narrow view of the challenges at stake. I think that we need more generalists who won't shy away from becoming engaged in a number of different topics and making their own decisions based on the available evidence. Since it is impossible to master several disciplines on the same level, one is bound to make mistakes in this pursuit. It makes sense to employ authorities on certain topics to one's benefit, yet we have to immerse ourselves into the topics to draw our own conclusions.

We come back to what you said initially when we began our conversations a few months ago, about how you learned the field by trying to absorb as much as possible on past cultures. This means one has to look at all the evidence that has been handed down to us and this, by definition, requires an interdisciplinary approach.

And it can take years to work yourself into a certain topic. You have to take for granted that one's later contributions will be better than the initial ones. So it is better to get going immediately!

Interview conducted on October 2, 2020.

Appendix

Endnotes

How Does Decipherment Work?
1. Drews 1988; 2017
2. Zangger 2017, 243
3. Ventris 1940
4. Robinson 2002, 95
5. Davis 2014
6. Homer, *Odyssey* 19.148

Waves of Indo-Europeanization across the Mediterranean
7. Kloekhorst 2019
8. Krahe 1964
9. Kuhn 1959
10. Woudhuizen 2018, 19
11. Bachhuber 2015
12. Drews 2017

The Earliest Cretan Scripts
13. *Histories* 2.106
14. Bietak 2003, 24 [table]
15. Bruins et al. 2009
16. Plato, *Timaeus* 25D

The Lasting Success of Luwian Hieroglyphic
17. Hawkins, Morpurgo-Davies and Neumann 1973, 155
18. Hawkins 2000, 434–435

Byblos Needs Its Own Script

A Cypriot Admiral Calls for Help
19. Ferrara 2012, 14
20. Ferrara 2012, 11
21. Sherratt 2013, 97
22. Woudhuizen 2017, 50
23. Enkomi inventory number 19.10
24. Kalavassos K-AD 389
25. Ugarit RS 20.25
26. Enkomi inventory number 1687

Origin and Motives of the Sea Peoples
27. Woudhuizen 2006
28. Zangger 1994
29. Redford 2017, 130–131
30. Hoffmeier 2018, 12–20
31. Champollion 1836
32. Jung 2009
33. Homer, *Iliad* 24.546; also Apollodorus of Athens, *Epitome* 3.33 and Eustathius of Thessalonica, *Commentary on the Iliad* 322.25

The Etruscans Came from Asia Minor
34. Herodotus, *Histories* 1.94; Dionysius of Halicarnassus, *Roman Antiquities* I, 25–30
35. Herbig 1914, 11, 12, 17, 20–21, 32
36. Herodotus, *Histories* 7.224
37. Frazer 1911
38. Plutarch, *On the Worship of Isis and Osiris*, 69 [378e]
39. Hesiod, *Works and Days*, 383–387
40. Herodotus, *Histories* 1.94

Other Luwian Dialects, Such as Lydian, Lycian and Carian
41. Kolb 2018
42. Strabo 13.4.17
43. Lydian no. 1 (LW 1)
44. Herodotus, *Histories* 1.171
45. Kaunos bilingual inscription C.Ka5
46. Waal 2018

Southwest Iberian Is Celtic
47. Herodotus, *Histories* 4.152

Etymology or No Etymology – That Is the Question
—

Further Reading

Research Means Looking at Things from a New Perspective
Zangger, Eberhard (2017): *Die Luwier und der Trojanische Krieg – Eine Entdeckungsgeschichte.* Zürich: Orell Füssli.

How Does Decipherment Work?
Best, Jan (1981): "Von Piktographisch zu Linear B – Beiträge zur Linear A-Forschung." *Supplementum Epigraphicum Mediterraneum ad Talanta – Proceedings of the Dutch Archaeological and Historical Society* 13: 7–47.

Davis, Brent (2014): *Minoan Stone Vessels with Linear A Inscriptions.* Aegeum 36. Leuven-Liège: Peeters.

Doblhofer, Ernst (2000): *Die Entzifferung alter Schriften und Sprachen.* Reclam-Bibliothek 1702. Leipzig: Reclam.

Drews, Robert (1988): *The Coming of the Greeks: Indo-European Conquests in the Aegean and the Near East.* Princeton: Princeton University Press.

Evans, Arthur (1895): *Cretan Pictographs and Prae-Phoenician Script.* London: G.P. Putnam's Sons.

Evans, Arthur (1909): *Scripta Minoa I, The Written Documents of Minoan Crete, With Special Reference to the Archives of Knossos; The Hieroglyphic and Primitive Linear Classes with an Account of the Discovery of the Pre-Phoenician Scripts.* Oxford: At the Clarendon Press.

Herbig, Gustav (1914): *Kleinasiatisch-etruskische Namengleichungen.* Sitzungsberichte der Bayerischen Akademie, Philosophisch-historische Klasse, 2. Abhandlung.

Krahe, Hans (1964): *Unsere ältesten Flussnamen.* Wiesbaden: Harrassowitz.

Pope, Maurice (1975): *The Story of Decipherment: From Egyptian Hieroglyphic to Linear B.* The world of archaeology. London: Thames & Hudson.

Robinson, Andrew (2012): *The Man Who Deciphered Linear B – The Story of Michael Ventris.* London: Thames & Hudson.

Ventris, Michael (1940): "Introducing the Minoan Language." *American Journal of Archaeology* 44: 494–520.
Woudhuizen, Frederik Christiaan (2004): *Selected Luwian Hieroglyphic Texts [1]*. Innsbrucker Beiträge zur Kulturwissenschaft, Sonderheft 120. Innsbruck: Institut für Sprachen und Literaturen der Universität Innsbruck.
Woudhuizen, Frederik Christiaan (2006): *The Earliest Cretan Scripts [1]*. Innsbrucker Beiträge zur Kulturwissenschaft, Sonderheft 125. Innsbruck: Institut für Sprachen und Literaturen der Universität Innsbruck.
Woudhuizen, Frederik Christiaan (2013): *The Liber Linteus: A Word for Word Commentary to and Translation of the Longest Etruscan Text*. Innsbrucker Beiträge zur Kulturwissenschaft, Neue Folge 5. Innsbruck: Institut für Sprachen und Literaturen der Universität Innsbruck.

Waves of Indo-Europeanization across the Mediterranean

Anthony, David W. (2007): *The Horse, the Wheel, and Language; How Bronze-Age Riders from the Eurasian Steppes Shaped the Modern World* Princeton: Princeton University Press.
Bachhuber, Christoph (2015): *Citadel and Cemetery in Early Bronze Age Anatolia*. Sheffield: Equinox.
Drews, Robert (2017): *Militarism and the Indo-Europeanizing of Europe*. London: Routledge.
Haak, Wolfgang et al. (2015): "Massive Migration from the Steppe Was a Source for Indo-European Languages in Europe." *Nature* 522 (7555).
Haarmann, Harald (2012): *Indo-Europeanization – Day One: Elite Recruitment and the Beginnings of Language Politics*. Wiesbaden: Harrassowitz.
Kloekhorst, Alwin (2019): *Kanišite Hittite – The Earliest Attested Record of Indo-European*. Handbook of Oriental Studies, Section 1, Ancient Near East 132. Leiden: Brill.
Krahe, Hans (1964): *Unsere ältesten Flussnamen*. Wiesbaden: Harrassowitz.

Kuhn, Hans (1959): "Vor- und frühgeschichtliche Ortsnamen in Norddeutschland und den Niederlanden." *Westfälische Forschungen, Mitteilungen des Provinzialinstituts für westfälische Landes- und Volkskunde* 12: 5–44.

Reich, David (2018): *Who We Are and How We Got Here – Ancient DNA and the New Science of the Human Past.* Oxford: Oxford University Press.

Woudhuizen, Frederik Christiaan (2018): *Indo-Europeanization in the Mediterranean: With Particular Attention to the Fragmentary Languages.* Papers in Intercultural Philosophy and Transcontinental Comparative Studies. Hoofddorp: Shikanda Press.

Yakubovich, Ilya (2010): *Sociolinguistics of the Luvian Language.* Brill's Studies in Indo-European Languages & Linguistics 2. Leiden: Brill.

The Earliest Cretan Scripts

Bietak, Manfred (2003): "Science Versus Archaeology: Problems and Consequences of High Aegean Chronology." In: *The Synchronisation of Civilisations in the Eastern Mediterranean in the Second Millennium B.C., Proceedings of the SCIEM 2000-EuroConference, Haindorf, 2nd of May – 7th of May 2001,* edited by Manfred Bietak, 23–33. Wien: Verlag der Österreichischen Akademie der Wissenschaften.

Bruins, Hendrik J., Johannes van der Plicht and J. Alexander MacGillivray (2009): "The Minoan Santorini Eruption and Tsunami Deposits in Palaikastro (Crete): Dating by Geology, Archaeology, 14C, and Egyptian Chronology." *Radiocarbon* 51 (2): 397–411.

Woudhuizen, Frederik Christiaan (2006): *The Earliest Cretan Scripts [1].* Innsbrucker Beiträge zur Kulturwissenschaft, Sonderheft 125. Innsbruck: Institut für Sprachen und Literaturen der Universität Innsbruck.

Woudhuizen, Frederik Christiaan (2009): *The Earliest Cretan Scripts 2.* Innsbrucker Beiträge zur Kulturwissenschaft, Sonderheft 129. Innsbruck: Institut für Sprachen und Literaturen der Universität Innsbruck.

Woudhuizen, Frederik Christiaan (2016): *Documents in Minoan Luwian, Semitic, and Pelasgian*. Publications of the Henri Frankfort Foundation. Amsterdam: Dutch Archaeological and Historic Society.

Zangger, Eberhard (1993): "Plato's Atlantis Account: A Distorted Recollection of the Trojan War." *Oxford Journal of Archaeology* 18 (1): 77–87.

Zangger, Eberhard (2001): *The Future of the Past – Archaeology in the 21st Century*. London: Weidenfeld & Nicolson.

The Lasting Success of Luwian Hieroglyphic

Bossert, Helmuth Theodor (1960): "Ist die B-L Schrift im wesentlichen entziffert?" *Orientalia Nova Series* 29 (4): 423–442.

Hawkins, John David, Anna Morpurgo-Davies and Günter Neumann (1973): *Hittite Hieroglyphs and Luwian: New Evidence for the Connection*. Nachrichten der Akademie der Wissenschaften in Göttingen, Philologisch-historische Klasse, 146–197. Göttingen: Vandenhoeck & Ruprecht.

Hawkins, John David (2000): *Corpus of Hieroglyphic Luwian Inscriptions, Vol 1. Inscriptions of the Iron Age. Part 1: Text: Introduction, Karatepe, Karkamiš, Tell Ahmar, Maraş, Malatya, Commagene*. Berlin: de Gruyter.

Mellaart, Arlette (2002): "Reflections on a Summerhouse – The Savfet Pasha Yalı in Kanlıca." *Cornucopia – Turkey for Connoisseurs* 5 (25): 106–122.

Woudhuizen, Frederik Christiaan (2011): *Selected Luwian Hieroglyphic Texts – The Extended Version*. Innsbrucker Beiträge zur Sprachwissenschaft 141. Innsbruck: Institut für Sprachen und Literaturen der Universität Innsbruck.

Woudhuizen, Frederik Christiaan (2017): "Selected Cuneiform Luwian Texts." *Talanta – Proceedings of the Dutch Archaeological and Historical Society* 48/49: 329–367.

Woudhuizen, Frederik Christiaan (2020): "Four Notes on Luwian Hieroglyphic." *Ancient West & East* 18, 245–264.

Woudhuizen, Frederik Christiaan and Eberhard Zangger (2018): "Arguments in Favour of the Authenticity of the Luwian Hieroglyphic Texts from the Mellaart Files." *Talanta – Proceedings of the Dutch Archaeological and Historical Society* 50: 183–212.

Zangger, Eberhard (2018): "James Mellaart's Fantasies." *Talanta – Proceedings of the Dutch Archaeological and Historical Society* 50: 125–182.

Zangger, Eberhard and Frederik Christiaan Woudhuizen (2018): "Rediscovered Luwian Hieroglyphic Inscriptions from Western Asia Minor." *Talanta – Proceedings of the Dutch Archaeological and Historical Society* 50: 9–56.

Byblos Needs Its Own Script

Best, Jan (2008): "Breaking the Code of the Byblos Script." *Ugarit-Forschungen* 40: 129–134.

Vita, Juan-Pablo and José Ángel Zamora (2018): "The Byblos Script." In: *Paths into Script Formation in the Ancient Mediterranean*, edited by Silvia Ferrara and Miguel Valério, Studie Micinei ed Egeo-Anatolici – Nuova Series Supplemento 1, 75–102. Rome: Edizioni Quasar di Severino Tognon.

Woudhuizen, Frederik Christiaan (2008): "On the Byblos Script." *Ugarit-Forschungen* 39: 689–766.

A Cypriot Admiral Calls for Help

Ferrara, Silvia (2012): *Cypro-Minoan Inscriptions*. Oxford: Oxford University Press.

Hiller, Stefan (1985): "Die kyprominoischen Schriftsysteme." *Archiv für Orientforschung, Beiheft* 20: 61–102.

Sherratt, Susan (2013): "Late Cypriot Writing in Context." In: *Syllabic Writing on Cyprus and Its Context*, edited by Philippa M. Steele, Cambridge Classical Studies, 77–105. Cambridge: Cambridge University Press.

Woudhuizen, Frederik Christiaan (2017): *The Language of Linear C and Linear D from Cyprus*. Publications of the Henri Frankfort Foundation 15. Amsterdam: Dutch Archaeological and Historical Society.

Origin and Motives of the Sea Peoples

Champollion, Jean François (1835–45): *Monuments de l'Egypte et la Nubie*, 4 volumes. Paris.

Champollion, Jean-François (1836): *Grammaire égyptienne, ou principes généraux de l'écriture sacrée Égyptienne appliquée à la représentation de la langue parlée*. Paris: Didot.

Hoffmeier, James K. (2018): "A Possible Location in Northwest Sinai for the Sea and Land Battles between the Sea Peoples and Ramesses III." *Bulletin of the American Schools of Oriental Research* 380: 1–25.

Jung, Reinhard (2009): "Pirates of the Aegean: Italy – the East Aegean – Cyprus at the End of the Second Millennium." In: *Cyprus and the East Aegean, International Contacts from 3000 to 500, An International Archaeological Symposium Held at Pythagoreion, Samos, October 17–18th 2008*, edited by Vassos Karageorghis and Ourania Kouka, 72–93. Nicosia.

Redford, Donald Bruce (2017): *The Medinet Habu Records of the Foreign Wars of Ramesses III*. Culture and History of the Near East 91. Leiden: Brill.

Wachsmann, Shelley (2013): *The Gurob Ship-Cart Model and Its Mediterranean Context: An Archaeological Find and Its Mediterranean Context*. College Station: Texas A&M University Press.

Woudhuizen, Frederik Christiaan (2006): *The Ethnicity of the Sea People*. PhD dissertation. Rotterdam: University of Rotterdam.

Zangger, Eberhard (1994). *Ein neuer Kampf um Troia – Archäologie in der Krise*. München: Droemer.

Zangger, Eberhard (2016): *The Luwian Civilization – The Missing Link in the Aegean Bronze Age*. Istanbul: Ege Yayınları.

The Etruscans Came from Asia Minor

Frazer, James George (1911): *The Golden Bough: A Study in Magic and Religion (Third Edition), Volume 4: The Dying God*. Reprint by Cambridge University Press, 2012.

Herbig, Gustav (1914): *Kleinasiatisch-etruskische Namengleichungen*. Sitzungsberichte der Bayerischen Akademie, Philosophisch-historische Klasse, 2. Abhandlung.

Woudhuizen, Frederik Christiaan (2008): *Etruscan as a Colonial Luwian Language*. Innsbrucker Beiträge zur Kulturwissenschaft. Innsbruck: Institut für Sprachen und Literaturen der Universität Innsbruck.

Woudhuizen, Frederik Christiaan (2013): *The Liber Linteus: A Word for Word Commentary to and Translation of the Longest Etruscan Text*. Innsbrucker Beiträge zur Kulturwissenschaft, Neue Folge 5. Innsbruck: Institut für Sprachen und Literaturen der Universität Innsbruck.

Zangger, Eberhard (2001): *The Future of the Past – Archaeology in the 21st Century*. London: Weidenfeld & Nicolson.

Other Luwian Dialects, Such as Lydian, Lycian and Carian

Adiego Lajara, Ignacio-Javier (2013): "Carian Identity and Carian Language." In: *4th Century Karia – Defining a Karian Identity under the Hekatomnids*, edited by Olivier Henry, Varia Anatolica 28, 15–20. Istanbul: Institut français d'études anatoliennes Georges-Dumezil.

Kolb, Frank (2018): *Lykien: Geschichte einer antiken Landschaft*. Darmstadt: wbg Philipp von Zabern.

Payne, Annick and Jorit Wintjes (2016): *Lords of Asia Minor – An introduction to the Lydians*. Philippika 93. Wiesbaden: Harrassowitz.

Waal, Willemijn (2018): "On the 'Phoenician Letters': The Case for an Early Transmission of the Greek Alphabet from an Archaeological, Epigraphic, and Linguistic Perspective." *Aegean Studies* 1: 83–125.

Woudhuizen, Frederik Christiaan (1985): "Origins of the Sidetic Script." *Talanta – Proceedings of the Dutch Archaeological and Historical Society* 16/17: 115–127.

Woudhuizen, Frederik Christiaan (1989): "The Recently Discovered Greek-Sidetic Bilingue from Seleucia." *Talanta – Proceedings of the Dutch Archaeological and Historical Society* 20/21: 87–96.

Woudhuizen, Frederik Christiaan (2012): "Lycian Forms of the Enclitic Pronoun of the 3rd Person: An Overview of the Relevant Data." *Colloquium Anatolicum* 11: 415–436.

Woudhuizen, Frederik Christiaan (2017): "Selected Cuneiform Luwian Texts." *Talanta – Proceedings of the Dutch Archaeological and Historical Society* 48/49: 329–367.

Woudhuizen, Frederik Christiaan (2019): "The Lydian *Yod*-Sign." In: *A Life Dedicated to Anatolian Prehistory: Festschrift for Jak Yakar*, edited by Barış Gür and Semra Dalkılıç, 465–477. Ankara: Bilgin.

Woudhuizen, Frederik Christiaan (2019): "A Carian Inscription from Mylasa." *Živa Antika* 69 (1/2): 5–10.

Woudhuizen, Frederik Christiaan (2020): "On the Reading and Interpretation of the Two Longer Sidetic Inscriptions S I.2.1 and S I.2.5." *Živa Antika* 70: 17–34.

Woudhuizen, Frederik Christiaan (in press): "Determining the Value of the Arrow-Sign in Phrygian and Lydian."

Southwest Iberian Is Celtic

Cunliffe, Barry and John T. Koch (eds.) (2019): *Exploring Celtic Origins – New Ways Forward in Archaeology, Linguistics, and Genetics*. Celtic Studies Publications. Oxford: Oxbow.

Koch, John T. (2019): *Common Ground and Progress on the Celtic of the South-Western (S.W.) Inscriptions*. Aberystwyth: Centre for Advanced Welsh and Celtic Studies. https://www.wales.ac.uk/Resources/Documents/Centre/2019/Koch-Celtic-of-the-SW-inscriptions-2019.pdf

Woudhuizen, Frederik Christiaan (2015): "Some Southwest Iberian Inscriptions." *Talanta – Proceedings of the Dutch Archaeological and Historical Society* 46/47: 299–334.

Picture Credits

Archaeological Museum in Zagreb: 164/165.

C. Messier: 60.

Department of Antiquities Cyprus: 3, 122, 128.

Isabelle Hattink: 14, 67, 103, 118, 171, 217.

Ivo Hajnal: 35.

Luwian Studies: 24 (#0515), 26 (#0537a), 32 (#0500), 34 (#0149), 37 (#0165a), 40 (#1061), 43 (#0158), 47 (#0125), 50 (#6330, #6331), 55 (#0146), 63 (#3122), 69 (#3121), 74 (#0309), 80/81 (#0147), 87 (#0173), 93 (#6028), 97 (#6029), 99 (#6031), 107 (#0164), 119 (#0537b), 122 (#0160), 125 (#1506), 130 (#0150), 136 (#1031), 138 (#4002), 140 (#0152), 142 (#4015), 143 (#6221), 144 (#6329), 149 (#0111), 158 (#0507), 163 (#0155), 168 (#0161), 174 (#0153), 175 (#0159), 184/185 (#0144), 194 (#0537c), 197 (#0154), 199 (#0156), 200 (#0162), 201 (#0163), 210/211 (#0148).

Museo Nazionale Etrusco di Villa Giulia. Archivio fotografico. Photo by Mauro Benedetti: 161.

Museu Regional de Beja, Portugal. Photo by António Cunha: 203.

National Archaeological Museum, Greece, Hellenic Ministry of Culture and Sports/Archaeological Resources Fund (Law 3028/2002): 167.

National Museum of Beirut: 107.

Olaf Tausch: 62.

Osborne et al. 2020, Fig. 17b, courtesy of the Türkmen-Karahöyük Intensive Survey Project. Photo by Jennifer Jackson: 101.

Paul Mellaart: 95.

Rosemary Robertson: 139, 146.

The Walters Art Museum, Baltimore: 17.

Trustees of the British Museum: 16, 116.

Index

A
abecedarium, 191
academic credibility, 215
academic freedom, 11–12
accounting system, 123, 126
    See also trade records
acrophonic principle, 83, 118
Adiego, Ignacio, 182–183
Adjusted Old Reading (Luwian hieroglyphic), 87, 90
admiral
    fleet's course of Cypriot, 130
    letter by Cypriot, 116, 127–129, 137
Aegean
    catacomb graves, 39
    migration of Pelasgians to, 36, 37
    See also Crete; Greece
Aegean Bronze Age, 13, 28, 29
    See also Minoan culture
aia- (verb), 21
Akamas of Ilion, 123–124, 137
Akkadian cuneiform
    invention, 26
    on Tarkondemos seal, 17, 73–74
Akrotiri, seals from, 69
Alaca Höyük, grave, 40
Aleppo, 89, 109–110
Almodôvar, Herdade da Abobada inscription, 203
alphabet values, 181
alphabetic letters, 180, 183, 187, 191
alphabets
    development, 208
    order of signs, 183

alphabets (*continued*)
    semi-syllabic, 192
    spread of, 194, 208–209
    See also Anatolian alphabets; Etruscan alphabet; Greek alphabet; Latin alphabet; Lycian alphabet; Phoenician alphabet; Sidetic alphabet; Southwest Iberian alphabet
Alps, migration to, 170
altar stone, from Malia, 61, 63
Amarna letters, 127
Amathus, bilingual document from, 121
Amenhotep III, Pharaoh, 75
Ammurapi, King of Ugarit, 137
Anatolia
    early period, 105
    migration from, 172, 178
    migration to, 39, 41, 49, 101, 145, 174
    script development, 55
    trade routes from Ugarit to, 124
    See also Alaca Höyük; Beycesultan; Beyköy; Gordion; Hittite Empire; Kayseri-Kululu; Kültepe-Kanesh; Lamiya; Latmos; Tarsus; Yalburt
Anatolian alphabets, 180, 209, 212
Anatolian languages, 159
animal head, as sign, 74
animals. *See* bird; cattle; horses
Ankara silver bowl, 22
Aramaic language, grave inscription, 179

archaeology
 and decipherments, 19–20
 and linguistics, 15
 See also excavations
Arganthonios, King of Tartessos, 195
Aritesup (personal name), 90
Arkalochori, double axe of, 61, 62
Armi, 32
arrow sign. *See* upward arrow sign
Arzawa, 75, 82, 177
Asherah inscription, 24
Asia (deity name), 171
Asia Minor. *See* Anatolia
Assyria, invasion of Hittite Empire, 134
Astarte (goddess), 59
Atlantis account, 70
atlunu (Atlantis), 66
attacks. *See* invasions; raids
axes. *See* double axe

B
Bachhuber, Christoph, 39
Balkan Peninsula, migration to, 49
Basque language, 198
Basques, 198, 199
battles
 of Cumae, 162
 of Kadesh, 134
 of Migdol, 138
 of Perire, 135
 of Troy, 154
 See also naval battles
Beekes, Robert, 167, 178

Best, Jan
 decipherment of Byblos script, 111, 112
 decipherment of Linear A, 24, 25, 56, 57
 decipherment of Linear C and D, 120
 decipherment of Phaistos disc, 61
 publications by, 64–65
Beycesultan, seal from, 32
"Beyköy 2" text, 129
"Beyköy text"
 cuneiform forgeries, 92, 96–97
 Luwian hieroglyphic, 91–92, 93–94, 95, 96, 97, 98
Bietak, Manfred, 66
bilateral agreements, in Iberia, 202
bilingual documents
 from Amathus, 121
 explained, 186
 grave inscription, 179
 See also Karatepe inscription; Kaunos bilingual inscription; Pyrgi tablets; Tarkondemos seal
bilingual evidence, 21–22
bird, looking backwards (design), 140
Black Sea, migration to and along, 34–35, 43
bookkeeping. *See* accounting system
border regions, languages affecting each other in, 206
Bossert, Helmuth, 84
bowls. *See* silver bowls
briga names, 198

Bronze Age
  Middle Chronology, 105
  See also Aegean Bronze Age
Bronze Age collapse, 148
  See also cultural collapse (after 1200)
burial sites. *See* graves
burials, single-horse, 39, 40
Byblos, 58, 106, 108, 189
Byblos script
  decipherment, 110, 111–113
  development, 112, 207
  direction of text, 108
  Linear A related to, 111–112, 119
  number of documents, 108
  punctuation marks, 107, 112
  in Semitic dialect, 107
  signs and sound values, 112, 211
  tablets, 107, 108–109

C
Cadmus, King of Thebes, 42
caldera, Thera as, 68
Canaanites, 42
captives, Sea Peoples as, 138
Carchemish, 148
Caria, 182
Carian language
  decipherment, 182–183
  Greek influence, 206
  Luwian, derived from, 172
  as Luwian dialect, 174, 189
  transcription in Kaunos bilingual inscription, 185, 186
Carians, 182
Carruba, Onofrio, 177–178
casidanos (noun), 194
catacomb graves, 36, 39

cattle, 50
Caucasus, Vladikavkaz disc, 61
celestial aspects, 11
Celtiberian script, 193
Celtic language, 193, 198, 217
Celts
  druids, 219
  Drynemeton, 202
  migration to Iberia, 197
centum languages, 216
chamber tombs, 169
Champollion, Jean-François, 16–17, 140
chariots, 41, 43, 106
Chian lid, 42
chronology
  incomplete Cretan, 71
  Middle, 105
Cibyra, 177
Cilicia. *See* Lamiya
citations, missing, 215
civil war, Greece, 154
clay balls, 121
climatic change, debate on migration triggered by, 46
clothes, 126
commodities. *See* goods
consonants, in decipherment, 18
copper, 126, 127, 144
Cornwall, 196
corpus, of Iron Age texts, 79
correspondence. *See* letters
credibility, academic, 215
Cretan hieroglyphic
  altar stone from Malia, 61, 63
  beginning of, 26, 53
  dating of documents, 61
  development, 207–208

Cretan hieroglyphic *(continued)*
    double axe of Arkalochori, 61, 62
    Egyptian and Luwian hieroglyphic, derived from, 26–27, 59
    logograms and sound values, 210
    number of documents, 26
    Phaistos disc, 61
    readability of documents, 62
    seals, 59, 62, 65
    translation, 61
Crete
    chronology, incomplete, 71
    destruction, supposed, 67
    Egyptian name for, 139
    eruption of Thera and its effects on, 66, 69
    influence in eastern Mediterranean, 69–70
    invasion by Greeks, 63–64, 70
    kingdoms, 45
    Linear A documents, 24, 27, 30
    Linear B documents, 30, 64
    migration to, 44, 58
    personal names, 28
    population, 28
    religion, 59
    research on, 65
    scarabs, 63, 139
    script development, 55, 207–208
    seals, 29, 54, 56, 69
    tablets, 24, 27, 30
    tin trade, 54, 56
    trade with Levant, 56
    tsunami deposits, no indication of, 67–68
    See also Arkalochori; Hagia Triada; Kato Zakros; Knossos; Malia; Phaistos; Sklavokampo
cult text, in Lydian language, 179

cultural collapse (after 1200), 133
Cumae, 162
cuneiform texts
    in Arzawa, 177
    Beyköy forgeries, 92, 96–97
    from Hattusa, 75
    seals with, 56
    See also Akkadian cuneiform; Hittite cuneiform; Luwian cuneiform
cuneiform writing, 53
curse formula, 78
cylinder seals, 56, 115, 121, 122, 123
Cypriot syllabary
    Linear B, comparison with, 18
    Linear C and D, evolved from, 121
    Southwest Iberian alphabet, influence on, 193, 200, 201
    tablet, 116
Cypro-Minoan 1 (CM1). *See* Linear C
Cypro-Minoan 2 (CM2). *See* Linear D
Cypro-Minoan syllabary
    dating, 116–117, 187
    in Kaunos bilingual inscription, 186
    in Sidetic alphabet, 180
    variants, 115, 120
Cyprus
    copper resources, 126, 127
    Hittite control, 147
    independence, 137
    invasions by Hittite Empire, 126
    place names, 150
    political status, 126–127
    script development, 55, 208
    trade, 115
    trade records, 123, 125
    See also Amathus; Enkomi

D

Danaïds, 186
Dark Age. *See* Bronze Age collapse
Davis, Brent, 28
decipherments
   acknowledgment, 120
   approaches, 29–30
   and archaeology, 19–20
   bilingual evidence, 21–22
   of Byblos script, 110, 111–113
   of Carian language, 182–183
   of Etruscan language, 9, 20, 157, 158, 160, 161, 168, 170–171
   internal and external approaches, 18, 111
   of Kaunos bilingual inscription, 183–186, 187
   of Lemnos stele, 166
   of Linear A, 24–25, 56–57
   of Linear B, 18–19, 29, 119
   of Linear C, 118–119, 120
   of Linear D, 118–119, 120
   of Luwian hieroglyphic, 17–18, 20–21, 77–78
   major successes, 15–16
   origin of signs, 187–188
   of Phaistos disc, 61
   of Sidetic language, 181
   of Southwest Iberian, 193, 194
   topics dealt with, 20
   See also doublets; triplets
declension, 18
dedications, 167, 181, 201–202, 203
deities. *See* gods and goddesses
Denyen, 141, 152
destruction
   of Crete, supposed, 67
   in eastern Mediterranean, 154
   of Gordion, 212
   of Knossos, 30
   by migration, 45–46
   of Minoan culture, 44
   of Ugarit, 137
dice, Tuscany, 158, 215
discs. *See* Magliano disc; Phaistos disc; Vladikavkaz disc
diseases. *See* plague
DNA analysis, 49–50
dogmatism, 23
domus (noun), 22, 83
double axe
   of Arkalochori, 61, 62
   as sign, 113
doublets, 18, 27, 111
Drews, Robert, 43
druids, 219
Drynemeton, 202
dying god, myth of, 165–166

E

early Mediterranean history. *See* Mediterranean pre- and protohistory
Early Mediterranean Scripts, in dialogue form, 12
East Iberian language, 198
Ebla tablets, 32
economy
   of Hittite Empire, 134–135
   See also trade
'Egel, King of Byblos, 110
Egypt
   Amarna letters, 127
   Byblos, influence on, 108
   Carian mercenaries, 182
   Gurob ship model, 144
   Hyksos rule, 106
   invasion by Indo-Aryans, 106

Egypt *(continued)*
  invasions by Sea Peoples, 150, 152, 155
  Libyans, conflict with, 135, 151–152
  migration of Indo-Aryans to, 41
  mummy wrapping, 164
  peace treaty with Hittite Empire, 134
  script development, 55
  shipment of grain to Hittite Empire, 135–136
  See also Medinet Habu temple; Migdol; Perire
Egyptian hieroglyphic
  beginning of, 53
  Byblos script related to, 111, 112
  Cretan hieroglyphic derived from, 26–27, 59
  Haunebut, 139
  invention, 26
  logograms and sound values, 210
  vs. Luwian hieroglyphic, 54
  on scarabs, 63
Egyptian language, vs. Luwian language, 53–54
Ekwesh, 141
enemy (noun). See *tíwaná*
England. See Cornwall
Enkomi, cylinder seal, 122
epistemological approach, 10
eruptions. *See* volcanic eruptions
Eteocypriot language, 121
ethnic names, 75, 102
ethnicity
  in battle of Kadesh, 134
  in battle of Perire, 135
  of Sea Peoples, 123, 133, 139, 140–141, 142–143, 149, 150, 152, 155
Etruria, chamber tombs, 169
Etruscan alphabet, 159
Etruscan language
  Anatolian connection, 159
  Asia (deity name), 171
  decipherment, 9, 20, 157, 158, 160, 161, 168, 170–171
  Indo-European Anatolian, derived from, 158
  Liber Linteus, 164–165
  Luwian, derived from, 172
  Luwian, related to, 160
  as Luwian dialect, 169, 170
  Magliano disc, 158
  number of documents, 157
  numerals, 157–158, 215
  in Pyrgi tablets, 161, 162
  translation, 163
Etruscans
  core region, 163
  origin of, 169
  religion, 165
  See also Tyrsenoi
etymological approach, 205, 206–207
Euboea, 159
Eurocentric scholarship, 217–218, 219
Evans, Arthur, 28–29
excavations, on Therasia, 69
expert's approach. *See* specialized approach
extinct languages. See *Trümmersprachen*

F

F sign, 159, 182
famines, in Hittite Empire, 135
feather headdresses, 139, 142, 145
Ferrara, Silvia, 117, 118, 119, 130
fictitious sources, 213
first person singular pronoun, 123
fleets
    course of Cypriot admiral, 130
    of Sea Peoples advancing into
        Mediterranean, 153
    of Sea Peoples advancing to
        Levant, 129
    See also naval battles; warships
forgeries, "Beyköy text," 92, 96–97
Forrer, Emil, 75, 78
fragmentary languages, 47
Frazer, James George, 165
Frei, Peter, 183

G

Gelb, Ignace, 21, 78
generalist's approach. *See* interdisciplinary approach
geographic names
    Haunebut, 139
    See also place names; river names
geological deposits, interpreted by
    archaeologists, 66, 67
gifts, to temple of Byblos, 108–109
Gimbutas, Marija, 33
give (verb). *See ya-ta-nū-tī*
gods and goddesses
    Asia (name), 171
    Astarte and Tinita, 59
    myth of dying, 165–166
Goedegebuure, Petra, 215
goods, 115, 125, 134
    See also clothes; grain; tin

Gordion, destruction, 212
grain, shipment to Hittite Empire,
    135–136
grave inscriptions, 176, 179
graves
    at Alaca Höyük, 40
    on Italic Peninsula, 48
    long swords in, 44
    Lycian, 175
    See also burials; catacomb graves;
        chamber tombs; shaft graves;
        tholos graves
"great prince" (sign), 98, 99
Greece
    civil war, 154
    migration from, 154
    migration to, 39, 43, 215
    Persian War, 162, 218
    script development, 55
    See also Euboea; Mycenae; Pylos
Greek alphabet
    dating, 180–181, 209
    perishable material, documents
        on, 189
    Phoenician alphabet, derived
        from, 180
    psi sign, 183
    sound values, 117
Greek language
    influence on Carian language, 206
    related to Phrygian language, 216,
        217
Greek mythology. *See* Scheria; Trojan
    War
Greeks
    arrival of, 42, 215
    in Iberia, 195, 197
    influence on Luwians, 188
    invasion of Crete, 63–64, 70

Greeks *(continued)*
   as Sea Peoples, 150
   See also Mycenaeans
Grey Ware, 41
Gurob ship model, 144
Gusmani, Roberto, 177
Gyges, King of Lydia, 178

H
Hagia Triada, Linear A documents, 30, 64
Hama(th), 73, 90
handmade burnished ware, 145
harbormaster, 124
Hartapus, King, 101
Hattic language, 75–76
Hattusa
   cuneiform texts, 75
   introduction of writing, 77
   Südburg and Nişantaş inscriptions, 136
   trade routes from Troy, 130
Hattusili I, Great King of Hittite Empire, 77, 105
Haunebut, 139
Hawkins, David, 79, 84–85, 89
helmets, with horns, 142, 145
Herbig, Gustav, 160
Herdade da Aboboda inscription, 203
Herodotus, 169, 177, 182, 195, 212
hieroglyphic scripts
   logograms and sound values, 210
   See also Cretan hieroglyphic; Egyptian hieroglyphic; Luwian hieroglyphic

historiographic accounts, 212–213
   See also Herodotus; Homer; Medinet Habu temple; Plato; Strabo
Hittite cuneiform, personal names, 21
Hittite Empire
   accounting system, 123, 126
   control of Cyprus, 147
   economy, 134–135
   end of, 173
   famines, 135
   invasion by Assyria of, 134
   invasions of Cyprus, 126
   Lycians as adversaries of, 124
   military, 152
   naval battles, 129, 137
   peace treaty with Egypt, 134
   shipment of grain to, 135–136
   See also Hattusa
Hittite language
   influence on Lydian, 23–24
   loanwords in Luwian hieroglyphic, 77
Homer, 70, 71, 150
horns, helmets with, 142, 145
horses, 41–42
   See also single-horse burials
house (noun). See *domus*; *parna*
Hout, Theo van den, 215
Houwink ten Cate, Philo, 79
Huelva, inscription from, 191
Hurrian language, 77
Hyksos, 41, 42, 106

I

Iberia
  bilateral agreements, 202
  early period, 48
  Greeks in, 195, 197
  migration to, 36, 37, 197, 198
  Phoenician alphabet introduction to, 197
  research on, 199–200
  river names, 198
  script development, 55
  See also Almodôvar; Huelva
Iberian languages, 199
  See also Basque language; East Iberian language; Southwest Iberian language
identical signs, 117, 118, 119
incised signs, of Byblos script, 108
Indo-Aryans
  invasion of Levant and Egypt by, 106
  migration of, 41
Indo-European Anatolian, 158
Indo-European languages
  centum and satem languages, 216
  development, 47
  earliest references to, 32–33
  etymological approach, 206
  misinterpreted, 48
  river names, 36
  See also individual languages
Indo-European studies, 31–32, 206–207
Indo-Europeans
  Group A and B, 38–39
  innovations of, 40
  migration from north Caspian steppes, 33–34
  migration in eastern Mediterranean, 42–43
  migration intervals, 45
  migration to Iberia, 198
  migration to Mediterranean, 36, 37–38, 39
  as product of Neolithic Revolution, 33
Indo-Germanic studies. *See* Indo-European studies
innovations
  chariots, 41
  of Indo-Europeans, 40
  by migration, 35–36
  past tense, 39
interdisciplinary approach, 13, 14, 15, 16, 219, 220
invasions
  of Crete by Greeks, 63–64, 70
  of Cyprus by Hittite Empire, 126
  of Egypt by Indo-Aryans, 106
  of Egypt by Sea Peoples, 150, 152, 155
  of Greece by Xerxes, 162
  of Hittite Empire by Assyria, 134
  of Levant by Indo-Aryans, 106
  of Luwian kingdoms by Mycenaeans, 153–154
  by Sea Peoples, 45, 46, 150, 152–153, 155
ī+r-ha-nu-a- (place name), 21
Iron Age, corpus of texts, 79
islands
  trade with Levant, 147
  See also Crete; Cyprus; Euboea; Lemnos; Sardinia; Thera; Therasia

Italic Peninsula
   graves, 48
   migration from, 48–49, 170
   migration to, 37, 48, 141, 145, 172
   river names, 48, 169
   script development, 55
   See also Cumae; Etruria; Tuscany
izi- (verb), 21

J
Jones, William, 31
Jung, Reinhard, 216

K
Kadesh, battle of, 134
Kaïkos valley. See Seha
Kameiros, 127
Karatepe inscription, 17, 18, 78, 86, 88
Kato Zakros, 64
Kaunos bilingual inscription, 183–186, 187, 206
Kayseri-Kululu, 123
Khvalynsk culture, migration of, 34–35
kingdoms, in Crete, 45
Kızıldağ 4 inscription, 215
Kizzuwatna, 150
Kloekhorst, Alwin, 33, 178
Knossos
   destruction, 30
   dominance of, 44, 45
   Linear B texts from, 64
   silver pins, 58
Kober, Alice, 18, 19, 130
Koch, John T., 193, 200
Kolaeus (merchant), 195
Kolb, Frank, 175
Krakatoa, eruption of, 68

Kültepe-Kanesh, 33
Kupantakurunta, Great King of Arzawa, 155

L
Lamiya, 124
languages
   in border regions affecting each other, 206
   closely related, 43–44
   connections between, 205–206
   fragmentary, 47
   of Iberia, 199
   of Lemnos stele, 167
   names, 75
   Trümmersprachen, 15, 188
   in Ugarit, 77
   See also Indo-European languages; non-Indo-European languages; Semitic languages; *individual languages*
Laroche, Emmanuel, 78–79, 85, 176
Latin, as transcription for Luwian, 22, 79–84
Latin alphabet, 192
Latmos inscription, 98, 99
Lemnos, inscription from, 168
Lemnos stele, 166–167, 168
Letoon trilingual text, 176
letters (correspondence)
   Amarna, 127
   by Ammurapi, 137
   by Cypriot admiral, 116, 127–129, 137
   from Mari, 54, 56
   Shikala, 144
   from Ugarit, 127
letters (signs). See alphabetic letters

Levant
  invasion by Indo-Aryans, 106
  migration from, 58
  migration to, 43
  place names, 147
  script development, 55
  Sea Peoples' advancement to, 129, 137
  Sea Peoples' settlements, 146–147, 148
  trade with islands, 56, 147
  See also Byblos; Syria
libation formula, 56
Liber Linteus, 164–165
Libyans, 135, 151–152
lids. *See* Chian lid
Ligurians, migration to Italic Peninsula, 37, 48
Limyra, 137
Linear A
  Asherah inscription, 24
  Byblos script related to, 111–112, 119
  Crete, documents from, 24, 27, 30, 64
  decipherment, 24–25, 56–57
  development, 57, 207–208
  Linear C and D derived from, 119, 121
  number of documents, 24
  personal names, 30, 64
  as Semitic language, 24, 25, 28, 56–57, 58
  signs and sound values, 117, 211
  Southwest Iberian alphabet, not related to, 193
  tablets, 24, 27, 30
  translation, 57
Linear B
  Crete, documents from, 30, 64
  Cypriot syllabary, comparison with, 18
  decipherment, 18–19, 29, 119
  Knossos, texts from, 64
  Linear C and D derived from, 121
  personal names, 30, 64
  quality of texts, 58
  signs and sound values, 117, 211
  tablets, 30
  vases, 41
Linear C
  cylinder seals, 115, 122
  Cypriot syllabary evolved from, 121
  decipherment, 118–119, 120
  Linear A and B, derived from, 119, 121
  vs. Linear D, 120
  research on, 129, 130
  signs and sound values, 211
Linear D
  Cypriot syllabary evolved from, 121
  decipherment, 118–119, 120
  letter by Cypriot admiral, 116, 127–129, 137
  Linear A and B, derived from, 119, 121
  vs. Linear C, 120
  research on, 129, 130
  signs and sound values, 211
linearized scripts, 208
"Linen Book of Zagreb." See *Liber Linteus*

linguistics
    and archaeology, 15
    See also consonants; declension; languages; names; plural; scripts; signs; sound values; syllables; vowels; word endings; words
Littmann, Enno, 178
loanwords, 76–77
local scripts, 54
logograms
    of Cretan hieroglyphic, 210
    of Egyptian hieroglyphic, 210
    of Luwian hieroglyphic, 80–81, 82, 86, 87, 210
    polyphonic, 84
long swords, in graves, 43, 44
Lukka, 135–136, 137, 139, 140
Lusitanian language, 47
Lusitanians, 36, 37, 47, 48
Luwian cuneiform, 11, 76
Luwian hieroglyphic
    Adjusted Old Reading, 87, 90
    amount of text in documents, 27
    beginning of, 26, 53, 207, 216
    "Beyköy text," 91–92, 93–94, 95, 96, 97, 98
    concluding period of use of, 172
    Cretan hieroglyphic derived from, 26–27, 59
    curse formula, 78
    decipherment, 17–18, 20–21, 77–78
    vs. Egyptian hieroglyphic, 54
    Etruscan, for understanding of, 170–171
    Kızıldağ 4 inscription, 215
    loanwords, 76–77
    logograms, 80–81, 82, 86, 87, 210
    vs. Luwian cuneiform, 76
    Lycian alphabet related to, 176–177
    New Reading, 10, 21, 84–85, 86, 87, 88–90, 91
    Nişantaş inscription, 136
    Old Reading, 85–86, 87
    perishable material, documents on, 188–189
    personal names, 21, 86, 88, 90
    Phrygians (noun), 215
    place names, 88, 89–90, 96
    plural, 76, 88
    seal from Beycesultan, 32
    Selected Luwian Hieroglyphic Texts, 79
    similarities to other scripts, 207
    sound values, 78, 79–82, 83, 85, 210
    stones of Hama, 73
    Südburg inscription, 136
    syllabograms, 82–83
    Tarkondemos seal, 17, 73–74
    tiwaná (noun), 214
    Tyszkiewicz seal, 74
    vowels, 89
    Yalburt inscription, 94, 125
    zi and *za* reading, 85
Luwian kingdoms, invasions by Mycenaeans, 153–154
Luwian language
    as centum language, 216
    deciphering of Etruscan with help of, 9
    dialects, 169, 170, 174, 176, 179, 180, 189
    vs. Egyptian language, 53–54
    Etruscan related to, 160

Kaunos bilingual inscription, role in, 206
languages derived from, 24, 172
Latin as transcription for, 22, 79–84
letters from Ugarit, 127
non-Eurocentric perspective, 218
parna (noun), 22, 83
personal names, 181
population speaking, 175
research on, 10, 11
types of scripts, 76
understanding, 10
use of, 188
Luwians
ethnic name for, 75
influence on Greeks, 188
migration to Anatolia, 39
Lycia
chamber tombs, 169
See also Limyra
Lycian alphabet, 175, 176
Lycian language, 172, 174, 176–177, 189
Lycians, 123, 124, 175, 176
Lydia
chamber tombs, 169
Mermnads (royal family), 179
as powerful kingdom, 177
See also Caria; Cibyra; Sardis
Lydian language
in Cibyra, 177
cult text, 179
Etruscan derived from, 159
grave inscription, 179
Hittite influence, 23–24
Luwian, derived from, 24, 172
as Luwian dialect, 174, 179, 189
number of documents, 23
research on, 177–178
signs with different readings, 178–179
word endings, 179
Lydians, 167–168, 169, 178, 197

M
Magliano disc, 158
make (verb). *See aia-*; *izi-*
Malia, altar stone from, 61, 63
Marek, Christian, 183
Mari, letters from, 54, 56
Masson, Emilia, 119, 120
Maykop region, 34, 35
Medinet Habu temple
countries mentioned, 148
discrepancies in inscriptions, 151
place names of Cyprus mentioned, 150
Sea Peoples, depictions of, 46, 138, 142, 145
Mediterranean pre- and protohistory, 9, 10, 14
See also Aegean Bronze Age
Melchert, Craig, 79, 80
Mellaart, James, 91, 92, 93, 94, 95, 96–97, 98
mēm sign, 191, 193
mercenaries, 135, 143, 182
Merenptah, Pharaoh, 135
Meriggi, Piero, 78, 177, 215
Mermnads (royal family), 179
Mesopotamia, 106
Messerschmidt, Leopold, 74
metals. *See* copper; tin
"Mid-Century Report, The," 19
Middle Chronology, 105
Migdol, battle of, 138

migration
- to Aegean, 36, 37
- to Alps, 170
- from Anatolia, 172, 178
- to Anatolia, 39, 41, 49, 101, 145, 174
- to Balkan Peninsula, 49
- to Black Sea, 34–35
- of Celts, 197
- from central Mediterranean, 145
- by climatic change, 46
- to Crete, 44, 58
- destruction by, 45–46
- in eastern Mediterranean, 42–43
- to Egypt, 41
- from Greece, 154
- to Greece, 39, 43, 215
- of Hittite ruling class, 173
- to Iberia, 36, 37, 197, 198
- of Indo-Aryans, 41
- of Indo-Europeans, 33–34, 36, 37–38, 39, 42–43, 45, 198
- innovations by, 35–36
- from Italic Peninsula, 48–49, 170
- to Italic Peninsula, 37, 48, 141, 145, 172
- of Khvalynsk culture, 34–35
- from Levant, 58
- to Levant, 43
- of Ligurians, 37, 48
- of Lusitanians, 36, 37
- of Luwians, 39
- of Lydians, 169, 178
- to Mediterranean, 36, 37–38, 39
- from north Caspian steppes, 33–34
- from northwestern Anatolia, 178
- of Pelasgians, 36, 37
- of Phrygians, 39, 41, 43, 49, 101, 145, 174
- problem-causing, 146
- at Sea Peoples' time, 48–49, 145
- at southern Black Sea, 43
- to Syria, 173
- of Thracians, 39
- to Tuscany, 169
- of *ūmman-manda*, 32
- of Urnfield culture, 141, 145

military
- of Hittite Empire, 152
- *See also* fleets; mercenaries; warriors; weapons

"milk stones." *See* seals

Minoan culture
- destruction and recovery, 44
- Semitic influence, 28
- trade, 44–45
- zenith, 63
- *See also* Crete

"Minoization," 42

Mira
- king of, 74
- Tarkondemos seal, 17

mistakes, in research, 213–214

Morpurgo-Davies, Anna, 84–85

mortuary temple of Ramesses III. *See* Medinet Habu temple

Muksus, 150

mummy wrapping, linen of *Liber Linteus* used as, 164

Muski, 173, 174

Mycenae, shaft graves, 15

Mycenaeans, 42, 147, 153–154

mystery cult, of Etruscans, 165

N

names
　ethnic, 75, 102
　of languages, 75
　See also geographic names; personal names
natural resources. See copper; tin
Naue-Type-II swords, 142
naval battles
　Sea Peoples vs. Egyptians, 142
　Sea Peoples vs. Hittites, 129
　Trojans vs. Hittites, 137
navy. See fleets
Neolithic Revolution, theory of Indo-Europeans as product of, 33
Neumann, Günter, 84–85
"new border" (place name), 86
"new frontier" (place name). See *ī+r-ha-nu-a-*
New Reading (Luwian hieroglyphic), 10, 21, 84–85, 86, 87, 88–90, 91
Nişantaş inscription, 136
non-Indo-European languages, 48, 167
　See also Basque language; Hattic language; Hurrian language; Semitic languages
north Caspian steppes, migration of Indo-Europeans from, 33–34
northern Caucasus. See Maykop region
nouns
　casidanos, 194
　parna/domus, 22, 83
　Phrygians, 215
　tíwaná, 214
-*nthos-* names, 40
numbers, alphabetic letters as, 183
numerals, in Etruscan, 157–158, 215
nuraghe, Santu Antine, 144

O

Old Reading (Luwian hieroglyphic), 85–86, 87
　See also Adjusted Old Reading

P

parna (noun), 22, 83
past tense, introduction, 39
Paulilatino. See Santa Cristina well
peace treaty, of Egypt and Hittite Empire, 134
Pelasgian language, 28
Pelasgians, 36, 37, 140
Peleset, 140
Perire, battle of, 135
perishable material, documents on, 188–189
Perrot, Georges, 94
Persian War, 162, 218
personal names
　Asia (deity), 171
　in Byblos script, 112
　on Crete, 28
　in Ebla tablets, 32
　in Etruscan, 160, 161
　in Hittite cuneiform, 21
　in Kaunos bilingual inscription, 183, 186
　in Linear A and B, 30, 64
　in Luwian hieroglyphic, 21, 86, 88, 90
　in Luwian language, 181
　polyphonic, 86, 88

personal names *(continued)*
   on seals from Tarsus, 124
   in Sidetic language, 181
   Tēreús, 41
Phaistos, seals from, 69
Phaistos disc
   about, 25, 26, 60
   dating, 27, 61, 62
   decipherment, 61
   doublets and triplets, 27
   side A, 60
Philistines, 140, 147
Phoenician alphabet
   in Anatolian alphabets, 180
   Byblos script, some similarities to, 110
   Greek alphabet derived from, 180
   Iberia, introduction to, 197
   mēm sign, 191, 193
   perishable material, documents on, 189
   Southwest Iberian alphabet derived from, 191, 212
   Southwest Iberian alphabet, related signs to, 200
Phoenician texts
   in Karatepe inscription, 18, 78
   in Pyrgi tablets, 161, 162
Phoenicians
   spread of alphabet by, 194
   tin trade, 195–196
   trade routes, 147, 196–197
   See also Canaanites
phonetic values. *See* sound values
Phrygia. *See* Gordion
Phrygian language, 216, 217
Phrygians
   dying god, 165
   ethnic names for, 102
   migration to Anatolia, 41, 49, 101, 145, 174
   migration to Greece, 39, 43
   as Sea Peoples, 155
Phrygians (noun), in Kızıldağ 4 inscription, 215
pins. *See* silver pins
place names
   of Cyprus, 150
   ending in *briga*, 198
   ending in *-nthos-*, 40
   ending in *-st-*, 38
   in Etruscan, 160
   ī+r-ha-nu-a-, 21
   of Levant, 147
   in Luwian hieroglyphic, 88, 89–90, 96
   "new border," 86
plague, 38
Plato, 69, 70
   See also Atlantis account
plural
   in Luwian, 76, 88
   in Lycian, 177
plus sign, 178
polyphonic logograms, 84
polyphonic names, 86, 88
polyphonic signs, 170–171
population
   of Crete, 28
   DNA analysis, 49–50
   Luwian-speaking, 175
   See also ethnicity
port towns, of Phoenicians, 196–197

pottery
    Grey Ware, 41
    handmade burnished ware, 145
    Philistine, 140
    See also vases
prehistory
    explained, 13
    See also Mediterranean pre- and protohistory
priests, manual for, 164
pronouns, first person singular, 123
pronunciation. *See* sound values
protohistory
    explained, 13
    See also Mediterranean pre- and protohistory
"Proto-Hittites," 34, 35
"Proto-Luwians," 34–35
Proto-Sinaitic inscriptions, 110–111
Proto-Villanovan culture, 48
psi sign, 183
punctuation marks
    in Byblos script, 107, 112
    See also *scriptio continua*
Pylos, 148
Pyrgi tablets, 161–162, 163
pyroclastic flows, tsunami by, 68

Q

questionnaire, "The Mid-Century Report," 19

R

raids, by Sea Peoples in eastern Mediterranean, 133, 196
Ramesses III, Pharaoh, 150, 155
    See also Medinet Habu temple
rapiers. *See* long swords
Ray, John D., 182
Ray-Adiego-Schürr system, 182–183
rebus, 82
religion
    of Crete, 59
    of Etruscans, 165
    See also gods and goddesses; priests
Renfrew, Colin, 33, 34
resurrection, of dying god, 165–166
Rhaetian language, 170
Rhodes. *See* Kameiros
rhotacism, 101
river names
    of Iberia, 198
    Indo-European, 36
    of Italic Peninsula, 48, 169
Robinson, Andrew, 19
root words, *sard-*, 142
Rosetta stone, 16

S

Samsat. *See* Armi
Sanskrit, 31
Santa Cristina well, 143
Santorini. *See* Thera
Santu Antine (nuraghe), 144
sard- (root word), 142
Sardinia, 142–144, 147
Sardis, 177
satem languages, 215
Sayce, Archibald, 73
scarabs, from Crete, 63, 139
Scheria, 213
Schürr, Diether, 182–183
scriptio continua, 200
    See also punctuation marks
scripts
    development, 55, 207–208
    different views on, 209, 212, 213

scripts *(continued)*
   linearized, 208
   local, 54
   mingled, 65, 187
   open questions, 209
   types of Luwian, 76
   in Ugarit, 77
   undeciphered, 117
   See also alphabets; cuneiform texts; hieroglyphic scripts
sea battles. *See* naval battles
Sea Peoples
   in battle of Perire, 135
   as captives, 138
   ethnicity, 123, 133, 139, 140–141, 142–143, 149, 150, 152, 155
   fleets, advancing, 129, 153
   invasions by, 45, 46, 150, 152–153, 155
   leadership question, 150–151
   Levant, advancement to, 129, 137
   Levant, settlements in, 146–147, 148
   migration at time of, 48–49, 145
   naval battles, 129, 142
   origin of, 143, 144, 145–146, 149, 216
   raids in eastern Mediterranean, 133, 196
   warriors, 138, 139, 140, 146
   warships, 142, 150
seals
   from Akrotiri, 69
   atlunu (Atlantis), 66
   from Beycesultan, 32
   Cretan hieroglyphic on, 59, 62, 65
   from Crete, 29, 54, 56, 69
   from Tarsus, 124

   See also cylinder seals; Tarkondemos seal; Tyszkiewicz seal
Seha, 96
Selected Luwian Hieroglyphic Texts, 79
semi-syllabic alphabets, 192
Semitic languages
   Byblos script as dialect of, 107
   Linear A as, 24, 25, 28, 56–57, 58
   See also Ugaritic language
shaft graves, 15, 43
Shekelesh, 123, 144
Sherden, 142, 144, 146
Shikala. *See* Shekelesh
Shikala letter, 144
ships
   Gurob model, 144
   for trade, 196
   See also warships
shipwreck, at Uluburun, 134
Sidetic alphabet, 180
Sidetic language, 174, 180, 181, 189
signs
   animal head, 74
   of Byblos script, 112, 211
   of Carian language, 182
   different for same sound values, 89
   double axe, 113
   of Etruscan alphabet, 159
   f, 159, 182
   "great prince," 98, 99
   identical, 117, 118, 119
   incised, 108
   of Linear A, 117, 211
   of Linear B, 117, 211
   of Linear C, 211
   of Linear D, 211
   of Lycian alphabet, 175

of Lydian language, 178–179
mēm, 191, 193
order of, 183
origin of, 187–188
plus, 178
polyphonic, 170–171
psi, 183
of Southwest Iberian alphabet, 200–201
upward arrow, 178
yod, 178–179
See also alphabetic letters; logograms
silver bowls, Ankara, 22
silver pins, from Knossos, 58
single-horse burials, 39, 40
Sipatba'al (harbormaster), 124
Sivas (functionary), 167
Sklavokampo, seals from, 69
soapstone, 99
sound values
of "Arzawa," 82
in Byblos script, 112, 211
change of, 117, 130, 200
in Cretan hieroglyphic, 210
different signs for same, 89
in Egyptian hieroglyphic, 210
in Greek alphabet, 117
in Linear A, 117, 211
in Linear B, 117, 211
in Linear C, 211
in Linear D, 211
in Luwian hieroglyphic, 78, 79–82, 83, 85, 210
need for, 19
in Southwest Iberian alphabet, 193, 200, 201
See also New Reading; Old Reading

Southwest Iberian alphabet
decipherment, 193, 194
Herdade da Abobada inscription, 203
introduction, 191
number of documents, 202
Phoenician alphabet, derived from, 191, 212
relationship to other scripts, 193, 200, 201
signs, 200–201
sound values, 193, 200, 201
syllables, 192, 201
vowels, 192
Southwest Iberian language, 191, 199, 217
Spain. *See* Iberia
specialized approach, 10, 15, 219
-*st*- names, 38
stamps, for producing Phaistos disc, 60
stelae. *See* Lemnos stele
steppes. *See* north Caspian steppes
stone (material). *See* soapstone
stones (objects)
Luwian hieroglyphic in Hama, 73
Türkmen-Karahöyük inscription, 99–101, 102–103
See also altar stone; Rosetta stone
Strabo, 177
Südburg inscription, 136
Suppiluliuma II, Great King of Hittite Empire, 136, 144
swords
long, 43, 44
Naue-Type-II, 142
syllabaries. *See* Cypriot syllabary; Cypro-Minoan syllabary

syllables, in Southwest Iberian alphabet, 192, 201
syllabograms, of Luwian hieroglyphic, 82–83
Syria
   migration of Hittite ruling class to, 173
   raids by Sea Peoples on port towns, 196
   See also Aleppo; Armi; Ebla; Hama(th); Kadesh; Mari; Ugarit

T
tablets
   in Byblos script, 107, 108–109
   from Crete, 24, 27, 30
   in Cypriot syllabary, 116
   Ebla, 32
   in Linear A, 24, 27, 30
   in Linear B, 30
   names of languages on, 75
   Pyrgi, 161–162, 163
   from Ugarit, 124
Tarhunt (name), 160
Tarkondemos seal, 17, 73–74
Tarquinia (name), 160
Tarsus, 124
Tartessian language. *See* Southwest Iberian language
Tartessos. *See* Huelva
temples
   of Byblos, 108–109
   at Cumae, 162–163
   See also Medinet Habu temple
Teresh, 140
Tēreús (name), 41
terminology, inconsistent, 120

Teukroi, 140
Thefarie Velianas (functionary), 161, 162
Thera
   as caldera, 68
   eruption of, 66, 68–69
   See also Akrotiri
Therasia, excavations on, 69
tholos graves, 36
Thracians, 39, 41, 43
tin trade
   of Crete, 54, 56
   of Minoan culture, 45
   of Phoenicians, 195–196
Tinita (goddess), 59
tin-master (noun). *See casidanos*
tíwaná (noun), 214
Tjeker. *See* Trojans
tombs. *See* graves
tombstones. *See* Lemnos stele
Topada inscription, 102
trade
   of Cyprus, 115
   of Levant and islands, 56, 147
   of Minoan culture, 44–45
   of Philistines, 147
   ships used for, 196
   See also goods; tin trade
trade records, 115, 121–123, 125, 126, 189
   See also accounting system
trade routes
   of Phoenicians, 147, 196–197
   from Troy to Hattusa, 130
   from Ugarit to Anatolia, 124
transcription
   of Carian in Kaunos bilingual inscription, 185, 186
   Latin for Luwian, 22, 79–84

See also New Reading; Old Reading
translation
  of Carian in Kaunos bilingual inscription, 185
  of Cretan hieroglyphic, 61
  of Etruscan documents, 163
  of *Liber Linteus*, 164–165
  of Linear A, 57
  of Pyrgi tablets, 162–163
treaties. *See* peace treaty
trilingual documents. *See* Letoon trilingual text; Rosetta stone
triplets, 18, 27, 111
Troad, assumed non-Indo-European language in, 167
Trojan War, 70–71, 147, 154
Trojans
  feather headdresses, 145
  naval battles vs. Hittites, 137
Troy
  battle of Mycenaeans vs. Luwians, 154
  early period, 40–41
  trade routes to Hattusa, 130
Trümmersprachen, 15, 188
tsunami, by pyroclastic flows, 68
tsunami deposits, no indication on Crete, 67–68
Tudhaliya IV, Great King of Hittite Empire, 134
Türkmen-Karahöyük inscription, 99–101, 102–103
Tuscany
  as core region of Etruscans, 163
  migration of Lydians to, 169
Tuscany dice, 158, 215
Tyrsenoi, 140
Tyszkiewicz seal, 74

U
Ugarit
  destruction, 137
  letters from, 127
  scripts and languages, 77
  tablet, 124
  texts, 78–79
  trade routes to Anatolia, 124
Ugaritic language, 109
Uluburun, shipwreck at, 134
ūmman-manda, 32
undeciphered scripts, 117
Untermann, Jürgen, 200
upward arrow sign, 178
Urnfield culture, 141, 145

V
values (linguistics). *See* alphabet values; sound values
vases, Linear B on, 41
vassals, of Hittite Empire, 134–135
vegetation histories, 46
Ventris, Michael, 18, 19, 29, 119, 130
verbs
  aia-/izi-, 21
  in Byblos script, 112–113
  write, 171
  ya-ta-nū-tī, 57
Vita, Juan-Pablo, 113
Vladikavkaz disc, 61
volcanic eruptions
  of Krakatoa, 68
  of Thera, 66, 68–69
vowels
  in decipherment, 18
  in Luwian hieroglyphic, 89
  in Southwest Iberian alphabet, 192

W

Waal, Willemijn, 188, 189
Wachsmann, Shelley, 144, 216
wagons, 36
  See also chariots
warriors
  with feather headdresses, 139, 142, 145
  Sea Peoples, 138, 139, 140, 146
  See also mercenaries
wars. *See* battles; civil war; invasions; Persian War; Trojan War
warships, of Sea Peoples, 142, 150
Wasusarma, Great King of Cappadocia, 102
water basin, Yalburt, 125
weapons
  chariots as, 43
  of Sherden, 142
  See also double axe; swords
well, Santa Cristina, 143
Weshesh, 141
western Asia Minor. *See* Luwian kingdoms
wheels, 36
word endings
  briga names, 198
  in Lydian language, 179
  -*nthos*- names, 40
  -*st*- names, 38
words
  doublets and triplets, 18, 27, 111
  loanwords, 76–77
  See also nouns; pronouns; root words; verbs
write (verb), 171
writing
  introduction in Hattusa, 77
  use of, 54

X

Xerxes, King of Persian Empire, 162

Y

Yakubovich, Ilya, 33, 179, 214–215
Yalburt inscription, 94, 125
Yarimlim of Aleppo, 109–110
ya-ta-nū-tī (verb), 57
yod sign, 178–179

Z

Zamora, José Ángel, 113
zi and *za* reading, 85
Zinko, Christian, 181
Zinko, Michaela, 181

About the Authors

Dr. Frederik Christiaan Woudhuizen (1959–2021) was an expert on ancient Indo-European languages, hieroglyphic Luwian and Mediterranean protohistory. He obtained a doctorate from Erasmus University Rotterdam with a dissertation on *The Ethnicity of the Sea Peoples*. Woudhuizen published 25 books and over 100 scholarly articles, primarily on the writing systems of the Late Bronze Age and Early Iron Age of the Mediterranean, including Luwian hieroglyphs, Cretan hieroglyphs, Linear A, Cypro-Minoan and the Byblos script. He has also dealt extensively with the Luwian language and with Lycian, Lydian, Sidetic, Carian, Etruscan and Southwest Iberian.

Dr. Eberhard Zangger (*1958) has been an expert in the reconstruction of archaeological landscapes since 1982 and has participated in many archaeological excavations and surveys in the countries around the eastern Mediterranean. His academic degrees include a PhD from Stanford University. He is the founder and president of the Luwian Studies foundation and has authored 6 books and over 50 scientific articles, most of which have appeared in international peer-reviewed journals.